Wiley CPAexcel® Exam Review
PRACTICE QUESTIONS
2019

REGULATION

Wiley CPAexcel® Exam Review

PRACTICE
QUESTIONS

2019

REGULATION

Gregory Carnes, Ph.D., CPA
Marianne M. Jennings, J.D.
Robert A. Prentice, J.D.

Wiley Efficient Learning™

Table of Contents

Multiple Choice Questions

Ethics, Professional Responsibilities, and Federal Tax Procedures

Ethics and Responsibility in Tax Practice

aicpa.aq.ethics.230.001_17

1. While reviewing a new client's prior-year tax returns, a CPA became aware that the client did not properly file all required federal income tax returns. Under Treasury Circular 230, what should the CPA do in this situation?

   A. Notify the AICPA of the situation and request a ruling of continuance.
   B. Notify the Internal Revenue Service of the client's noncompliance.
   C. Resign from the engagement.
   D. Advise the client of the consequences of the noncompliance.

assess.AICPA.100985REG-SIM

2. Under Circular 230, it is proper to delay as long as possible in fulfilling an IRS request for records or information if:

   A. You have investigated and believe in good faith that the information is privileged.
   B. It would benefit your client strategically in his tax dispute with the IRS.
   C. A and B
   D. None of the above.

assess.AICPA.100986REG-SIM

3. If you learn that the tax return that you prepared for your client last year contained a material error, you should:

   A. Promptly inform your client.
   B. Inform the IRS even before informing your client.
   C. A and B.
   D. None of the above.

assess.AICPA.101157REG

4. Pursuant to Treasury Circular 230, which of the following statements about the return of a client's records is correct?

   A. The client's records are to be destroyed upon the submission of a tax return.
   B. The practitioner may retain copies of the client's records.
   C. The existence of a dispute over fees generally relieves the practitioner of responsibility to return the client's records.
   D. The practitioner does **not** need to return any client records that are necessary for the client to comply with the client's federal tax returns.

assess.AICPA.120604REG

5. Under Treasury Circular 230, which of the following actions of a CPA tax advisor is characteristic of a best practice in rendering tax advice?

   A. Requesting written evidence from a client that the fee proposal for tax advice has been approved by the board of directors.
   B. Recommending to the client that the advisor's tax advice be made orally instead of in a written memorandum.
   C. Establishing relevant facts, evaluating the reasonableness of assumptions and representations, and arriving at a conclusion supported by the law and facts in a tax memorandum.
   D. Requiring the client to supply a written representation, signed under penalties of perjury, concerning the facts and statements provided to the CPA for preparing a tax memorandum.

assess.AICPA.130704REG

6. Under Circular 230, which of the following describes improper activity by a CPA giving federal tax advice?

   A. The CPA takes into account the possibility that a tax return will **not** be audited.
   B. The CPA reasonably relies upon representations of the client.
   C. The CPA considers all relevant facts that are known.
   D. The CPA takes into consideration assumptions about future events related to the relevant facts.

assess.AICPA.REG.ethics.230-0001

7. While preparing a tax return for a new client and reviewing the client's prior-year return, a CPA noticed an error made by the client's former tax preparer. According to Treasury Department Circular 230, which of the following is the CPA specifically required to do in this case?

   A. Contact the tax preparer who made the error and suggest that an amended return be prepared for the client.
   B. Inform the client of the error and insist that the return be amended.
   C. Inform the client of the error and advise of the consequences.
   D. Advise the client to contact the tax preparer of the prior-year return.

Internal Revenue Code and Regulations Related to Tax Return Preparers

aicpa.aq.irs.1986.001_17

8. With respect to any given tax return, which of the following statements is correct?

   A. More than one person may be deemed to be a preparer of a tax return.
   B. The final reviewer of a tax return is automatically considered the preparer of the return.
   C. Only one person may be deemed to be a preparer of a tax return.
   D. The two individuals who have done the most work in preparing the return will be deemed to be the only preparers.

aicpa.aq.irs.1986.002_17

9. A tax preparer filed a return for a taxpayer and used the taxpayer's detailed check register containing both business and personal expenses. If the tax preparer knowingly included personal expenses as deductible business expenses on the taxpayer's business, then the

   A. Tax preparer will be liable only for penalties for taking an unreasonable position that led to an understatement.
   B. Taxpayer will be liable for penalties for taking an unreasonable position that led to an understatement.
   C. Tax preparer will be liable for penalties arising from an understatement due to willful or reckless conduct.
   D. Taxpayer will be liable for penalties attributable to transactions lacking economic substance.

assess.AICPA.100991REG-SIM

10. Which of the following will not get CPA Sandy in trouble with the IRS?

    A. Failing to furnish copies of returns to her clients.
    B. Failing to sign returns she prepares and files.
    C. Failure to furnish her preparer's identifying number to her clients.
    D. Failure to keep copies of the returns she prepares.

assess.AICPA.100992REG-SIM

11. Pak worked for EPS marketing trusts and other asset protection devices through a nationwide multi-level marketing network of financial planners. The IRS labeled the trusts illicit tax shelters. EPS then started calling the trusts by new names but continued to market them. Pak was EPS's executive vice president, spoke at its public events, and received sales overrides from agents he recruited as sales representatives for EPS. As Pak explained them, the trusts allowed clients to transfer all their income to a "donor-directed" trust from which they could spend the money on anything they wanted, without paying taxes on it. The IRS brought an action against Pak, seeking to fine him for promoting an abusive tax shelter in violation of 26 U.S.C. 6700. Which of the following is true?

    A. Pak is probably liable.
    B. Pak is probably not liable, because he did not organize or participate in sale of the shelters.
    C. Pak is probably not liable, because he did not make any materially false statements that affect tax liability.
    D. B and C.

assess.AICPA.100993REG-SIM

12. Under which of the following scenarios will Jenny be in trouble under Section 6713's confidentiality provisions?

    A. When she sells a celebrity client's confidential tax information to a tabloid newspaper.
    B. When she discloses a rich client's confidential tax information pursuant to court order.
    C. When she shows several of her clients' tax returns to another accountant performing a peer review of Jenny's firm.
    D. All of the above.

assess.AICPA.100995REG-SIM

13. CPA Monrew induced several rich tax clients to invest in a domesticated beaver tax shelter device. When the IRS sought to audit one of Monrew's clients, he realized that among other difficulties, he had not had the client sign proper documentation. While an IRS agent sat in the waiting room of one of his clients, Monrew slipped in a back door and had the client sign a backdated document. When the government discovered all this, Monrew was indicted for tax fraud in violation of Section 7206. Which of the following is true?

   A. Monrew is probably guilty.
   B. Monrew is probably not guilty, because the client bears the blame here.
   C. Monrew is probably not guilty because his actions, while not praiseworthy, do not violate the statute.
   D. B and C.

assess.AICPA.101155REG

14. Louis, the volunteer treasurer of a nonprofit organization and a member of its board of directors, compiles the data and fills out its annual Form 990, *Return of Organization Exempt from Income Tax*. Under the Internal Revenue Code, Louis is **not** considered a tax return preparer because:

   A. He is a member of the board of directors.
   B. The return does **not** contain a claim for a tax refund.
   C. He is **not** compensated.
   D. Returns for nonprofit organizations are exempt from the preparer rules.

assess.AICPA.120606REG

15. Tax return preparers can be subject to penalties under the Internal Revenue Code for failure to do any of the following *except*

   A. Sign a tax return as a preparer.
   B. Disclose a conflict of interest.
   C. Provide a client with a copy of the tax return.
   D. Keep a record of Returns prepared.

Licensing and Disciplinary Systems

aicpa.aq.lic.disp.syst.001_17

16. Which agency is responsible for determining the continuing professional education requirements for licensed CPAs?

   A. The Securities and Exchange Commission
   B. The board of accountancy for the state in which the licensed CPA practices

   C. The American Institute of Certified Public Accountants
   D. The National Association of State Boards of Accountancy

aicpa.aq.lic.disp.syst.002_17

17. To whom must a CPA pay license fees in order to maintain a CPA license?

   A. The Public Company Accounting Oversight Board
   B. The American Institute of Certified Public Accountants
   C. The state board of accountancy of the CPA's state of licensure
   D. The state society of certified public accountants of the CPA's state of licensure

assess.AICPA.081903REG-1D

18. When an ethics complaint carrying national implications arises, which entity typically handles it?

   A. SEC.
   B. PCAOB.
   C. State CPA society.
   D. AICPA.

assess.AICPA.081904REG-1D

19. What is JEEP?

   A. Joint Energy Equity Program.
   B. Junior Emergency Enforcement Program.
   C. Joint Ethics Enforcement Program.
   D. None of the above.

assess.AICPA.081907REG-1D

20. CPA Smithers has had some professional difficulties. Which of the following is true?

   A. If the state board of accountancy revokes Smithers' CPA license, s/he will be automatically expulsed from the AICPA.
   B. If the state society of CPAs expulses Smithers, the state board of accountancy will automatically revoke his/her CPA license.
   C. Both A and B.
   D. Neither A nor B.

assess.AICPA.100996REG-SIM

21. Which of the following can grant a CPA license?

   A. A state board of accountancy.
   B. The AICPA.
   C. The Securities Exchange Commission.
   D. All of the above.

assess.AICPA.100997REG-SIM

22. Cherokee wants to know which of the following is a requirement to earn a CPA license:

    A. 150 hours of college education.
    B. Passing the CPA examination.
    C. One year of work experience.
    D. All of the above.

assess.AICPA.100999REG-SIM

23. Iola has had a few serious professional problems. Which of the following will probably cause a state board of accountancy to revoke her license or order a lesser punishment?

    A. Failing to complete required continuing professional education.
    B. Failing to pay her own income tax.
    C. Violating professional standards.
    D. All of the above.

assess.AICPA.960502REG-BL

24. Which of the following bodies ordinarily would have the authority to suspend or revoke a CPA's license to practice public accounting?

    A. The SEC.
    B. The AICPA.
    C. A state CPA society.
    D. A state board of accountancy.

Federal Tax Practice and Procedures

Substantiation and Disclosure of Tax Positions

sub.disc.tax.pos.001

25. Taxpayer Clegg would certainly like to take a particular deduction that is barred by an IRS regulation. However, after considerable research Clegg's tax attorney believes that there is a one-third chance that a court would overturn the regulation as invalidly promulgated by the IRS. What should Clegg do?

    A. Take the deduction without disclosure.
    B. Take the deduction, but disclose it.
    C. Not take the deduction.
    D. All of the above.

sub.disc.tax.pos.002

26. Fitely hired a tax accountant whom his attorney recommended. The accountant, Tilder, recommended that Fitely take a particular tax position that resulted in an understatement of taxes and the IRS is now seeking to penalize Fitely. In order to establish a good faith defense against the 20% understatement penalty, which of the following does Fitely need to establish:

    A. That Tilder was a competent professional.
    B. That Fitely gave Tilder all necessary and accurate information.
    C. That Fitely actually relied in good faith on Tilder's judgment.
    D. All of the above.

sub.disc.tax.pos.003

27. Which of the following burdens of proof must be met when a disclosed position regarding a particular individual deduction is evaluated to determine whether it was taken in good faith.

    A. ≥ 10% chance of being sustained
    B. ≥ 20% chance of being sustained
    C. ≥ 40% chance of being sustained
    D. >50% chance of being sustained

aq.sub.disc.tax.pos.005_071

28. For taxpayers who are trying to get things right when facing difficult tax questions, what two key words they should keep in mind?

    A. Reasonable cause and good faith
    B. Good faith and no fraud
    C. Reasonable cause and attention to detail
    D. Attention to detail and no fraud

Taxpayer Penalties

aq.tax.pen.001_2017

29. Tribble carelessly filed his taxes four months late. He owed $60,000 in taxes. What is his late filing penalty?

    A. $120,000
    B. $60,000
    C. $12,000
    D. $9,500

aq.tax.pen.002_2017

30. Xina carelessly filed her taxes 10 months late. She owed $100,000 in taxes. What is Xina's late filing penalty?

    A. $100,000
    B. $75,000
    C. $50,000
    D. $25,000

aq.tax.pen.003_2017

31. Tera filed her tax return on time but did not pay her taxes until four months after they were due. She owed $20,000. What is her late payment penalty amount?

    A. $400
    B. $600
    C. $4,000
    D. $60,000

aq.tax.pen.004_2017

32. Omar's correct tax amount is $500,000, but he filed a form reporting that it was only $400,000. There is no claim of fraud. Is this a "substantial understatement" that will subject him to the 20% understatement penalty?

   A. Yes, and his penalty will be $100,000.
   B. Yes, and his penalty will be $20,000.
   C. Yes, and his penalty will be $5,000.
   D. No.

aq.tax.pen.005_2017

33. ABC Corporation, a Chapter C corporation, had a correct tax amount of $1,000,000 but reported only $800,000. There is no claim of fraud. Is this a "substantial understatement" that will subject ABC to the 20% understatement penalty?

   A. Yes, and its penalty will be $40,000.
   B. Yes, and its penalty will be $20,000.
   C. Yes, and its penalty will be $10,000.
   D. No.

aq.tax.pen.006_2017

34. Slim is considering taking an aggressive tax position on his income tax return. His experienced tax CPA has evaluated the position carefully and determined that there is a one in four chance that it will, if challenged, be sustained. What should Slim do?

   A. Take the position but not disclose it.
   B. Take the position and disclose it.
   C. Not take the position.
   D. All of the choices.

Sources of Tax Authority and Research

assess.AICPA.060811REG-P2-AR

35. In evaluating the hierarchy of authority in tax law, which of the following carries the greatest authoritative value for tax planning of transactions?

   A. Internal Revenue Code.
   B. IRS regulations.
   C. Tax court decisions.
   D. IRS agents' reports.

assess.AICPA.101091REG-SIM

36. Which of the following type of regulations cannot be cited as authority to support a tax position?

   A. Legislative regulations.
   B. Interpretive regulations.
   C. Procedural regulations.
   D. Proposed regulations.

assess.AICPA.101092REG-SIM

37. Which of the following courts is not a court of original jurisdiction?

   A. United States Tax Court.
   B. United States District Court.
   C. United States Court of Appeals.
   D. United States Court of Federal Claims.

assess.AICPA.101093REG-SIM

38. All of the following are administrative sources of the tax law except:

   A. Private letter rulings.
   B. Technical advice memoranda.
   C. Revenue rulings.
   D. Committee reports.

assess.AICPA.120713REG

39. Which Senate committee considers new tax legislation?

   A. Budget.
   B. Finance.
   C. Appropriations.
   D. Rules and Administration.

assess.AICPA.120719REG

40. Which of the following is NOT considered a primary authoritative source when conducting tax research?

   A. Internal Revenue Code.
   B. Tax Court cases.
   C. IRS publications.
   D. Treasury regulations.

assess.AICPA.REG.sources.tax-0007

41. A CPA is researching a tax issue and is attempting to understand the intent of Congress. Which of the following would generally be **least** useful for that purpose?

   A. Committee Report of the House Ways and Means Committee
   B. A Notice of Proposed Rulemaking
   C. A Senate Finance Committee Report
   D. *The Congressional Record*

assess.AICPA.REG.sources.tax-0013

42. Which of the following is a list of courts that are referred to as courts of original jurisdiction, or trial courts, for tax matters?

   A. The Tax Court, the U.S. District Court, and the U.S. Court of Federal Claims.
   B. The Tax Court, the U.S. District Court, and the U.S. Bankruptcy Court.
   C. The Tax Court, the U.S. Court of Federal Claims, and the U.S. Court of Appeals.
   D. The U.S. District Court, the U.S. Court of Federal Claims, and the U.S. Court of Appeals.

Tax Practice and Procedure

assess.AICPA.101118REG-SIM

43. If a taxpayer receives a *30-day letter* from the Internal Revenue Service, the taxpayer:

    A. Must pay the tax deficiency or respond to the issues raised through written correspondence to the IRS within 30 days of the date of the letter.
    B. May ignore the letter and take no action.
    C. Must pay the tax deficiency or file a petition with the Tax Court within 30 days of the date of the letter.
    D. Must pay the tax deficiency and file a petition with the District Court within 30 days of the date of the letter.

assess.AICPA.101119REG-SIM

44. Which of the following documents does NOT govern the conduct of a CPA who is engaged in providing tax services?

    A. AICPA's Code of Professional Conduct
    B. AICPA's Statements on Standards for Tax Services
    C. Circular 230
    D. Internal Revenue Service Audit Guides

assess.AICPA.120726REG

45. An IRS agent has just completed an examination of a corporation and issued a "no change" report. Which of the following statements about that situation is correct?

    A. The taxpayer may **not** amend the tax return for that taxable year.
    B. The IRS generally does **not** reopen the examination except in cases involving fraud or other similar misrepresentation.
    C. The IRS may **not** reopen the examination.
    D. The IRS may **not** examine any other tax return of the corporation for a period of one year.

assess.AICPA.951125REG-AR

46. A corporation's tax year can be reopened after all statutes of limitations have expired if

    I. The tax return has a 50% nonfraudulent omission from gross income.
    II. The corporation prevails in a determination allowing a deduction in an open tax year that was taken erroneously in a closed tax year.

    A. I only.
    B. II only.
    C. Both I and II.
    D. Neither I nor II.

Compliance Responsibilities

aicpa.aq.compl.respon.001_17

47. A C corporation had a federal income tax liability of $40,000 for each of the last five years, each covering a 12-month period. The tax for the current year is $48,000. What is the lowest amount that must have been paid as estimated taxes for the current year so that **no** penalty for underpayment is applicable?

    A. $40,000
    B. $44,000
    C. $48,000
    D. $52,800

assess.AICPA.010505REG-AR

48. A taxpayer filed his income tax return after the due date but neglected to file an extension form. The return indicated a tax liability of $50,000 and taxes withheld of $45,000.

    On what amount would the penalties for late filing and late payment be computed?

    A. $0
    B. $5,000
    C. $45,000
    D. $50,000

assess.AICPA.940519REG-AR

49. A tax return preparer may disclose or use tax return information without the taxpayer's consent to

    A. Facilitate a supplier's or lender's credit evaluation of the taxpayer.
    B. Accommodate the request of a financial institution that needs to determine the amount of taxpayer's debt to it, to be forgiven.
    C. Be evaluated by a quality or peer review.
    D. Solicit additional nontax business.

assess.AICPA.940520REG-AR

50. Which, if any, of the following could result in penalties against an income tax return preparer?

    I. Knowing or reckless disclosure or use of tax information obtained in preparing a return.
    II. A willful attempt to understate any client's tax liability on a return or claim for refund.

    A. Neither I nor II.
    B. I only.
    C. II only.
    D. Both I and II.

assess.AICPA.950516REG-AR

51. An accuracy-related penalty applies to the portion of tax underpayment attributable to

    I.   Negligence or a disregard of the tax rules or regulations.
    II. Any substantial understatement of income tax.

    A. I only.
    B. II only.
    C. Both I and II.
    D. Neither I nor II.

assess.AICPA.950519REG-AR_2-18

52. Chris Baker's adjusted gross income on her 2018 tax return was $160,000. The amount covered a 12-month period. For the 2019 tax year, Baker may avoid the penalty for the underpayment of estimated tax if the timely estimated tax payments equal the required annual amount of

    I.   90% of the tax on the return for the current year paid in four equal installments.
    II. 100% of prior year's tax liability paid in four equal installments.

    A. I only.
    B. II only.
    C. Both I and II.
    D. Neither I nor II.

assess.AICPA.951116REG-AR

53. A civil fraud penalty can be imposed on a corporation that underpays tax by

    A. Omitting income as a result of inadequate recordkeeping.
    B. Failing to report income it erroneously considered not to be part of corporate profits.
    C. Filing an incomplete return with an appended statement, making clear that the return is incomplete.
    D. Maintaining false records and reporting fictitious transactions to minimize corporate tax liability.

assess.AICPA.951124REG-AR_1808

54. Edge Corp., a calendar-year C corporation, had a net operating loss and zero tax liability for its 2018 tax year. To avoid the penalty for underpayment of estimated taxes, Edge could compute its first-quarter 2019 estimated income tax payment using the

	Annualized income method	Preceding-year method
A.	Yes	Yes
B.	Yes	No
C.	No	Yes
D.	No	No

assess.AICPA.951126REG-AR

55. A penalty for understated corporate tax liability can be imposed on a tax preparer who fails to

    A. Audit the corporate records.
    B. Examine business operations.
    C. Copy all underlying documents.
    D. Make reasonable inquiries when taxpayer information appears incorrect.

assess.AICPA.970511REG-AR_1808

56. Morgan, a sole practitioner CPA, prepares individual and corporate income tax returns. What documentation is Morgan required to retain concerning each return prepared?

    A. An unrelated party compliance statement.
    B. Taxpayer's name and identification number or a copy of the tax return.
    C. Workpapers associated with the preparation of each tax return.
    D. A power of attorney.

Legal Duties and Responsibilities

Common Law Duties and Liabilities to Clients and Third Parties

assess.AICPA.060649REG

57. An accounting firm was hired by a company to perform an audit. The company needed the audit report in order to obtain a loan from a bank. The bank lent $500,000 to the company based on the auditor's report. Fifteen months later, the company declared bankruptcy and was unable to repay the loan. The bank discovered that the accounting firm failed to discover a material overstatement of assets of the company.

    Which of the following statements is correct regarding a suit by the bank against the accounting firm? The bank

    A. Cannot sue the accounting firm because of the statute of limitations.
    B. Can sue the accounting firm for the loss of the loan because of negligence.
    C. Cannot sue the accounting firm because there was no privity of contact.
    D. Can sue the accounting firm for the loss of the loan because of the rule of privilege.

assess.AICPA.081909REG-1E1

58. CPA Fatjo agreed to prepare Tacko's individual tax return. However, two months before the return was due, Fatjo had the opportunity to take an around-the-world cruise with a rich uncle. Fatjo called up Tacko and said: "Keep your fee and find yourself another accountant. I'm going to cruise

the world." Tacko found another accountant who would prepare his tax return, but would charge $300 more than Fatjo. Tacko was extraordinarily upset that Fatjo intentionally breached a signed contract contained in their engagement letter and added a punitive damages claim for $5,000. Tacko sued Fatjo for breach of contract. Which of the following is true?

A. Tacko will probably lose.
B. Tacko will probably win $300.
C. Tacko will probably win $10,000.
D. Tacko will probably win $10,300.

assess.AICPA.081910REG-1E1

59. CPA Crane agreed to audit Banner Co. The audit did not go well, especially because Crane did not audit Banner's subsidiary, which created various problems for Banner. Banner sued Crane for breach of contract, because Crane allegedly did not comply with the engagement letter. Which of the following might Crane successfully raise in defense?

A. Evidence that Banner did not provide Crane with all the records needed to successfully complete the audit.
B. A provision in the engagement letter that provided that Crane would audit Banner, but not its subsidiaries.
C. A provision in the engagement letter that provided that Crane would not be liable for any errors it made in the audit.
D. A and B.

assess.AICPA.081911REG-1E1

60. Bosco Corporation had a very complicated tax situation. It hired CPA Arnold to prepare its corporate income tax return. Arnold made an error that caused Bosco to overpay its taxes by $3,000. The payment could have been avoided had Arnold advised Bosco to structure a particular transaction in a slightly different way. Bosco paid $233,000 rather than the $230,000 that it might have paid. Upset with Arnold's error, Bosco refused to pay the $20,000 fee specified in the engagement letter on grounds that Arnold had breached the contract by giving inaccurate advice. Which of the following is true regarding Arnold's fee?

A. Because he breached the contract by giving defective advice, Arnold cannot recover his fee.
B. Because he substantially performed the contract, Arnold will recover his fee minus the damages his breach caused Bosco ($20,000 – $3,000 = $17,000).
C. A and B.
D. None of the above.

assess.AICPA.081912REG-1E1

61. A CPA who has agreed to prepare a corporation's taxes and to provide tax advice will generally be liable for breaching:

A. Promises made in the written engagement letter.
B. Promises made orally.
C. A and B.
D. None of the above.

assess.AICPA.101158REG

62. A company engaged a CPA to perform the annual audit of its financial statements. The audit failed to reveal an embezzlement scheme by one of the employees. Which of the following statements best describes the CPA's potential liability for this failure?

A. The CPA's adherence to generally accepted auditing standards (GAAS) may prevent liability.
B. The CPA will not be liable if care and skill of an ordinary reasonable person was exercised.
C. The CPA may be liable for punitive damages if due care was not exercised.
D. The CPA is liable for any embezzlement losses that occurred before the scheme should have been detected.

assess.AICPA.101160REG

63. Under the position taken by a majority of the courts, to which third parties will an accountant who negligently prepares a client's financial report be liable?

A. Only those third parties in privity of contract with the accountant.
B. All third parties who relied on the report and sustained injury.
C. Any foreseen or known third party who relied on the report.
D. Any third party whose reliance on the report was reasonably foreseeable.

assess.AICPA.901105REG-BL

64. Mix and Associates, CPAs, issued an unqualified opinion on the financial statements of Glass Corp. for the year ended December 31, 2005. It was determined later that Glass's treasurer had embezzled $300,000 from Glass during 2005. Glass sued Mix because of Mix's failure to discover the embezzlement. Mix was unaware of the embezzlement.

Which of the following is Mix's best defense?

A. The audit was performed in accordance with GAAS.

B. The treasurer was Glass's agent and, therefore, Glass was responsible for preventing the embezzlement.

C. The financial statements were presented in conformity with GAAP.

D. Mix had no actual knowledge of the embezzlement.

assess.AICPA.911102REG-BL

65. When performing an audit, a CPA

A. Must exercise the level of care, skill, and judgment expected of a reasonably prudent CPA under the circumstances.

B. Must strictly adhere to generally accepted accounting principles.

C. Is strictly liable for failing to discover client fraud.

D. Is not liable unless the CPA commits gross negligence or intentionally disregards generally accepted auditing standards.

assess.AICPA.931104REG-BL.wpqti

66. While conducting an audit, Larson Associates, CPAs, failed to detect material misstatements included in its client's financial statements. Larson's unqualified opinion was included with the financial statements in a registration statement and prospectus for a public offering of securities made by the client. Larson knew that its opinion and the financial statements would be used for this purpose.

In a suit by a purchaser against Larson for common law negligence, Larson's best defense would be that the

A. Audit was conducted in accordance with generally accepted auditing standards.

B. Client was aware of the misstatements.

C. Purchaser was not in privity of contract with Larson.

D. Identity of the purchaser was not known to Larson at the time of the audit.

Privileged Communications, Confidentiality, and Privacy Acts

aicpa.aq.prvlg.comm.001_17

67. A husband prepared his own tax return as married filing separately. His wife hired a CPA to prepare her tax return as married filing separately and asked the CPA not to disclose the information to anyone. The CPA was not retained by the husband for any tax work. The husband believed that his wife's tax return was negligently prepared and that he was financially harmed. He hired an attorney, without his wife's consent, to pursue a negligence claim against

the CPA. The CPA hired an attorney to defend against the negligence claim. To which party, if any, may the CPA disclose the wife's tax return information without the wife's consent?

A. The husband, for the evaluation of the negligence claim

B. The CPA's attorney, for the evaluation of the negligence claim

C. The husband's attorney, for the evaluation of the negligence claim

D. No one, because all disclosures must be made with the wife's consent

assess.AICPA.101025REG-SIM

68. Salina wants to know which of the following recognizes an accountant-client testimonial privilege:

A. Federal courts creating procedural rules.

B. Congress for very limited purposes when tax practitioners are involved.

C. Approximately 15 state legislatures.

D. B and C.

assess.AICPA.101026REG-SIM

69. Girard gave tax advice to Frontenac Corporation. The Department of Justice and IRS are now investigating certain tax shelter transactions that Frontenac Corp. entered into. Girard is resisting their requests for information by citing the tax practitioner's privilege of §7525 of the I.R.C. To which of the following would that privilege be inapplicable?

A. Criminal proceedings.

B. Written advice in connection with promotion of a tax shelter.

C. A and B.

D. None of the above.

assess.AICPA.101027REG-SIM

70. Lakin is a CPA whose client, Sublette, is being sued by a state government in state court for evasion of state income taxes. Sublette does not want Lakin to testify against him regarding information that Sublette communicated to Lakin. Which of the following is true in a state with a statutory version of the accountant-client testimonial privilege?

A. Only Lakin can invoke the testimonial privilege.

B. Sublette can invoke the privilege as to parts of the communications he had with Lakin, while asking Lakin to testify as to other parts.

C. If the suit was in federal court, the state privilege would not apply even though the communication took place in the state.

D. A and B.

assess.AICPA.101043REG-SIM

71. Which of the following are recognized exceptions that allow disclosure of confidential information?

    A. An enforceable subpoena has been served on the CPA.

    B. An ethical examination is being conducted regarding the CPA's conduct.

    C. A peer review is occurring.

    D. All of the above.

assess.AICPA.101044REG-SIM

72. Trego is a CPA. Under which of the following circumstances would it be permissible for Trego to share confidential client information?

    A. He has been hospitalized on April 14 and needs to share information with his partner, Tandy, who will complete a client's tax return before the April 15 deadline.

    B. A client has filed a complaint with the State Board of Accountancy about Trego's work, and he needs to show the Board confidential information to prove that he acted professionally throughout the engagement.

    C. None of the above.

    D. A and B.

assess.AICPA.101045REG-SIM

73. Powhattan was surprised to learn how much income his tax client, Absurdco, Inc., was making. He thought that Absurdco's competitors might be interested in the information, so he sold it to one of them. When Absurdco found this out, it started investigating what consequences it might visit upon Powhattan. Which of the following is true?

    A. Powhattan may lose his CPA license.

    B. Powhattan may be sued civilly by the IRS.

    C. Powhattan may be prosecuted criminally by the Department of Justice.

    D. All of the above.

assess.AICPA.101046REG-SIM

74. Colby is the managing partner of a small accounting firm. He has heard of the Generally Accepted Privacy Principles (GAPP) and wants to know what his responsibilities are regarding client information. Among others, Colby's firm must:

    A. Provide its clients notice of its privacy policies and procedures.

    B. Collect information only in compliance with its policies and procedures.

    C. Provide clients with access to their personal information for review and update.

    D. All of the above.

assess.AICPA.101047REG-SIM

75. Jetmore was surprised to learn how much income his tax client, Quantilco, Inc., was making. He thought that Quantilco's competitors might be interested in the information, so he sold it to one of them. When Quantilco found this out, it started investigating what consequences it might visit upon Jetmore. Which of the following is true?

    A. He may be sued civilly by the IRS.

    B. He may be prosecuted criminally by the Department of Justice.

    C. A and B.

    D. None of the above.

assess.AICPA.101095REG

76. In which of the following situations is there a violation of client confidentiality under the AICPA Code of Professional Conduct?

    A. A member discloses confidential client information to a court in connection with arbitration proceedings relating to the client.

    B. A member discloses confidential client information to a professional liability insurance carrier after learning of a potential claim against the member.

    C. A member whose practice is primarily bankruptcy discloses a client's name.

    D. A member uses a records retention agency to store clients' records that contain confidential client information.

assess.AICPA.101097REG

77. Which of the following is a correct statement about the circumstances under which a CPA firm may or may **not** disclose the names of its clients without the clients' express permission?

    A. A CPA firm may disclose this information if the practice is limited to bankruptcy matters, so that prospective clients with similar concerns will be able to contact current clients.

    B. A CPA firm may disclose this information if the practice is limited to performing asset valuations in anticipation of mergers and acquisitions.

    C. A CPA firm may disclose this information **unless** disclosure would suggest that the client may be experiencing financial difficulties.

    D. A CPA firm may **not** disclose this information because the identity of its clients is confidential information.

Business Law

Contracts

Introduction and Classification

Applicable Laws

aq.app.laws.001_2017

78. On March 13, Ike contracted with Turner for Turner to perform in Ike's club, exclusively, for four weeks beginning June 2 for $10,000 per week. Which of the following statements is correct?

    A. The contract is governed by the UCC.
    B. The contract is governed by common law.
    C. Turner's services are governed by common law, and the payment is governed by the UCC.
    D. Because the contract does not begin immediately, it is governed by the UCC.

aq.app.laws.002_2017

79. Janice Gwinn is having an in-floor vacuum system put in her new home. The cost of the components for the system and installation is $22,000. She has signed a contract with Jill's Permanent Vacuum Systems for that amount with installation to be completed as the phases of construction of the home proceed and allow. Which of the following statements is correct about this contract?

    A. Because the contract is one for the purchase of a vacuum, it is the sale of a good and is governed by the UCC.
    B. Because the contract involves real estate, it is governed by common law.
    C. Because the contract is a sale by a merchant, it is governed by the UCC.
    D. Because the contract is one predominantly for installation, it is governed by common law.

aq.app.laws.003_2017

80. Gwyneth's grandmother asks Gwyneth to come to her house on Tuesday evening for a visit and promised that Gwyneth would be glad that she came. Gwyneth did go to her grandmother's house on Tuesday evening, but she arrived late. Gwyneth's grandmother said, "Well, I was going to give you my car since I can't drive anymore, but since you cannot even show up on time, I have changed my mind."

Which of the following statements is correct?

A. There is no contract between Gwyneth and her grandmother for the car.
B. There is a contract between Gwyneth and her grandmother, and it is governed by the UCC.
C. There was a contract, but Gwyneth did not perform properly, so the grandmother can refuse to honor the contract.
D. The contract is for Gwyneth's services in coming over and is governed by common law.

Types of Contracts

aq.type.contract.003_0718

81. Jeff Rosenstein had an oral contract with Jennifer Howard to install new landscape lighting at Jennifer's home. Jennifer paid Jeff a $4,500 deposit on the $9,000 contract. Jeff dug trenches for the lighting wires and then abandoned the project. Which of the following statements is correct?

    A. The contract is partially executed on Jeff's part and executed on Jennifer's part.
    B. The contract is partially executed on both sides.
    C. The contract is governed by the UCC because it involves the sale of lights.
    D. The contract is neither partially executed nor executed.

assess.AICPA.082067REG-I.A_2-18

82. Mary offers to buy Hal's desktop computer for $400. Hal sends Mary an e-mail of acceptance. The $400 is to be paid upon Hal's delivery of the computer. Which of the following properly classifies this contract?

    A. This is a bilateral, valid, executory contract.
    B. This is a bilateral, valid, executed contract.
    C. This is a unilateral, express, executory contract.
    D. This is a unilateral, implied-in-fact, executed contract.

assess.AICPA.111181REG_2-18

83. The text of the letter from Bridge Builders, Inc. to Allied Steel Co. is as follows:

> We offer to purchase 10,000 tons of No. 4 steel pipe at today's quoted price for delivery two months from today. Your acceptance must be received in five days.

> Bridge Builders intended to create a (an)

A. Option contract.
B. Unilateral contract.
C. Bilateral contract.
D. Joint contract.

assess.AICPA.910516REG-BL_2-18

84. Kay, an art collector, promised Hammer, an art student, that if Hammer could obtain certain rare artifacts within two weeks, Kay would pay for Hammer's postgraduate education. At considerable effort and expense, Hammer obtained the specified artifacts within the two-week period. When Hammer requested payment, Kay refused. Kay claimed there was no consideration for the promise. Hammer would prevail against Kay based on

A. Unilateral contract.
B. Unjust enrichment.
C. Public policy.
D. Quasi contract.

Formation

Offer and Acceptance

aq.form.off.acc.001_2017

85. Barron offers in writing to sell her 13,000‡acre cattle ranch to Reese for $5 million, the offer to remain open until March 15. On March 1, Goad offers Barron $5.8 million for the ranch. Reese hears of this offer on March 11 and faxes his unqualified acceptance of Barron's offer. Barron's offer to Reese

A. Is revoked if Reese, before accepting, learned that Barron has sold the ranch to Goad.
B. Can be withdrawn any time prior to March 15.
C. May be withdrawn only in writing.
D. Cannot be withdrawn since it is a firm offer involving the sale of land.

aq.form.off.acc.002_2017

86. Which is correct?

	Acceptances must be communicated in the same manner as offers.	Revocation of an acceptancer equires consideration.
A.	No	No
B.	No	Yes
C.	Yes	No
D.	Yes	Yes

assess.AICPA.921111REG-BL

87. On February 12, Harris sent Fresno a written offer to purchase Fresno's land. The offer included the following provision: "Acceptance of this offer must be by registered or certified mail, received by Harris no later than February 18 by 5:00 p.m. CST." On February 18, Fresno sent Harris a letter accepting the offer by private overnight delivery service. Harris received the letter on February 19.

Which of the following statements is correct?

A. A contract was formed on February 19.
B. Fresno's letter constituted a counteroffer.
C. Fresno's use of the overnight delivery service was an effective form of acceptance.
D. A contract was formed on February 18 regardless of when Harris actually received Fresno's letter.

Consideration

aq.consideration.001_2017

88. Explain what consideration is and why it is a requirement for a valid contract. Prince hired Jank to remove asbestos from a warehouse that Prince was expanding. The written contract provided a fee of $3,500 payable to Jank upon "completion as certified by the architect." Jank had estimated that the project would take three weeks. Jank was not aware that the state required special breathing gear, which was more costly than that mandated by local building authorities. Because of this, Jank incurred unforeseen costs of $575. Jank

A. Must perform for the agreed price.
B. Can reform the contract under the UCC.
C. Can void the contract because of the price increase.
D. Can demand the additional $575 be paid by Prince.

assess.AICPA.901121REG-BL

89. Which of the following requires consideration to be binding on the parties?

    A. Material modification of a contract involving the sale of real estate.
    B. Ratification of a contract by a person after reaching the age of majority.
    C. A written promise signed by a merchant to keep an offer to sell goods open for 10 days.
    D. Material modification of a sale of goods contract under the UCC.

assess.AICPA.REG.consideration-0036

90. Kelly owed Connor $500. Connor agreed to accept Kelly's microwave oven instead of the money. Kelly immediately delivered the oven to Connor. Which of the following terms correctly describes this agreement?

    A. Mutual rescission
    B. Accord and satisfaction
    C. Novation
    D. Material alteration

Writing and Records: The Statute of Frauds

aicpa.aq.stat.frad.rec.002_17

91. Which of the following statements is correct regarding the parol evidence rule?

    A. It applies only in cases involving an oral contract.
    B. It applies only to subsequent written modifications to a written contract.
    C. It applies to subsequent oral agreements that contradict the terms of a final written agreement.
    D. It applies to prior or contemporaneous oral agreements that contradict the terms of final written agreements.

aq.stat.frad.rec.001_2017

92. Tate signs an all-inclusive written agreement whereby he undertakes to "fully refurbish Bond's 1981 Porsche 911." Tate later asserts that the contract did not include rechroming any of the chrome parts. Bond wishes to introduce evidence that rechroming is part of the agreement. Which of the following will not be permitted as evidence under the parol evidence rule?

    A. All of these forms of evidence would be admissible.
    B. A piece of paper in which Tate, just prior to signing the contract, illustrated which Porsche parts needed chrome plating.

C. A telephone call from Tate to Bond, after work had begun, requesting more money "since chrome plating has gone way up in price".
D. Testimony of an industry expert that the term "fully refurbish" generally includes chrome plating as needed.

assess.AICPA.050903-REG

93. Kram sent Fargo, a real estate broker, a signed offer to sell a specific parcel of land to Fargo for $250,000. Kram, an engineer, had inherited the land. On the same day that Kram's letter was received, Fargo telephoned Kram and accepted the offer. Which of the following statements is correct under the common law Statute of Frauds?

    A. No contract could be formed because Fargo's acceptance was oral.
    B. No contract could be formed because Kram's letter was signed only by Kram.
    C. A contract was formed and would be enforceable against both Kram and Fargo.
    D. A contract was formed but would be enforceable only against Kram.

Defenses to Formation

aq.def.form.001_2017

94. Fritz, a minor who actually appeared to be in his early 20s, purchased from Mills a used Jet Ski for $2,750 in cash. Fritz ran the Jet Ski aground the first week he used it, causing it considerable damage. Fritz

    A. Can return the Jet Ski to Mills, without repairs, for a full refund.
    B. Can return the Jet Ski to Mills for a partial refund only.
    C. Can return the Jet Ski to Mills for a full refund if he first has it repaired.
    D. Cannot cancel his contract with Mills.

assess.AICPA.050905-REG

95. On May 25, Fresno sold Bronson, a minor, a used computer. On June 1, Bronson reached the age of majority. On June 10, Fresno wanted to rescind the sale. Fresno offered to return Bronson's money and demanded that Bronson return the computer. Bronson refused, claiming that a binding contract existed. Bronson's refusal is:

    A. Not justified because Fresno is not bound by the contract unless Bronson specifically ratifies the contract after reaching the age of majority.

B. Not justified, because Fresno does not have to perform under the contract if Bronson has a right to disaffirm the contract.

C. Justified, because Bronson and Fresno are bound by the contract as of the date Bronson reached the age of majority.

D. Justified, because Fresno must perform under the contract regardless of Bronson's minority.

assess.AICPA.130707REG

96. What type of conduct generally will make a contract voidable?

A. Fraud in the execution.
B. Fraud in the inducement.
C. Physical coercion.
D. Contracting with a person under guardianship.

Performance

Defining Performance and Breach

assess.AICPA.921119REG-BL

97. The statute of limitations for an alleged breach of contract

A. Does not apply if the contract was oral.
B. Requires that a lawsuit is commenced and a judgment rendered within a prescribed period of time.
C. Is determined on a case by case basis.
D. Generally commences on the date of the breach.

assess.AICPA.921125REG-BL

98. On June 15, 2004, Alpha, Inc., contracted with Delta Manufacturing, Inc., to buy a vacant parcel of land Delta owned. Alpha intended to build a distribution warehouse on the land because of its location near a major highway. The contract stated that: "Alpha's obligations hereunder are subject to the vacant parcel being rezoned to a commercial zoning classification by July 31, 2005." Which of the following statements is correct?

A. If the parcel is not rezoned by July 31, and Alpha refuses to purchase it, Alpha would not be in breach of contract.

B. If the parcel is rezoned by July 31, and Alpha refuses to purchase it, Delta would be able to successfully sue Alpha for specific performance.

C. The contract is not binding on either party because Alpha's performance is conditional.

D. If the parcel is rezoned by July 31, and Delta refuses to sell it, Delta's breach would not discharge Alpha's obligation to tender payment.

assess.AICPA.931122REG-BL

99. Teller brought a lawsuit against Kerr ten years after an oral contract was made and eight years after it was breached. Kerr raised the statute of limitations as a defense.

Which of the following allegations would be most important to Kerr's defense?

A. The contract was oral.
B. The contract could not be performed within one year from the date made.
C. The action was not timely brought because the contract was entered into ten years prior to the commencement of the lawsuit.
D. The action was not timely brought because the contract was allegedly breached eight years prior to the commencement of the lawsuit.

assess.AICPA.950525REG-BL

100. Ordinarily, in an action for breach of a construction contract, the statute of limitations time period would be computed from the date the

A. Contract is negotiated.
B. Contract is breached.
C. Construction is begun.
D. Contract is signed.

Discharge of Performance

aq.discharg.perf.003_2017

101. Which of the following statements correctly applies to a typical statute of limitations?

A. The statute requires that a legal action for breach of contract be commenced within a certain period of time after the breach occurs.
B. Must have signed the contract.
C. The statute limits the right of a party to recover damages for misrepresentation unless the false statements were intentionally made.
D. The statute prohibits the admission into evidence of proof of oral statements about the meaning of a written contract.

assess.AICPA.911125REG-BL

102. On May 25, 20x5, Smith contracted with Jackson to repair Smith's cabin cruiser. The

work was to begin on May 31, 20x5. On May 26, 20x5, the boat, while docked at Smith's pier, was destroyed by arson. Which of the following statements is correct with regard to the contract?

A. Smith would not be liable to Jackson because of mutual mistake.
B. Smith would be liable to Jackson for the profit Jackson would have made under the contract.
C. Jackson would not be liable to Smith because performance by the parties would be impossible.
D. Jackson would be liable to repair another boat owned by Smith.

assess.AICPA.950523REG-BL

103. Which of the following actions could result in the discharge of a party to a contract?

	Prevention of performance	Accord and satisfaction
A.	Yes	Yes
B.	Yes	No
C.	No	Yes
D.	No	No

assess.AICPA.950524REG-BL

104. Under a personal services contract, which of the following circumstances will cause the discharge of a party's duties?

A. Death of the party who is to receive the services.
B. Cost of performing the services has doubled.
C. Bankruptcy of the party who is to receive the services.
D. Illegality of the services to be performed.

Issues of Passage of Title and Risk of Loss

assess.AICPA.020516REG-BL

105. Under the Sales Article of the UCC, which of the following statements is correct regarding a seller's obligation under a F.O.B. destination contract?

A. The seller is required to arrange for the buyer to pick up the conforming goods at a specified destination.
B. The seller is required to tender delivery of conforming goods at a specified destination.
C. The seller is required to tender delivery of conforming goods at the buyer's place of business.

D. The seller is required to tender delivery of conforming goods to a carrier who delivers to a destination specified by the buyer.

assess.AICPA.120612REG

106. When do title and risk of loss for conforming goods pass to the buyer under a shipment contract covered by the Sales Article of the UCC?

A. When the goods are identified and designated for shipment.
B. When the goods are given to a common carrier.
C. When the goods arrive at their destination.
D. When the goods are tendered to the buyer at their destination.

assess.AICPA.990515REG-BL

107. Under the Sales Article of the UCC, when a contract for the sale of goods stipulates that the seller ship the goods by common carrier "F.O.B. purchaser's loading dock," which of the parties bears the risk of loss during shipment?

A. The purchaser, because risk of loss passes when the goods are delivered to the carrier.
B. The purchaser, because risk of loss passes with the title.
C. The seller, because risk of loss passes only when the goods reach the purchaser's loading dock.
D. The seller, because risk of loss remains with the seller until the goods are accepted by the purchaser.

Remedies

Types of Remedies

aq.types.remedies.001_2-18

108. Carson agreed orally to repair Ives's rare book for $450. Before the work was started, Ives asked Carson to perform additional repairs to the book and agreed to increase the contract price to $650. After Carson completed the work, Ives refused to pay and Carson sued. Ives's defense was based on the Statute of Frauds. What total amount will Carson recover?

A. $650
B. $0
C. $200
D. $450

aq.types.remedies.005_2-18

109. Jane hired Delta to cut and remove nine trees from Jane's lot for $1,000. Delta cut all of the trees but only removed about half of the debris. Will Jane be successful if she asks a court to force Delta to finish removing the debris since Jane has already paid Delta the $1,000?

   A. Jane cannot force Delta to remove the debris.
   B. Jane is entitled to a refund of her $1,000.
   C. Jane is entitled to specific performance for removal of the debris.
   D. Jane is entitled to a refund of her $1,000 and specific performance for removal of the debris.

testbank.CONT-0102

110. For which of the following contracts will a court generally grant the remedy of specific performance?

   A. A contract for the sale of a patent.
   B. A contract of employment.
   C. A contract for the sale of fungible goods.
   D. A contract for the sale of stock that is traded on a national stock exchange.

Formulas for Damages

aicpa.aq.form.damage.001_2-18

111. Dunlap contracted to work exclusively for Foster during June for $5,000. On May 31, Foster canceled the contract. Dunlap found another job during June for $3,000. Dunlap filed suit against Foster for breach of contract. Dunlap should recover what amount of compensatory damages?

   A. $8,000
   B. $5,000
   C. $3,000
   D. $2,000

aq.form.damages.002_2-18

112. Myers entered into a contract to purchase a valuable rare coin from Eisen. Myers tendered payment which was refused by Eisen. Upon Eisen's breach, Myers brought suit to obtain the coin. The court will grant Myers

   A. Compensatory damages.
   B. Specific performance.
   C. Reformation.
   D. Restitution. This remedy will restore the funds expended but not the true value and is insufficient.

aq.form.damages.003_2-18

113. Under the UCC Sales Article, which of the following legal remedies would a buyer not have when a seller fails to transfer and deliver goods identified to the contract?

   A. Suit for specific performance.
   B. Suit for punitive damages.
   C. Purchase substitute goods (cover).
   D. Recover the identified goods (replevin).

supplemental.SALE-0024B_2-18

114. Under the Sales Article of the UCC, which of the following rights is (are) available to the buyer when a seller commits an anticipatory breach of contract?

	Recover damages	Cancel the contract	Collect punitive damages
A.	Yes	Yes	Yes
B.	Yes	Yes	No
C.	Yes	No	Yes
D.	No	Yes	Yes

Third-Party Rights

assess.AICPA.050906-REG

115. West, Inc., and Barton entered into a contract. After receiving valuable consideration from Egan, West assigned its rights under the Barton contract to Egan. In which of the following circumstances would West not be liable to Egan?

   A. West released Barton.
   B. West breached the contract.
   C. Egan released Barton.
   D. Barton paid West.

assess.AICPA.950522REG-BL

116. One of the criteria for a valid assignment of a sales contract to a third party is that the assignment must

   A. Be supported by adequate consideration from the assignee.
   B. Be in writing and signed by the assignor.
   C. Not materially increase the other party's risk or duty.
   D. Not be revocable by the assignor.

assess.AICPA.REG.part.rights-0002

117. Under which of the following circumstances would an assignment of rights under a contract be invalid?

   A. The assignment was made without notice to the obligor.
   B. The assignment was made without the assignor's intent to transfer.
   C. The assignment was made without delivery of an evidentiary document.
   D. The assignment was made without notice to the assignee.

assess.AICPA.REG.part.rights-0005

118. Contracts to purchase which of the following cannot be assigned without consent of the other party to the contract?

   A. Vehicles
   B. Real estate
   C. Businesses
   D. Personal services

Agency

Types of Agency Relationships and Creation

aq.types.agency.001_2017

119. A principal and agent relationship requires a

   A. Meeting of the minds and consent to act.
   B. Written agreement.
   C. Power of attorney.
   D. Specified consideration.

aq.types.agency.002_2017

120. Which of the following actions requires an agent for a corporation to have a written agency agreement?

   A. Purchasing an interest in undeveloped land for the principal
   B. Purchasing office supplies for the principal's business
   C. Hiring an independent general contractor to renovate the principal's office building
   D. Retaining an attorney to collect a business debt owed the principal

aq.types.agency.003_2017

121. Noll gives Carr a written power of attorney. Which of the following statements is correct regarding this power of attorney?

   A. It may limit Carr's authority to specific transactions.
   B. It may continue in existence after Noll's death.
   C. It must be signed by both Noll and Carr.
   D. It must be for a definite period of time.

assess.AICPA.101007REG-SIM

122. Which of the following would **not** have capacity to create an agency relationship?

   A. An unincorporated association
   B. A corporation
   C. An individual
   D. A government agency

assess.AICPA.101100REG

123. Which of the following terms best describes the relationship between a corporation and the CPA it hires to audit corporate books?

   A. Employer and employee
   B. Employer and independent contractor
   C. Master and servant
   D. Employer and principal

assess.AICPA.130710REG

124. Which of the following conditions must be met to form an agency?

   A. An agency agreement must be in writing.
   B. An agency agreement must be signed by both parties.
   C. The principal must furnish legally adequate consideration for the agent's services.
   D. The principal must possess contractual capacity.

Duties of Agents and Principals

aq.duties.agents.001_2-18

125. Ozgood is a principal and Flood is his agent. Ozgood is totally dissatisfied with the agency relationship and wishes to terminate it. In which of the following situations does Ozgood not have the power to terminate the relationship?

   A. Ozgood and Flood have agreed that their agency is irrevocable.
   B. Flood has been appointed as Ozgood's agent pursuant to a power of attorney.
   C. Flood is an agent coupled with an interest.
   D. The agency agreement is in writing and provides for a specific duration, which has not elapsed.

aq.types.agency.004_2017

126. Thorp was a purchasing agent for Ogden, a sole proprietor, and had express authority to place purchase orders with Ogden's suppliers. Thorp placed an order with Datz, Inc. on Ogden's behalf after Ogden was declared incompetent in a judicial proceeding. Thorp was aware of Ogden's incapacity. Which of the following statements is correct concerning Ogden's liability to Datz?

   A. Ogden will not be liable because Thorp's agency ended when Ogden was declared incompetent.
   B. Ogden will be liable because Datz was not informed of Ogden's incapacity.
   C. Ogden will be liable because Thorp acted with express authority.
   D. Ogden will not be liable because Ogden was a nondisclosed principal.

assess.AICPA.051148REG

127. Under the agent's duty to account, which of the following acts must a gratuitous agent perform?

	Commingle funds	Account for the principal's property
A.	Yes	Yes
B.	Yes	No
C.	No	Yes
D.	No	No

assess.AICPA.081939REG-2A.2

128. The Silvas wish to sell their house and they talk to Bisbee, a real estate agent. Bisbee convinces the Silvas to form a joint venture with him. He would take responsibility for selling the property in exchange for 10% of the proceeds. The Silvas want at least $80,000. Bisbee tells the Silvas that he has sold the property for $100,000 and delivers to them a check for $90,000. The Silvas are pleased until they learn that Bisbee was an owner of the corporation that bought the property and that Bisbee thought it was worth more than $100,000. The Silvas wish to sue Bisbee. Which of the following is true?

   A. Since the Silvas got more than they were expecting, they have no valid lawsuit.
   B. Because Bisbee had an undisclosed conflict of interest, the Silvas can win.
   C. A and B.
   D. None of the above.

assess.AICPA.REG.duties.agents-0037

129. Baker sold an automobile to Bob's Old Autos, where Fuller is a manager. Fuller took $100 from Baker for encouraging the sale. What duty to Bob's Old Autos did Fuller violate?

   A. Reasonable care.
   B. Reimbursement.
   C. Obedience.
   D. Loyalty.

Contract Liability of Agents and Principals

aq.contract.liab.005_0818

130. Rod Rosen was hired by Andrea Albemarle (a famous actress) to find her a house in the Brentwood area of Los Angeles. Andrea instructed Rod to not disclose her name or that he was working for someone else to make the purchase. Rod was able to find a house that Andrea approved, and Rod signed a contract to purchase the home for $4.7 million. Andrea experienced some setbacks in her career and lost two movies contracts. Andrea refused to close on the house. The seller has brought suit against Rod for breach of contract.

   A. Only Rod's name is on the contract, not Andrea's, so he is liable, and the introduction of Andrea's relationship with Rod would violate the parol evidence rule.
   B. Only Rod is liable to the seller because he withheld information from the seller in entering into the contract.
   C. Both Rod and Andrea are liable to the seller for breach of contract.
   D. Rod has committed fraud, and he is liable for the fraud, not Andrea.

aq.contract.liab.002_2-18

131. Jason Manufacturing Company wished to acquire a site for a warehouse. Knowing that if it negotiated directly for the purchase of the property, the price would be substantially increased, it employed Kent, an agent, to secure lots without disclosing that he was acting for Jason. Kent's authority was evidenced by a writing signed by the proper officers of Jason. Kent entered into a contract in his own name to purchase Peter's lot, giving Peter a negotiable note for $1,000 signed by Kent as first payment. Jason wrote Kent acknowledging the purchase.

Jason also disclosed his identity as Kent's principal to Peter. In respect to the rights and liabilities of the parties, which of the following is a correct statement?

A. Peter is not bound on the contract since Kent's failure to disclose he was Jason's agent was fraudulent.
B. Jason, Kent, and Peter are potentially liable on the contract.
C. Unless Peter formally ratifies the substitution of Jason for Kent, he is not liable.
D. Kent has no liability since he was acting for and on behalf of an existing principal.

aq.contract.liab.003_2-18

132. Magnus Real Estate Developers Inc. wanted to acquire certain tracts of land in Marshall Township in order to build a shopping center complex. To accomplish this goal, Magnus engaged Dexter, a sophisticated real estate dealer, to represent them in the purchase of the necessary land without revealing the existence of the agency. Dexter began to slowly but steadily acquire the requisite land. Which of the following is correct under these circumstances?

A. The use of an agent by Magnus, an undisclosed principal, is manifestly illegal.
B. Either Magnus or Dexter may be held liable on the contracts for the land.
C. An undisclosed principal such as Magnus can have no liability under the contract since the third party believed he was dealing with Dexter as a principal.
D. An agent for an undisclosed principal assumes no liability as long as he registers his relationship to the principal with the clerk of the proper county having jurisdiction.

assess.AICPA.051141REG

133. Food Corp. owns a restaurant called The Ambers. The corporation president, T.J. Jones, hires a contractor to make repairs at the restaurant, signing the contract "T.J. Jones for The Ambers." Two invoices for restaurant repairs were paid by Food Corp. with corporate checks. Upon presenting the final invoice, the contractor was told that it would not be paid. The contractor sued Food Corp. Which of the following statements is correct regarding the liability of Food Corp.?

A. It is not liable, because Jones is liable.
B. It is not liable, because the corporation was an undisclosed principal.

C. It is liable, because Jones is not liable.
D. It is liable, because Jones had authority to make the contract.

Tort Liability of Agents and Principals

assess.AICPA.081942REG-2A.3

134. Baker (P) leaves her two-month-old daughter, Summer, at the Ave Maria Child Care Center (D). Because Summer will not stop crying, one of D's employees, Davis, hits Summer's head against the corner of a shelf, causing major brain injury. Davis later pleads guilty to injury to a child and goes to jail. P sues D for Davis's tort. Which of the following is true?

A. A principal is never liable for an agent's intentional tort.
B. D is not liable, because Davis was not acting within the scope of employment—she was hired to help children, not to injure them.
C. P will probably recover.
D. Because Davis is only an employee, she cannot be liable.

assess.AICPA.101011REG-SIM

135. Your client, Sanitary Dairies, Inc., employs Harold Stone as a milk-truck driver. Stone negligently runs the truck into the car of Ronald Green, injuring Green, his wife, and damaging Green's car. Stone is also injured in the collision. Which of the following is correct?

A. If Stone had never had a previous accident, Sanitary Dairies would not be liable.
B. Stone can avoid liability, because he was engaged in the performance of his principal's business.
C. If Green is shown to have been contributorily negligent, he cannot recover for his injuries, or for the damage to the car.
D. Stone is not entitled to receive worker's compensation.

assess.AICPA.931113REG-BL

136. Generally, a disclosed principal will be liable to third parties for its agent's unauthorized misrepresentations, if the agent is an

	Employee	Independent Contractor
A.	Yes	Yes
B.	Yes	No
C.	No	Yes
D.	No	No

Debtor-Creditor Relationships

Rights, Duties, and Liabilities of Debtors, Creditors, Sureties, and Guarantors

Suretyship—Introduction, Creation, and Types

assess.AICPA.090593REG-II-C-1

137. Camp orally guaranteed payment of a loan Camp's cousin Wilcox had obtained from Camp's friend Main. The loan was to be repaid in 10 monthly payments. After making 6 payments, Wilcox defaulted on the loan and Main demanded that Camp honor the guarantee. Regarding Camp's liability to Main, Camp is

   A. Liable under the oral surety agreement because the loan would be paid within one year.

   B. Liable under the oral surety agreement because Camp benefited by maintaining a personal relationship with Main.

   C. Not liable under the oral surety agreement because Camp's surety agreement must be in writing to be enforceable.

   D. Not liable under the oral surety agreement because of failure of consideration.

assess.AICPA.910526REG-BL

138. Edwards Corp. lent Lark $200,000. At Edwards's request, Lark entered into an agreement with Owen and Ward for them to act as compensated co-sureties on the loan in the amount of $200,000 each.

If Edwards releases Ward without Owen's or Lark's consent, and Lark later defaults, which of the following statements is correct?

   A. Lark will be released for 50% of the loan balance.

   B. Owen will be liable for the entire loan balance.

   C. Owen will be liable for 50% of the loan balance.

   D. Edwards's release of Ward will have no effect on Lark's and Owen's liability to Edwards.

assess.AICPA.931125REG-BL

139. Nash, Owen, and Polk are co-sureties with maximum liabilities of $40,000, $60,000, and $80,000, respectively. The amount of the loan on which they have agreed to act as co-sureties is $180,000. The debtor defaulted at a time when the loan balance was $180,000. Nash paid the lender $36,000 in full settlement of all claims against Nash, Owen, and Polk.

The total amount that Nash may recover from Owen and Polk is

   A. $0

   B. $24,000

   C. $28,000

   D. $140,000

Suretyship—Rights of Parties

assess.AICPA.941131REG-BL

140. Ingot Corp. lent Flange $50,000. At Ingot's request, Flange entered into an agreement with Quill and West for them to act as compensated co-sureties on the loan in the amount of $100,000 each. Ingot released West without Quill's or Flange's consent, and Flange later defaulted on the loan.

Which of the following statements is correct?

   A. Quill will be liable for 50% of the loan balance.

   B. Quill will be liable for the entire loan balance.

   C. Ingot's release of West will have no effect on Flange's and Quill's liability to Ingot.

   D. Flange will be released for 50% of the loan balance.

assess.AICPA.950526REG-BL

141. Green was unable to repay a loan from State Bank when due.

State refused to renew the loan unless Green provided an acceptable surety. Green asked Royal, a friend, to act as surety on the loan. To induce Royal to agree to become a surety, Green fraudulently represented Green's financial condition and promised Royal discounts on merchandise sold at Green's store. Royal agreed to act as surety and the loan was renewed. Later, Green's obligation to State was discharged in Green's bankruptcy. State wants to hold Royal liable.

Royal may avoid liability

   A. If Royal can show that State was aware of the fraudulent representations.

   B. If Royal was an uncompensated surety.

   C. Because the discharge in bankruptcy will prevent Royal from having a right of reimbursement.

   D. Because the arrangement was void at the inception.

assess.AICPA.950527REG-BL

142. Wright cosigned King's loan from Ace Bank. Which of the following events would release Wright from the obligation to pay the loan?

   A. Ace seeking payment of the loan only from Wright.
   B. King is granted a discharge in bankruptcy.
   C. Ace is paid in full by King's spouse.
   D. King is adjudicated mentally incompetent.

assess.AICPA.951129REG-BL

143. Which of the following acts will always result in the total release of a compensated surety?

   A. The creditor changes the manner of the principal debtor's payment.
   B. The creditor extends the principal debtor's time to pay.
   C. The principal debtor's obligation is partially released.
   D. The principal debtor's performance is tendered.

Article 9—UCC Secured Transactions

Introduction and Creation of Security Interests

assess.AICPA.090595REG_2-18

144. Under the Secured Transactions Article of the UCC, all of the following are needed to create enforceable security interest except

   A. A security agreement must exist.
   B. The secured party must give value.
   C. The debtor must have rights in the collateral.
   D. A financing statement must be filed.

assess.AICPA.101170REG_2-18

145. Under the Secured Transactions Article of the UCC, which of the following statements is correct regarding a security interest that has not attached?

   A. It is effective against the debtor, but not against third parties.
   B. It is effective against both the debtor and third parties.
   C. It is effective against third parties with unsecured claims.
   D. It is not effective against either the debtor or third parties.

assess.AICPA.120613REG_2-18

146. Under the Secured Transactions article of the UCC, when does a security interest become enforceable?

   A. A contract is executed between a debtor and a secured party under which the debtor gives the secured party rights in collateral if the debtor violates any of the terms contained in the contract.
   B. The debtor and the secured party execute a security agreement describing the transfer of the collateral and, after doing so, the secured party files it with the requisite agency.
   C. The debtor and the secured party execute a security agreement describing the transfer of collateral from seller to buyer and the secured party retains possession of the agreement.
   D. The value has been given, the secured party receives a security agreement describing the collateral authenticated by the debtor, and the debtor has rights in the collateral.

Perfection of Security Interests

assess.AICPA.071203REG-BL

147. Jones lives in Oklahoma and is the owner of a large number of valuable antiques. Treasures Delight, located in Arkansas, is a seller of antiques. Treasures Delight is owned by Sally Delight. Delight offers to purchase all of the antiques owned by Jones paying 60% of the agreed price and, by agreement, signs a security agreement for the balance putting up her entire inventory as security. The security agreement provides for monthly payments. Which of the following is correct?

   A. Since this is a purchase money security interest, Jones is automatically perfected without a filing.
   B. Although this is a purchase money security interest, Jones must file to have a perfected security interest.
   C. There is not a purchase money security interest because being antiques for resell classifies the collateral as inventory.
   D. If Jones decides to file for perfection of his security interest, Jones would file a financing statement in Oklahoma.

assess.AICPA.120609REG

148. Under the Secured Transactions Article of the UCC, which of the following items can usually be *excluded* from a filed original financing statement?

   A. The name of the debtor.
   B. The address of the debtor.
   C. A description of the collateral.
   D. The amount of the obligation secured.

assess.AICPA.931159REG-BL

149. Grey Corp. sells computers to the public. Grey sold and delivered a computer to West on credit. West executed and delivered to Grey a promissory note for the purchase price and a security agreement covering the computer. West purchased the computer for personal use. Grey did not file a financing statement.

    Is Grey's security interest perfected?

    A. Yes, because Grey retained ownership of the computer.
    B. Yes, because it was perfected at the time of attachment.
    C. No, because the computer was a consumer good.
    D. No, because Grey failed to file a financing statement.

assess.AICPA071204REG-BL

150. Which of the following requires a filing for perfection?

    A. A purchase money security interest in consumer goods.
    B. A purchase money security interest in equipment.
    C. A security interest in negotiable promissory notes.
    D. None of the above.

Priorities in Security Interests

assess.AICPA.921149REG-BL

151. On July 8, Ace, a refrigerator wholesaler, purchased 50 refrigerators. This comprised Ace's entire inventory and was financed under an agreement with Rome Bank that gave Rome a security interest in all refrigerators on Ace's premises, all future acquired refrigerators, and the proceeds of sales. On July 12, Rome filed a financing statement that adequately identified the collateral. On August 15, Ace sold one refrigerator to Cray for personal use and four refrigerators to Zone Co. for its business.

    Which of the following statements is correct?

    A. The refrigerators sold to Zone will be subject to Rome's security interest.
    B. The refrigerator sold to Cray will not be subject to Rome's security interest.
    C. The security interest does not include the proceeds from the sale of the refrigerators to Zone.
    D. The security interest may not cover after-acquired property even if the parties agree.

assess.AICPA.940549REG-BL

152. Under the UCC Secured Transactions Article, which of the following after-acquired property may be attached to a security agreement given to a secured lender?

	Inventory	Equipment
A.	Yes	Yes
B.	Yes	No
C.	No	Yes
D.	No	No

assess.AICPA.940552REG-BL

153. Under the UCC Secured Transactions Article, what is the order of priority for the following security interests in store equipment?

    I. Security interest perfected by filing on April 15, 2016.
    II. Security interest attached on April 1, 2016.
    III. Purchase money security interest attached April 11, 2016, and perfected by filing on April 20, 2016.

    A. I, III, II.
    B. II, I, III.
    C. III, I, II.
    D. III, II, I.

Rights of Secured Parties and Debtors

assess.AICPA.082076REG-II.E.

154. A debtor is in default. The collateral consists of 100 cows described in the security agreement. Thirty cows were stolen through no fault of the debtor. Which of the following statements is correct concerning the secured party's rights due to the debtor's default?

    A. The secured party must take the peaceful possession of the 70 remaining cows before s/he can pursue any remedies.
    B. If the secured party takes possession, the secured party cannot keep the cows in full satisfaction of the debt, if the debtor has paid 60% or more of the debt.
    C. If the secured party takes possession and sells the 70 cows. Proceeds will be applied to expenses incurred in the keeping of the cows. The costs of sale, and any balance, will be applied to the debt. The debt will then be discharged, even if the proceeds are insufficient to cover the costs and the debt.
    D. Upon default, the secured party can proceed to recover under the Uniform Commercial Code or proceed with any judicial remedy (such as get a judgment and levy on the debtor's non-exempt property).

assess.AICPA.101012REG-SIM

155. A debtor purchased an LCD television from BestBuy for $1,000. BestBuy financed the transaction. With finance charges, the total cost of the financing is $1,200. After the debtor has paid $600, he defaults on the payment and BestBuy repossesses the TV. BestBuy has decided to keep the TV as a floor display model. The debtor believes it would be best if BestBuy sold the TV.

   A. Under Article 9, BestBuy must sell the TV.
   B. Under Article 9, BestBuy is not required to sell the TV.
   C. Under Article 9, the debtor has no control over the creditor's actions once there has been a default.
   D. Under Article 9, the decision to sell or retain is always within the discretion of the creditor.

assess.AICPA.941160REG-BL

156. Under the Secured Transactions Article of the UCC, which of the following remedies is available to a secured creditor when a debtor fails to make a payment when due?

	Proceed against the collateral	Obtain a general judgment against the debtor
A.	Yes	Yes
B.	Yes	No
C.	No	Yes
D.	No	No

Bankruptcy and Insolvency

Prebankruptcy Options, and Introduction to and Declaration of Bankruptcy

assess.AICPA.082053REG-II.C.I

157. Green is heavily in debt to numerous creditors. Green does have some assets, including an antique car that he drives in parades and to other functions. Green is looking for a method that will allow him to get out of debt without going into bankruptcy, and will allow him to continue to drive his antique car. Green sells the antique car to a friend living in another city at a price estimated at 70% of the car's actual value. The friend has agreed to allow Green to keep the car and use it as before the sale. Green then gets all other creditors, except Sharp, to sign an agreement that, upon selling all of his remaining non-exempt assets, and with an appropriate division of proceeds, they would release him from his debts. Which of the following is correct?

   A. Since the vast majority of creditors signed the Composition of Creditor's Agreement, Sharp is also bound by the agreement.
   B. The above agreement is called an Assignment for the Benefit of Creditors.
   C. If Sharp cannot prove the transfer of the antique car as fraud-in-fact, Sharp has virtually no remedy available.
   D. Sharp can pursue an action based on fraud-in-law to set aside the sale to Green's friend.

assess.AICPA.940523REG-BL

158. Which of the following methods will allow a creditor to collect money from a debtor's wages?

   A. Arrest.
   B. Mechanic's lien.
   C. Order of receivership.
   D. Writ of garnishment.

assess.AICPA.951126REG-BL

159. Which of the following statements is (are) correct regarding debtors' rights?

   I. State exemption statutes prevent all of a debtor's personal property from being sold to pay a federal tax lien.
   II. Federal Social Security benefits received by a debtor are exempt from garnishment by creditors.

   A. I only.
   B. II only.
   C. Both I and II.
   D. Neither I nor II.

assess.AICPA.951127REG-BL

160. Which of the following liens generally require(s) the lienholder to give notice of legal action before selling the debtor's property to satisfy the debt?

	Mechanic's lien	Artisan's lien
A.	Yes	Yes
B.	Yes	No
C.	No	Yes
D.	No	No

Bankruptcy Process

aq.bankrupt.proc.001_2-18

161. Which of the following transfers by a debtor within 90 days of filing for bankruptcy could be set aside as a preferential payment?

    A. Making a gift to charity
    B. Paying a business utility bill
    C. Borrowing money from a bank secured by giving a mortgage on business property
    D. Prepaying an installment loan on inventory

aq.bankrupt.proc.002_2-18

162. Which of the following is **not** allowed as a federal exemption under the Federal Bankruptcy Code?

    A. Some specified amount of equity in one motor vehicle
    B. Unemployment compensation
    C. Some specified amount of value in books and tools of one's trade
    D. All of the above options are allowed.

assess.AICPA.050902-REG

163. Under the federal Bankruptcy Code, which of the following rights or powers does a trustee in bankruptcy not have?

    A. The power to prevail against a creditor with an unperfected security interest.
    B. The power to require persons holding the debtor's property at the time the bankruptcy petition is filed to deliver the property to the trustee.
    C. The right to use any grounds available to the debtor to obtain the return of the debtor's property.
    D. The right to avoid any statutory liens against the debtor's property that were effective before the bankruptcy petition was filed.

assess.AICPA.990510REG-BL

164. Under the liquidation provisions of Chapter 7 of the federal Bankruptcy Code, certain property acquired by the debtor after the filing of the petition becomes part of the bankruptcy estate.

An example of such property is

    A. Municipal-bond interest received by the debtor within 180 days of the filing of the petition.
    B. Alimony received by the debtor within one year of the filing of the petition.
    C. Social Security payments received by the debtor within 180 days of the filing of the petition.
    D. Gifts received by the debtor within one year of the filing of the petition.

Distribution of Debtor's Estate

aq.distrib.debt.001_2-18

165. On April 15, 2017 Wren Corp., an appliance wholesaler, was petitioned involuntarily into bankruptcy under Chapter 7. When the petition was filed, Wren's creditors included:

Fifth Bank—first mortgage on warehouse owned by Wren: $50,000

Hart Manufacturing Corporation—perfected purchase money security interest in inventory: $30,000

TVN Computers, Inc.—perfected security interest in office computers: $15,000

Wren's other creditors include:

IRS—2016 federal income tax: $20,000

Acme Office Cleaners—services for January, February, and March 2017: $750

Ted Smith (employee)—February and March wages: $4,400

Joan Sims (employee)—March 2017 commissions: $1,500

Power Electric—electricity charges for January, February, and March 2017: $600

Soft Office Supplies for supplies purchased during 2016: $2,000

The following transactions occurred before the bankruptcy petition was filed:

- On December 31, 2016, Wren paid off a $5,000 loan from Mary Lake, the sister of one of Wren's directors.
- On January 30, 2017, Wren donated $2,000 to Universal Charities.
- On February 1, 2017, Wren gave Young Finance Co. a security agreement covering Wren's office fixtures to secure a loan previously made by Young.
- On March 1, 2017, Wren made the final $1,000 monthly payment to Integral Appliance Corp. on a two-year note.
- On April 1, 2017, Wren purchased from Safety Co. a new burglar alarm system for its factory, for $5,000 cash.

All of Wren's assets were liquidated. The warehouse was sold for $75,000, the computers were sold for $12,000, and the inventory was sold for $25,000. After paying the bankruptcy administration expenses of $8,000, secured creditors, and priority general creditors, there was enough cash to pay each nonpriority general creditor 50 cents on the dollar.

Which of the following would **not** be set aside by the trustee as a voidable preference?

A. Payment to Mary Lake
B. Payment to Integral Appliance Corp.
C. Purchase from Safety Co.
D. All of the above would be set aside.

aq.distrib.debt.002_2-18

166. On April 15, 2017 Wren Corp., an appliance wholesaler, was petitioned involuntarily into bankruptcy under Chapter 7. When the petition was filed, Wren's creditors included:

Fifth Bank—first mortgage on warehouse owned by Wren: $50,000

Hart Manufacturing Corporation—perfected purchase money security interest in inventory: $30,000

TVN Computers, Inc.—perfected security interest in office computers: $15,000

Wren's other creditors include:

IRS—2016 federal income tax: $20,000

Acme Office Cleaners—services for January, February, and March 2017: $750

Ted Smith (employee)—February and March wages: $4,400

Joan Sims (employee)—March 2017 commissions: $1,500

Power Electric—electricity charges for January, February, and March 2017: $600

Soft Office Supplies for supplies purchased during 2016: $2,000

The following transactions occurred before the bankruptcy petition was filed:

- On December 31, 2016, Wren paid off a $5,000 loan from Mary Lake, the sister of one of Wren's directors.

- On January 30, 2017, Wren donated $2,000 to Universal Charities.

- On February 1, 2017, Wren gave Young Finance Co. a security agreement covering Wren's office fixtures to secure a loan previously made by Young.

- On March 1, 2017, Wren made the final $1,000 monthly payment to Integral Appliance Corp. on a two-year note.

- On April 1, 2017, Wren purchased from Safety Co. a new burglar alarm system for its factory, for $5,000 cash.

All of Wren's assets were liquidated. The warehouse was sold for $75,000, the computers were sold for $12,000, and the inventory was sold for $25,000. After paying the bankruptcy administration expenses of $8,000, secured creditors, and priority general creditors, there was enough cash to pay each nonpriority general creditor 50 cents on the dollar.

Which of the following claims would be paid first by the trustee?

A. Bankruptcy administration expense
B. Acme Office Cleaners
C. Fifth Bank
D. Joan Sims

assess.AICPA.950533REG-BL

167. Dart Inc., a closely held corporation, is petitioned involuntarily into bankruptcy under the liquidation provisions of Chapter 7 of the Federal Bankruptcy Code. Dart contests the petition.

Dart has not been paying its business debts as they become due, has defaulted on its mortgage-loan payments, and owes back-taxes to the IRS. The total cash value of Dart's bankruptcy estate after the sale of all assets and payment of administration expenses is $100,000.

Dart has the following creditors:

- Fracon Bank is owed $75,000 principal and accrued interest on a mortgage loan secured by Dart's real property. The property was valued at and sold, in bankruptcy, for $70,000.
- The IRS has a $12,000 recorded judgment for unpaid corporate income tax.
- JOG Office Supplies has an unsecured claim of $3,000 that was filed in a timely fashion.
- Nanstar Electric Co. has an unsecured claim of $1,200 that was not filed in a timely fashion.
- Decoy Publications has a claim of $14,000, of which $2,000 is secured by Dart's inventory that was valued and sold, in bankruptcy, for $2,000. The claim was filed in a timely fashion.

Assume that the bankruptcy estate was distributed.

What dollar amount would the IRS receive?

A. $0
B. $8,000
C. $10,000
D. $12,000

Discharge and Reaffirmation Agreements

assess.AICPA.020505REG-BL

168. Under Chapter 7 of the Federal Bankruptcy Code, what affect does a bankruptcy discharge have on a judgment creditor when there is no bankruptcy estate?

   A. The judgment creditor's claim is non-dischargeable.
   B. The judgment creditor retains a statutory lien against the debtor.
   C. The debtor is relieved of any personal liability to the judgment creditor.
   D. The debtor is required to pay a liquidated amount to vacate the judgment.

assess.AICPA.941134REG-BL

169. Under the liquidation provisions of Chapter 7 of the Federal Bankruptcy Code, which of the following statements applies to a person who has voluntarily filed for and received a discharge in bankruptcy?

   A. The person will be discharged from all debts.
   B. The person can obtain another voluntary discharge in bankruptcy under Chapter 7 after three years have elapsed from the date of the prior filing.
   C. The person must surrender for distribution to the creditors amounts received as an inheritance, if the receipt occurs within 180 days after filing the bankruptcy petition.
   D. The person is precluded from owning or operating a similar business for two years.

assess.AICPA.970512REG-BL

170. Under the liquidation provisions of Chapter 7 of the Federal Bankruptcy Code, a debtor will be denied a discharge in bankruptcy if the debtor

   A. Fails to list a creditor.
   B. Owes alimony and child support payments.
   C. Cannot pay administration expenses.
   D. Refuses satisfactorily to explain a loss of assets.

Government Regulation of Business

Federal Securities Regulation

Defining a Security

assess.AICPA.081944REG-2.D.1

171. Sam, a Harlingen business owner, sues a local shopping mall, accusing it of conspiring with a former partner of Sam's to put Sam out of business. Sam lacks resources to pay his lawyers and otherwise fund the lawsuit. Sternberg forms Plaintiff's Funding Corp. (PFC) and comes to Sam's aid. Sternberg and PFC induce ten people to put up $5,000 each to buy an 11% stake in the litigation. Sam uses the $50,000 to fund the lawsuit, which recovers $5.4mn. The ten investors were entitled to $594,000, but were never paid. They sued Sternberg and PFC for securities fraud. Defendants claimed that no "securities" were involved in this case. Which is true?

   A. The defendants are correct; there were no "securities" involved in this case.
   B. The investors should win; these were securities in the form of an "investment contract."
   C. These interests were securities, because they were stock-derivative option-equity contracts.
   D. None of the above.

assess.AICPA.081945REG-2.D.1

172. Alliance Leasing Corp. locates and recruits more than 1,500 investors from all over the U.S. to invest in an enterprise that uses investor money to buy commercial office or kitchen equipment, that was then leased out to third-party lessees. Investors' funds are to be placed in special accounts at either Wells Fargo Bank or Merrill Lynch, and Alliance is to use the capital to "engage in a single or multiple transactions with a lessee." In several cases, Alliance bundles the leases together in packages of several million dollars each, which were purchased by institutional investors. The lease payments by the lessees are then to be paid to the investors on a monthly basis for two years, with a balloon payment at the end of the two-year period. Alliance represents that investors would earn a return of 14% per year (as would Alliance, which was splitting the profits with investors 50/50) and that the investment is "low risk." After Alliance goes bankrupt, investors sue its principals for securities fraud. Defendants claimed that no "securities" were involved. Which of the following is true?

   A. These interests are "securities."
   B. These interests are not securities, because the interests were not bought over an organized stock market.
   C. These interests are not securities, because there is no common interest.
   D. B and C.

assess.AICPA.101171REG

173. Which of the following transactions is subject to registration requirements of the Securities Act of 1933?

   A. The public sale of stock of a trucking company regulated by the Interstate Commerce Commission.
   B. A public sale of municipal bonds issued by a city government.
   C. The issuance of stock by a publicly traded corporation to its existing shareholders because of a stock split.
   D. The public sale by a corporation of its negotiable ten-year notes.

The Registration Process

assess.AICPA.051149REG

174. Under the Securities Act of 1933, which of the following statements is (are) correct regarding the purpose of registration?

   I. The purpose of registration is to allow the detection of management fraud and prevent a public offering of securities when management fraud is suspected.
   II. The purpose of registration is to adequately and accurately disclose financial and other information upon which investors may determine the merits of securities.

   A. I only.
   B. II only.
   C. Both I and II.
   D. Neither I nor II.

assess.AICPA.940532REG-BL

175. A preliminary prospectus, permitted under SEC regulations, is known as the

   A. Unaudited prospectus.
   B. Qualified prospectus.
   C. "Blue-sky" prospectus.
   D. "Red herring" prospectus.

assess.AICPA.940533REG-BL

176. A tombstone advertisement

   A. May be substituted for the prospectus under certain circumstances.
   B. May contain an offer to sell securities.
   C. Notifies prospective investors that a previously offered security has been withdrawn from the market and is therefore effectively "dead."
   D. Makes known the availability of a prospectus.

Exempt Transactions and Securities

aq.exempt.trans.001_2-18

177. Hamilton Corporation is making a $4.5 million securities offering under Rule 504 of the Securities Act of 1933. Under this regulation, Hamilton is

   A. Required to provide full financial information to accredited investors only.
   B. Allowed to make the offering through general solicitation in all states.
   C. Limited to selling to no more than 35 non-accredited investors.
   D. Allowed to sell to an unlimited number of investors, both accredited and non-accredited.

aq.exempt.trans.002_2-18

178. Walpole Corporation is considering making an offering without filing a registration statement with the SEC pursuant to Regulation A. Which of the following is **not** true regarding Reg A?

   A. No information is required to be provided to investors.
   B. General solicitation is permitted.
   C. Walpole could raise as much as $50 million in a 12-month period.
   D. Reg A allows potential issuers to "test the waters" by approaching investors to gauge their interest in investing before launching the offering.

assess.AICPA.060652REG

179. Which of the following securities is exempt from registration under the Securities Act of 1933?

   A. Municipal bonds.
   B. Securities sold by a discount broker.
   C. Pre-incorporation stock subscriptions.
   D. One-year notes issued to raise working capital.

assess.AICPA.082102REG-II.D.I

180. Which of the following transactions is subject to registration requirements of the Securities Act of 1933?

   A. The public sale by a corporation of its negotiable ten-year notes.
   B. The public sale by a charitable organization of 10-year bearer bonds.
   C. The sale across state lines of municipal bonds issued by a city.
   D. Issuance of stock by a publicly traded corporation to its shareholders, because of a stock split.

aq.exempt.trans.004_2-18

181. Sloban Corporation wishes to raise a lot of money without filing a registration statement with the SEC. It is interested in knowing more about Rule 506 of Regulation D. Which of the following is true?

    A. Firms may raise up to $50 million in a 12-month period under Rule 506.
    B. General solicitation is never allowed under Rule 506.
    C. Investors' resale of securities purchased under Rule 506 is restricted.
    D. Unlike under Rule 504, issuers need not file a Form D.

aq.exempt.trans.005_2-18

182. Noxious Corporation is located in Idaho and wishes to sell securities to Idaho residents without filing a registration statement. Noxious would like to know more about the difference between Rule 147 and Rule 147A. Which of the following is **not** the same under both rules?

    A. There is no limit on the amount of money that can be raised in a 12-month period.
    B. There is no requirement that specified information be disclosed to investors.
    C. All offerees must be reasonably believed to be Idaho residents.
    D. Resale to non-Idaho residents by investors will be restricted.

aq.exempt.trans.007_2-18

183. Pix Corporation needs to raise $7.5 million within the next 12 months. It wishes to do so without filing a registration statement with the SEC. It will need to raise money in more than one state. Which of the following is the best option for Pix?

    A. Rule 504
    B. Rule 506
    C. Regulation Crowdfunding
    D. Rule 147A

Liability Provisions—1933 Act

assess.AICPA.090601REG-II-D-1

184. Under the liability provisions of Section 11 of the Securities Act of 1933, a CPA who certifies financial statements included in a registration statement generally will not be liable to a purchaser of the security

    A. Unless the purchaser can prove scienter on the part of the CPA.
    B. Unless the purchaser can prove privity with the CPA.

    C. If the CPA can prove due diligence.
    D. If the financial statements were materially misleading.

assess.AICPA.101159REG

185. In which of the following types of action, brought against a CPA who issues an audit report containing an unqualified opinion on materially misstated financial statements, may a plaintiff prevail without proving reliance on the audit report?

    A. An action for common-law fraud.
    B. An action for common-law breach of contract.
    C. An action brought under Section 11 of the Securities Act of 1933.
    D. An action brought under Rule 10b-5 of the Securities Exchange Act of 1934.

assess.AICPA.941113REG-BL

186. Under the liability provisions of Section 11 of the Securities Act of 1933, a CPA may be liable to any purchaser of a security for certifying materially misstated financial statements that are included in the security's registration statement.

Under Section 11, which of the following must be proven by a purchaser of the security?

	Reliance on the financial statements	Fraud by the CPA
A.	Yes	Yes
B.	Yes	No
C.	No	Yes
D.	No	No

assess.AICPA.951112REG-BL

187. Under Section 11 of the Securities Act of 1933, which of the following standards may a CPA use as a defense?

	Generally accepted accounting principles	Generally accepted detection standards
A.	Yes	Yes
B.	Yes	No
C.	No	Yes
D.	No	No

Purposes, Requirements, and Provisions of the 1934 Act

assess.AICPA.051135REG

188. Under the liability provisions of Section 18 of the Securities Exchange Act of 1934, for which of the following actions would an accountant generally be liable?

    A. Negligently approving a reporting corporation's incorrect internal financial forecasts.
    B. Negligently filing a reporting corporation's tax return with the IRS.
    C. Intentionally preparing and filing with the SEC a reporting corporation's incorrect quarterly report.
    D. Intentionally failing to notify a reporting corporation's audit committee of defects in the verification of accounts receivable.

assess.AICPA.081934REG-1E2

189. Ted buys Synchotic Corporation shares based on Synchotic's announcement of record earnings. But just a few days later, on July 1, 2010, Synchotic admits that its earnings had been artificially inflated via fraudulent earnings management. Its stock price drops dramatically that day, and Ted makes a significant loss. Ted wishes to bring a 1934 Act securities-fraud lawsuit against Synchotic. In terms of the statute of limitations, when must Ted bring his lawsuit?

    A. Within one year of when he should have discovered the fraud or within three years of the fraud.
    B. Within one year of when he should have discovered the fraud and within three years of the fraud.
    C. Within two years of when he should have discovered the fraud or within five years of the fraud.
    D. Within two years of when he should have discovered the fraud and within five years of the fraud.

assess.AICPA.101150REG

190. Which defense must an accountant establish to be absolved from civil liability under Section 18 of the Securities Exchange Act of 1934 for false or misleading statements made in reports or documents filed under the Act?

    A. Lack of gross negligence.
    B. Exercise of due care.
    C. Good faith and lack of knowledge of the statement's falsity.
    D. Lack of privity with an injured party.

assess.AICPA.REG.purp.req.pay-0019

191. Under the Section 10(b) Rule 10b-5 antifraud provisions of the Securities Exchange Act of 1934, which of the following conditions must a plaintiff prove to recover damages from an accountant?

    A. The plaintiff is in privity of contract with the accountant.
    B. The plaintiff relied on the accountant's intentional misstatement of material facts.
    C. The plaintiff is free from contributory negligence.
    D. The accountant acted without due diligence.

Criminal Liability

assess.AICPA.060654REG

192. Under the Securities Exchange Act of 1934, which of the following penalties could be assessed against a CPA who intentionally violates the provisions of Section 10(b), Rule 10b-5 of the Act?

	Civil liability of monetary damages	Criminal liability of a fine
A.	Yes	Yes
B.	Yes	No
C.	No	Yes
D.	No	No

assess.AICPA.081957REG-2.D.1

193. Seimone, an auditor for the ABC accounting firm, learns that her audit client, Bupkis Co., is about to announce a record profit. She buys Bupkis shares in a fake name and profits upon the public announcement. Which of the following is true?

    A. The SEC may bring civil charges against Seimone.
    B. The SEC may bring criminal charges against Seimone.
    C. A and B.
    D. None of the above.

assess.AICPA.081960REG-2.D.1

194. CPA Sobel engages in insider trading of the shares of an audit client. She is caught. The SEC brings a civil action and forces Sobel to give up her insider-trading profits and pay a civil fine of three times the amount of the profits. Sobel thought she had been punished sufficiently, but then the DOJ began an investigation. Which of the following is true?

   A. DOJ cannot bring criminal charges because Sobel has been punished enough.
   B. The DOJ can choose to bring criminal charges to supplement the SEC's civil action.
   C. To bring criminal charges would amount to double jeopardy.
   D. A and C.

assess.AICPA.081959REG-2.D.1

195. Willful violations of which of the following acts can create the basis for federal criminal liability?

   A. The 1933 Securities Act.
   B. The 1934 Securities Exchange Act.
   C. A and B.
   D. None of the above.

Other Federal Laws and Regulations

Employment Tax

aicpa.aq.fed.unemploy.001_17

196. Juan recently started operating a flower shop as a proprietorship. In its first year of operations, the shop had a taxable income of $60,000. Assuming that Juan had no other employment-related earnings,

   A. The flower shop must withhold FICA taxes from Juan's earnings.
   B. Juan must pay self-employment tax on the earnings of the business.
   C. Juan will be exempt from self-employment taxes for the first three years of operations.
   D. Juan will be exempt from the Medicare tax because the business earnings are below the threshold amount.

aq.fed.unemploy.json.001_17

197. The Model Bakery Corporation (MBC) has not been withholding and remitting its federal taxes as it should have. The federal government is considering suing some of MBC's employees under 26 U.S.C. Sec. 6672 in order to hold them personally liable to pay these taxes. Which of the following persons, all of whom knew that MBC was not withholding as it should have, is

most likely to be deemed a "responsible person" for purposes of Sec. 6672?

   A. Sally is MBC's bookkeeper. She has been with the company for 20 years and is very meticulous and precise. Her job is to pay the bills that MBC's CFO, Telford, tells her to pay, and she does so, promptly and accurately.
   B. Bobbert is an accountant with MBC's tax accounting firm, Dimble & Facet LLC. Once when MBC's bookkeeper, Sally, was ill for a month, Bobbert stepped in and helped MBC by paying the bills that MBC's CFO, Telford, told him to pay.
   C. Telford is MBC's CFO. He never pays any bills himself. He typically instructs MBC's bookkeeper, Sally, as to which bills to pay.
   D. Emily is an outside director on MBC's board. She attends semiannual meetings and votes on the big-picture items that are brought up at directors' meetings, such as whether MBC should agree to be purchased by XYZ Corporation. It didn't.

aq.fed.unemploy.json.002_17

198. The Blazing Saddles Corporation (BSC) is covered by the Federal Unemployment Tax Act (FUTA). Several of its workers have left BSC lately. Which one of the next workers is entitled to collect unemployment compensation benefits from BSC?

   A. Toddrick had worked for BSC for seven years as a welder in its trailer division but was let go when BSC decided to stop making trailers because that division was losing money.
   B. Elaine had worked for BSC for 20 years and was so bored that she felt her mental health was threatened if she did not retire. So she quit. Because her retirement savings were limited, she applied for unemployment compensation to carry her a few months before she began dipping into her savings.
   C. Ming had worked for BSC for 15 years in its internal audit department. Because of some new software that it acquired, BSC was able to downsize the number of internal auditors it had. BSC offered Ming a transfer to its tax department, but Ming hated taxes and refused the transfer. BSC therefore laid Ming off.
   D. Danny had worked for BSC for 22 years. Over the years, seven different women had filed sexual harassment complaints against him. The seventh complaint was the last straw. BSC fired Danny. Danny is entitled to unemployment compensation.

assess.AICPA.951132REG-BL

199. Taxes payable under the Federal Unemployment Tax Act (FUTA) are

   A. Calculated as a fixed percentage of all compensation paid to an employee.
   B. Deductible by the employer as a business expense for federal income-tax purposes.
   C. Payable by employers for all employees.
   D. Withheld from the wages of all covered employees.

Affordable Care Act

aq.aca.0001

200. Which of the following is typically **not** a medical care expense that may be deducted if the taxpayer meets the applicable threshold?

   A. Payment for diagnosis of disease.
   B. Payment for treatment of disease.
   C. Payment for prevention of disease.
   D. Payment for nicotine patches

aq.aca.0002

201. In 2019, thirty-something Tessa had an AGI of $75,000. She had some severe dental problems and paid her dentist $10,000 that was not covered by insurance. How much may Tessa deduct from her income tax form under the ACA?

   A. $10,000
   B. $7,500
   C. $2,500
   D. $4,375

aq.aca.0007

202. Under his health care plan, Tran has a deductible of $1,200, a coinsurance of 20%, and an out-of-pocket limit that matches the federal maximum of $6,850 (in 2016). Tran has significant surgery for which his bill is $5,000, hospitalization for which his bill is $40,000, and home health care after he leaves the hospital which comes to $4,000. How much of the hospital bill will Tran pay, assuming he pays the three bills in the order mentioned?

   A. $40,000
   B. $6,850
   C. $3,425
   D. $4,890

Worker Classification Laws and Regulations

worker.law.reg.001

203. Tim works alongside three other workers at ABC Co. They all do the same work. They all work 8–5 most days and are required to work occasionally in the evening or on a weekend. They are all paid on an hourly basis. The other three workers are labeled and treated as employees, but Tim signed a contract saying that he is an *independent contractor*. Later, litigation arose regarding Tim's status. Which of the following is **true**?

   A. Because Tim signed the contract, he is indeed an independent contractor rather than an employee of ABC.
   B. Signing the contract is not the most important factor in this scenario, but Tim is nonetheless an independent contractor.
   C. A court will probably disregard the contract and hold that Tim is an employee.
   D. Choices 1 and 2.

worker.law.reg.002

204. Tilly's roof was damaged in a hail storm. She went on line, read the reviews, and hired Ahmad's Roofing Co. (ARC) to fix her roof, agreeing to pay $2,500 for the job. Ahmad sent its best worker, Shanline, over to work on Tilly's roof. This was a relatively minor job that Ahmad had Shanline fit in between two commercial roofing jobs it had gotten. Which of the following is probably **true**?

   A. ARC is probably an employee of Tilly's.
   B. Shanline is probably an employee of Tilly's.
   C. Shanline is probably an employee of ARC's.
   D. ARC and Shanline are both probably employees of Tilly's.

worker.law.reg.003

205. TUV Company owns a tall office building. Once every two months for many years, the Quixotic Window Washing Co. (QWW) has sent its workers to the building to wash its windows using QWW's equipment. In return, TUV pays QWW $1,000 bi-monthly. One time, one of QWW's employees carelessly dropped a squeegee which landed on a pedestrian below, injuring him. The employee had not been following QWW's safety protocols. The pedestrian sued TUV in negligence. Which of the following is **true**?

   A. The pedestrian can probably recover from TUV because the QWW employee, it is specified in the facts, dropped the squeegee carelessly.
   B. The QWW worker is probably an independent contractor of TUV's and of QWW.
   C. TUV is probably liable because its relationship with QWW has lasted many years.
   D. TUV is probably not liable because too many other factors point toward QWW being an independent contractor.

worker.law.reg.005

206. XYZ Corporation classified large numbers of its workers as independent contractors, but in litigation brought by the IRS, the court held that they were actually employees who had been deprived of their rightful benefits. Which of the following is likely **true** if XYZ's classification was erroneous, but not intentional?

   A. An unintentional error is not punished in this context.
   B. Even an unintentional error will result in XYZ paying stiff fines.
   C. XYZ's unintentional error will probably not be punished if its decision had a reasonable basis within the meaning of the *safe harbor* that exists of these decisions.
   D. All of the above.

Business Structure

Selection and Formation of Business Entity and Related Operation and Termination

Selection of a Business Entity

aicpa.aq.select.bus.ent.001_17

207. A corporation that intends to make an election to become an S corporation seeks advice. An accountant would most appropriately make which of the following recommendations?

   A. Limit the number of shareholders to 120 unrelated individuals.
   B. Limit the issuance of stock to common and preferred.
   C. Ensure that **no** shareholders are resident aliens.
   D. Evaluate the eligibility of all shareholders.

assess.AICPA.048283REG-SIM

208. Tim and Sarah wish to form an accounting firm. They are not confident in their own abilities and wish to choose a form of organization that will shield them from personal liability for their own malpractice.

   Which of the following would succeed for them?

   A. LLP
   B. LLC
   C. Both of the above.
   D. Neither of the above.

assess.AICPA.082094BEC-I.A.2

209. The owners of a limited-liability company are known as which of the following

   A. Partners.
   B. Members.
   C. Stockholders.
   D. Shareholders.

assess.AICPA.090609BEC-I-D

210. Which of the following forms of business generally provides all owners with limited liability, while avoiding federal taxation of income at the entity level?

   A. A Subchapter C corporation.
   B. A Subchapter S corporation.
   C. Partnership.
   D. Limited partnership.

Formation

assess.AICPA.051132BEC

211. Following the formation of a corporation, which of the following terms best describes the process by which the promoter is released from, and the corporation is made liable for, pre-incorporation contractual obligations?

   A. Assignment.
   B. Novation.
   C. Delegation.
   D. Accord and satisfaction.

assess.AICPA.051133BEC

212. Under the Revised Model Business Corporation Act (RMBCA), which of the following items of information must be included in a corporation's articles of incorporation (charter)?

   A. Name and address of each incorporator.
   B. Nature and purpose of the corporation's business.
   C. Name and address of the corporation's promoter.
   D. Election of either C corporation or S corporation status.

assess.AICPA.090615BEC-I-A

213. Under the Revised Uniform Limited Partnership Act, which of the following statements is correct regarding limited partnerships?

   A. Limited partners may lose limited liability if they participate in management activities.
   B. Limited partnerships may legally exist without filing a certificate of limited partnership.

C. Limited partners have the same rights, responsibilities, and authority as general partners.
D. Limited partners may contribute cash only and may not contribute services as their capital contributions.

assess.AICPA.940511BEC-BL
214. Under the Revised Model Business Corporation Act (RMBCA), which of the following must be contained in a corporation's articles of incorporation?

A. Quorum voting requirements.
B. Names of stockholders.
C. Provisions for issuance of par and non-par shares.
D. The number of shares the corporation is authorized to issue.

Operations: Nonfinancial Factors

assess.AICPA.080922BEC-1B
215. Elmo forms a corporation to run a retail store. He buys $100,000 worth of its stock, as does his mother. They are the only two shareholders. The store's location was not favorable and the business does not take off. Over the course of five years, Elmo slowly burns through the $200,000 in capital, as the store posts losses every year. Near the end of the sixth year, the corporation takes bankruptcy, leaving creditors on the hook for $40,000; they had delivered inventory to the store for which the corporation had been unable to pay. The creditors sue Elmo and his mother personally. Given the facts presented, what should happen?

A. The court should pierce the corporate veil, because the store was obviously undercapitalized.
B. The court should pierce the corporate veil, because the creditors failed to have Elmo or his mother personally guarantee their extensions of credit.
C. The court should not pierce the corporate veil.
D. A and B.

assess.AICPA.101002REG-SIM
216. Sal wishes to form a business entity that he will own and control all by himself. Which of the following is not a good choice for him?

A. Sole proprietorship.
B. General partnership.
C. LLC.
D. Corporation.

assess.AICPA.120601REG
217. Which of the following statements is correct regarding a limited liability company's operating agreement?

A. It must be filed with a central state agency.
B. It must be in writing.
C. It is designed to forestall and resolve disputes among the owners.
D. It is necessary for a limited liability company to exist.

Financial Structure

assess.AICPA.051140BEC
218. Which of the following decreases stockholder equity?

A. Investments by owners.
B. Distributions to owners.
C. Issuance of stock.
D. Acquisition of assets in a cash transaction.

assess.AICPA.082085BEC-I.BEC.I.C
219. Which of the following statements is (are) correct regarding corporate debt and equity securities?

I. Both debt and equity security holders have an ownership interest in the corporation.
II. Both debt and equity securities have an obligation to pay income.

A. I only.
B. II only.
C. Both I and II.
D. Neither I nor II.

assess.AICPA.090610BEC-I-D
220. Under the RMBCA, which of the following dividends is not defined as a distribution?

A. Cash dividend.
B. Property dividends.
C. Liquidating dividends.
D. Stock dividends.

assess.AICPA.101004REG-SIM

221. Ed, Fred, and Ned form the EFN general partnership. Ed and Fred each contribute $50,000 to start the business. Ned contributes $25,000. Ed and Fred both work 20 hours a week for the business, while Ned works 40 hours a week. After capital contributions are repaid, the firm starts turning a profit. The partners had not expressly agreed how those profits should be shared. Which of the following is true?

   A. The profits should be shared equally.
   B. Ed and Fred should receive more of the profits than Ned, because they put more capital into the partnership.
   C. Ned should receive a greater share of the profits than Ed and Fred, because he is contributing more labor to the business.
   D. None of the above.

Termination

aq.termination.001_17

222. The Maglie Corporation has been doing business for many years, but it has had some difficulties lately. Which of the following is true about the rules for *involuntary* dissolution for Maglie?

   A. If Maglie fraudulently obtained approval for its articles of incorporation, creditors may sue to dissolve it.
   B. If Maglie has failed to pay its franchise taxes, it may be involuntarily dissolved in an action by its shareholders.
   C. A vote of Maglie's shareholders can involuntarily dissolve Maglie.
   D. If Maglie has admitted in writing that a creditor's claim is due and owing and that Maglie is insolvent, the creditor could sue for an involuntary judicial dissolution of Maglie.

aq.termination.002_17

223. Amanda is a member of the Ames Network LLC. She has had some conflict with other members of the LLC and is seeking your advice. Please tell Amanda which of the following is true.

   A. Agreeing to become the member of an LLC is a very important commitment, and Amanda must remain a member until either she dies or the LLC dissolves.
   B. If Amanda seeks to dissolve the LLC and can obtain the agreement of a majority of other LLC members, the LLC will dissolve under the Revised Uniform Limited Liability Company Act (RULLCA).

   C. If Amanda can prove that she is a minority member of the LLC and that the members in control of the LLC are looting the LLC's assets for their own personal benefit, she can likely successfully sue for dissolution.
   D. Amanda should avoid loaning any money to the LLC, because if it dissolves she cannot possibly get any of that money back.

assess.AICPA.941124REG-BL

224. The partners of College Assoc., a general partnership, decide to dissolve the partnership and agree that none of the partners will continue to use the partnership name.

   Under the Uniform Partnership Act, which of the following events will occur on dissolution of the partnership?

	Each partner's existing liability will be discharged.	Each partner's apparent authority will continue.
A.	Yes	Yes
B.	Yes	No
C.	No	Yes
D.	No	No

assess.AICPA.970503BEC-BL

225. Which of the following actions may be taken by a corporation's Board of Directors without stockholder approval?

   A. Purchasing substantially all of the assets of another corporation.
   B. Selling substantially all of the corporation's assets.
   C. Dissolving the corporation.
   D. Amending the articles of incorporation.

Rights, Duties, Legal Obligations, and Authority of Owners and Management

Rights and Duties

assess.AICPA.048294REG-SIM

226. Slinger, Hurl, and Macomb are partners in a small real estate business. The three partners discuss whether to purchase a vacant strip mall and attempt to renovate it. Slinger and Macomb vote against, because the partnership already owns a strip mall across the highway from this one, so the purchase does not occur. However, a week later, Hurl purchases the land in his own name.

Which of the following is true?

A. Hurl has wrongfully misappropriated a partnership business opportunity.
B. Hurl has wrongfully gone into competition with the partnership.
C. A and B.
D. Hurl has not breached any duty to the partnership.

assess.AICPA.080907BEC-1A1

227. Tilda, Max, and Boniface form an equal partnership that manufactures batteries for solar-powered cars. Unfortunately, their ambition exceeds their technology and the partnership is unable to pay several contractual obligations entered into in its name. A supplier, Sims Co., is owed $400,000 on materials it delivered to the partnership. Sims has sued and received a judgment against the three partners and the partnership. Sims should begin its quest to satisfy the judgment by proceeding against the assets of:

A. Tilda.
B. Max.
C. Boniface.
D. The partnership.

assess.AICPA.101006REG-SIM

228. Sam is a member of a member-managed LLC. The other partners have agreed to make Sam the sole manager of the firm. Sam is worried about his liability, should he make any mistakes. Which protections would not be proper for Sam to ask the other members to approve?

A. A provision in the operating agreement that specifies that it is permissible for Sam to contract to buy paper products from his wife's stationery store, so long as he does so at the same price paid by other customers.
B. A provision in the operating agreement providing that Sam cannot be liable to the firm or to other members for his carelessness, unless it rises to the level of, at least, recklessness.
C. A provision in the operating agreement indicating that Sam is not liable to the firm for money damages resulting from his knowing violation of the law.
D. All of the above (would not be proper).

assess.AICPA.101161REG

229. Which of the following positions best describes the nature of relationship of the Board of Directors of XYZ Co to the company as a whole?

A. Agent.
B. Executive.
C. Fiduciary.
D. Representative.

assess.AICPA.REG.rights.duties-0020

230. Peters owned 500 shares of common stock in Kidsmart, Inc. Accordingly, Peters had the right to

A. Automatically receive a dividend in any quarter in which the corporation made a profit.
B. Inspect the corporate records on demand.
C. Vote for the election and removal of the board of directors.
D. Vote for and remove the corporate officers and set their compensation.

Authority of Owners and Managers

assess.AICPA.060646BEC

231. Which of the following actions is required to ensure the validity of a contract between a corporation and a director of the corporation?

A. An independent appraiser must render to the Board of Directors a fairness opinion on the contract.
B. The director must disclose the interest to the independent members of the Board and refrain from voting.
C. The shareholders must review and ratify the contract.
D. The director must resign from the Board of Directors.

assess.AICPA.082087BEC-I.BEC.I.D

232. The principle that protects corporate directors from personal liability for acts performed in good faith on behalf of the corporation is known as

A. The "clean hands doctrine."
B. The "full-disclosure rule."
C. The "responsible person doctrine."
D. The "business-judgment rule."

assess.AICPA.951117REG-BL

233. Which of the following statements is (are) usually correct regarding general partners' liability?

   I. All general partners are jointly and severally liable for partnership torts.

   II. All general partners are liable only for those partnership obligations they actually authorized.

   A. I only.
   B. II only.
   C. Both I and II.
   D. Neither I nor II.

assess.AICPA.960511REG-BL

234. Under the Uniform Partnership Act, which of the following statements concerning the powers and duties of partners in a general partnership is (are) correct?

   I. Each partner is an agent of every other partner and acts as both a principal and an agent in any business transaction within the scope of the partnership agreement.

   II. Each partner is subject to joint liability on partnership debts and contracts.

   A. I only.
   B. II only.
   C. Both I and II.
   D. Neither I nor II.

assess.AICPA.960512BEC-BL

235. Under the Revised Model Business Corporation Act (RMBCA), a corporate director is authorized to

   A. Rely on information provided by the appropriate corporate officer.
   B. Serve on the Board of Directors of a competing business.
   C. Self control of the corporation.
   D. Profit from insider information.

Federal Taxation of Property Transactions

Property Transactions

Sales and Dispositions of Assets

aicpa.aq.sales.dispos.001_17

236. A married couple abandoned their principal residence in May. They had purchased the house five years ago for $350,000. The house had a current fair market value of $300,000. What is the maximum loss, if any, that they are allowed to deduct on the current-year's tax return for the abandoned property?

   A. $0
   B. $50,000
   C. $300,000
   D. $350,000

aicpa.aq.sales.dispos.002_17

237. Talbot purchased a laptop for $1,500 and a television for $1,300. The laptop is used solely for business and the television solely for personal entertainment. During the same year, Talbot experienced serious financial difficulty and sold the television for $300 and the laptop for $1,000. What amount, if any, is Talbot entitled to deduct as a loss relating to the sale of the television and laptop?

   A. $0
   B. $500
   C. $1,000
   D. $1,500

assess.AICPA.060801REG

238. Carter purchased 100 shares of stock for $50 per share. Ten years later, Carter died on February 1 and bequeathed the 100 shares of stock to a relative, Boone, when the stock had a market price of $100 per share. One year later, on April 1, the stock split 2 for 1.

   Boone gave 100 shares of the stock to another of Carter's relatives, Dixon, on June 1 that same year, when the market value of the stock was $150 per share.

   What was Dixon's basis in the 100 shares of stock when acquired on June 1?

   A. $5,000
   B. $5,100
   C. $10,000
   D. $15,000

assess.AICPA.090855REG

239. Bluff purchases equipment for business use for $35,000 and makes $1,000 of improvements to the equipment. After deducting depreciation of $5,000, Bluff gives the equipment to Russett for business use. At the time the gift is made, the equipment has a fair market value of $32,000. Ignoring gift-tax consequences, what is Russett's basis in the equipment?

   A. $31,000
   B. $32,000
   C. $35,000
   D. $36,000

assess.AICPA.120702REG_2-18

240. Upon her grandfather's death, Jordan inherited 10 shares of Universal Corp. stock that had a fair market value of $5,000. Her grandfather acquired the shares in 1996 for $2,500. Four months after her grandfather's death, Jordan sold all her shares of Universal for $7,500. What was Jordan's recognized gain in the year of sale?

   A. $2,500 long-term capital gain
   B. $2,500 short-term capital gain
   C. $5,000 long-term capital gain
   D. $5,000 short-term capital gain

assess.AICPA.130911REG

241. For an individual business owner, which of the following would typically be classified as a capital asset for federal income tax purposes?

   A. Accounts receivable
   B. Marketable securities
   C. Machinery and equipment used in a business
   D. Inventory

Capital Gains and Losses

aicpa.aq.cap.gain.loss.001_17

242. An individual taxpayer reported the following net long-term capital gains and losses:

The amount of capital gain that the individual taxpayer should report in Year 3 is

Year	Gain (loss)
1	($5,000)
2	1,000
3	4,000

A. $0
B. $1,000
C. $3,000
D. $4,000

assess.AICPA.020501REG-AR

243. Jackson, a single individual, inherits Bean Corp. common stock from his parents. Bean is a qualified small business corporation under Code Section 1244. The stock costs Jackson's parents $20,000 and has a fair market value of $25,000 at the parents' date of death. During the year, Bean declares bankruptcy and Jackson is informed that the stock is worthless.

What amount may Jackson deduct as an ordinary loss in the current year?

A. $0
B. $3,000
C. $20,000
D. $25,000

assess.AICPA.120722REG

244. On February 1, year 1, a taxpayer purchased an option to buy 1,000 shares of XYZ Co. for $200 per share. The taxpayer purchased the option for $50,000, which was to remain in effect for six months. The market declined, and the taxpayer let the option lapse on August 1, year 1. The taxpayer would report which of the following as a capital loss on the year 1 income tax return?

A. $50,000 long term.
B. $50,000 short term.
C. $150,000 long term.
D. $200,000 short term.

assess.AICPA.130915REG

245. Summer, a single individual, had a net operating loss of $20,000 three years ago. A Code Sec. 1244 stock loss made up three-fourths of that loss. Summer had no taxable income from that year until the current year. In the current year, Summer has gross income of $80,000 and sustains another loss of $50,000 on Code Sec. 1244 stock. Assuming that Summer can carry the entire $20,000 net operating loss to the current year, what is the amount and character of the Code Sec. 1244 loss that Summer can deduct for the current year?

A. $35,000 ordinary loss.
B. $35,000 capital loss.
C. $50,000 ordinary loss.
D. $50,000 capital loss.

assess.AICPA.REG.capital.gain.loss-0011

246. On year 1, Janice had the following transactions in Jacky, Inc., common stock:

	Shares	Price
Jan. 01—Purchase	500	$25
May 12—Sale	500	$23
May 28—Purchase	250	$22
Oct. 15—Sale	100	$18

What is Janice's deductible capital loss?

A. $400
B. $700
C. $1,100
D. $1,400

Section 1231 Assets

assess.AICPA.101125REG-SIM_2-18

247. On August 22, 2018 Martha purchases a computer to use in her childcare business. She sells the computer on December 28, 2018 for $2,000 when the machine has an adjusted tax basis of $1,700. What is the amount and character of the gain on the sale?

A. $300 short-term capital gain
B. $300 long-term capital gain
C. $300 ordinary income
D. $300 Section 1231 gain

assess.AICPA.101126REG-SIM

248. The results of UNA Corporation's first six years of operations are presented below.

Year	Results of Operations
1	Section 1231 losses of $50,000
2	Section 1231 losses of $30,000
3	Section 1231 gains of $75,000
4	Section 1231 losses of $20,000
5	Section 1231 losses of $30,000
6	Section 1231 gain of $80,000

UNA corporation's year-six Section 1231 gain can best be characterized as

A. $80,000 Section 1231 gain.
B. $50,000 ordinary income; $30,000 Section 1231 gain.
C. $80,000 ordinary income.
D. $55,000 ordinary income; $25,000 Sec. 1231 gain.

assess.AICPA.120731REG_2-18

249. Decker sold equipment for $200,000. The equipment was purchased for $160,000 and had accumulated depreciation of $60,000. What amount is reported as ordinary income under Code Sec. 1245?

A. $0
B. $40,000
C. $60,000
D. $100,000

assess.AICPA.120732REG

250. Lobster, Inc. incurs the following losses on disposition of business assets during the year:

Loss on the abandonment of office equipment	$25,000
Loss on the sale of a building (straight-line depreciation taken in prior years of $200,000)	250,000
Loss on the sale of delivery trucks	15,000

What is the amount and character of the losses to be reported on Lobster's tax return?

A. $40,000 Section 1231 loss only
B. $40,000 Section 1231 loss, $50,000 long-term capital loss
C. $40,000 Section 1231 loss, $250,000 long-term capital loss
D. $290,000 Section 1231 loss

Section 1231 Assets—Cost Recovery

aicpa.aq.sec1231.as.costs.001_17

251. Lobster, Inc. purchased the following assets during Year 1:

Computers	$35,000
Computer desks	22,000
Office furniture	4,000
Delivery trucks	25,000
Building	425,000

What should be reported as the cost basis for a MACRS seven-year property?

A. $26,000
B. $86,000
C. $451,000
D. $511,000

aicpa.aq.sec1231.as.costs.002_17

252. A calendar-year taxpayer purchases a new business on July 1. The contract provides the following price allocation: customer list, $100,000; trade name, $50,000; goodwill, $90,000. What is the amortization deduction for the current year?

A. $3,000
B. $6,000
C. $8,000
D. $16,000

assess.AICPA.101108REG_2-18

253. On August 1, 2018, Graham purchases and places into service an office building costing $264,000, including $30,000 for the land. What was Graham's MACRS deduction for the office building in 2018?

A. $9,600
B. $6,000
C. $3,600
D. $2,250

assess.AICPA.120730REG

254. As part of a business acquisition, on January 1, Fast, Inc. entered into a covenant not to compete with Swift, Inc. for a period of five years, with an option by Swift to extend it to seven years. What is the amortization period of the covenant for tax purposes?

A. 5 years
B. 7 years
C. 15 years
D. 17 years

Like-Kind Exchanges and Involuntary Conversions

assess.AICPA.090845REG_2-18

255. A heavy equipment dealer would like to trade some business assets in a nontaxable exchange. Which of the following exchanges would qualify as nontaxable in 2018?

   A. The company jet for a large truck to be used in the corporation
   B. Investment securities for antiques to be held as investments
   C. A road grader held in inventory for another road grader
   D. A corporate office building for a vacant lot

assess.AICPA.120745REG

256. Hogan exchanged a business-use machine having an original cost of $100,000 and accumulated depreciation of $30,000 for business-use equipment owned by Baker having a fair market value of $80,000 plus $1,000 cash. Baker assumed a $2,000 outstanding debt on the machine. What taxable gain should Hogan recognize?

   A. $0
   B. $3,000
   C. $10,000
   D. $11,000

assess.AICPA.REG.like.exchange-0012

257. Dawson, Inc.'s warehouse (with an adjusted tax basis of $75,000) was destroyed by fire. The following year, Dawson received insurance proceeds of $195,000 and acquired a new warehouse for $167,000. Dawson elected to recognize the minimum gain possible. What is Dawson's basis in the new warehouse?

   A. $47,000
   B. $75,000
   C. $139,000
   D. $167,000

Other Nonrecognition Transactions

assess.AICPA.090838REG

258. Sands purchased 100 shares of Eastern Corp. stock for $18,000 on April 1 of the prior year. On February 1 of the current year, Sands sold 50 shares of Eastern for $7,000. Fifteen days later, Sands purchased 25 shares of Eastern for $3,750. What is the amount of Sands's recognized gain or loss?

   A. $0
   B. $500 loss
   C. $1,000 loss
   D. $2,000 loss

assess.AICPA.090847REG

259. Wynn, a single individual age 60, sold Wynn's personal residence for $450,000. Wynn had owned Wynn's residence, which had a basis of $250,000, for six years. Within eight months of the sale, Wynn purchased a new residence for $400,000. What is Wynn's recognized gain from the sale of Wynn's personal residence?

   A. $0
   B. $50,000
   C. $75,000
   D. $200,000

assess.AICPA.120728REG

260. In the current year, Essex sold land with a basis of $80,000 to Yarrow for $100,000. Yarrow paid $25,000 down and agreed to pay $15,000 per year, plus interest, for the next five years, beginning in the second year. Under the installment method, what gain should Essex include in gross income for the year of sale?

   A. $25,000
   B. $20,000
   C. $15,000
   D. $5,000

assess.AICPA.950504REG_2-18

261. Conner purchases 300 shares of Zinco stock for $30,000 in 2003. On May 23, 2017, Conner sells all the stock to his daughter, Alice, for $20,000, its then fair market value. Conner realizes no other gain or loss during 2017. On July 26, 2018, Alice sells the 300 shares of Zinco for $25,000.

What is Alice's recognized gain or loss on her sale?

   A. $0
   B. $5,000 long-term gain
   C. $5,000 short-term loss
   D. $5,000 long-term loss

Federal Taxation of Individuals

Income

Gross Income—General Concepts and Interest

aicpa.aq.gross.income.con.001_17

262. Parents lend $2,000,000 to their child to start a business. The loan is interest-free and is payable on demand. The imputed interest is subject to

   A. The gift tax only in the year the parents lend the money.
   B. The generation-skipping transfer tax, but **not** the gift tax.
   C. The gift tax each year the loan is outstanding.
   D. An excise tax.

assess.AICPA.931133REG_2-18

263. In 2017, Farb, a cash-basis individual taxpayer, received an $8,000 invoice for personal property taxes.

   Believing the amount to be overstated by $5,000, Farb paid the invoiced amount under protest and immediately started legal action to recover the overstatement. In November 2018, the matter was resolved in Farb's favor, and he received a $5,000 refund. Farb itemizes his deductions on his tax returns.

   Which of the following statements is correct regarding the deductibility of the property taxes?

   A. Farb should deduct $8,000 in his 2017 income tax return and should report the $5,000 refund as income in his 2018 income tax return.
   B. Farb should not deduct any amount in his 2017 income tax return and should deduct $3,000 in his 2018 income tax return.
   C. Farb should deduct $3,000 in his 2017 income tax return.
   D. Farb should not deduct any amount in his 2017 income tax return when originally filed, and should file an amended 2017 income tax return in 2018.

assess.AICPA.951110REG_2-18

264. In 2017, Stewart Corp. properly accrued $5,000 for an income item on the basis of a reasonable estimate. In 2018, after filing its 2017 federal income tax return, Stewart determined that the exact amount was $6,000.

   Which of the following statements is correct?

   A. No further inclusion of income is required as the difference is less than 25% of the original amount reported and the estimate had been made in good faith.
   B. The $1,000 difference is includible in Stewart's income tax return.
   C. Stewart is required to notify the IRS within 30 days of the determination of the exact amount of the item.
   D. Stewart is required to file an amended return to report the additional $1,000 of income.

Gross Income—Other Inclusions

assess.AICPA.060804REG_2-18

265. Porter was unemployed for part of the year in 2018. Porter received $35,000 in wages, $4,000 from a state unemployment compensation plan, and $2,000 from his former employer's company-paid supplemental unemployment benefit plan. What is the amount of Porter's gross income in 2018?

   A. $35,000
   B. $37,000
   C. $39,000
   D. $41,000

assess.AICPA.090854REG

266. An individual received $50,000 during the current year pursuant to a divorce decree. A check for $25,000 was identified as annual alimony, checks totaling $10,000 as annual child support, and a check for $15,000 as a property settlement. What amount should be included in the individual's gross income?

   A. $50,000
   B. $40,000
   C. $25,000
   D. $0

assess.AICPA.130912REG

267. Randolph is a single individual who always claims the standard deduction. Randolph received the following in the current year:

Wages	$22,000
Unemployment compensation	6,000
Pension distribution (100% taxable)	4,000
A state tax refund from the previous year	425

What is Randolph's gross income?

A. $22,000
B. $28,425
C. $32,000
D. $32,425

assess.AICPA.931124REG_2-18

268. John and Mary were divorced in 2017. The divorce decree provides that John pay alimony of $10,000 per year, to be reduced by 20% on their child's 18th birthday. During 2018, John paid $7,000 directly to Mary and $3,000 to Spring College for Mary's tuition.

What amount of these payments should be reported as income in Mary's 2018 income tax return?

A. $5,600
B. $8,000
C. $8,600
D. $10,000

assess.AICPA.REG.gross.income.oth-0014

269. In a divorce settlement, the ex-husband was required by court order to pay his ex-wife $36,000 in alimony. She received $25,000 in cash, a painting valued at $10,000, and the use of his beach house, valued at $3,000. What amount of gross income should she report as alimony?

A. $25,000
B. $35,000
C. $36,000
D. $38,000

Gross Income—Exclusions

assess.AICPA.020503REG-AR

270. Fuller was the owner and beneficiary of a $200,000 life insurance policy on a parent. Fuller sold the policy to Decker, for $25,000. Decker paid a total of $40,000 in premiums.

Upon the death of the parent, what amount must Decker include in gross income?

A. $0
B. $135,000
C. $160,000
D. $200,000

assess.AICPA.081201REG_2-18

271. In 2018, Joan accepted and received a $10,000 award for outstanding civic achievement. Joan was selected without any action on her part, and no future services are expected of her as a condition of receiving the award. What amount should Joan include in her 2018 adjusted gross income in connection with this award?

A. $0
B. $4,000
C. $5,000
D. $10,000

assess.AICPA.970501REG-AR

272. Klein, a master's degree candidate at Briar University, was awarded a $12,000 scholarship from Briar. The scholarship was used to pay Klein's university tuition and fees. Klein also received $5,000 for teaching two courses at a nearby college.

What amount is includible in Klein's gross income?

A. $0
B. $5,000
C. $12,000
D. $17,000

Taxation of Income from Business Entities

supplemental.ITAX-0009B

273. During the current year, Gail Judd received the following dividends from

Benefit Life Insurance Co., on Gail's life insurance policy (Total dividends received have not yet exceeded accumulated premiums paid)	$100
Safe National Bank, on bank's common stock	300
Roe Mfg. Corp., a Delaware corporation, on preferred stock	500

What amount of dividend income should Gail report in her current-year income tax return?

A. $900
B. $800
C. $500
D. $300

supplemental.ITAX-0010B_2-18

274. Amy Finch had the following cash receipts during 2018:

Dividend from a mutual insurance company on a life insurance policy	$500
Dividend on listed corporation stock; payment date by corporation was 12/30/17, but Amy received the dividend in the mail on 1/2/18	875

Total dividends received to date on the life insurance policy do not exceed the aggregated premiums paid by Amy. How much should Amy report for dividend income for 2018?

A. $1,375
B. $875
C. $500
D. $0

supplemental.TPRO-0013B_2-18

275. In January 2018, Joan Hill bought one share of Orban Corp. stock for $300. On March 1, 2018, Orban distributed one share of preferred stock for each share of common stock held. This distribution was nontaxable. On March 1, 2018, Joan's one share of common stock had a fair market value of $450, while the preferred stock had a fair market value of $150. The holding period for the preferred stock starts in

A. January 2018.
B. March 2018.
C. September 2018.
D. December 2018.

supplemental.TPRO-0014B_2-18

276. On July 1, 2012, Lila Perl paid $90,000 for 450 shares of Janis Corp. common stock. Lila received a nontaxable stock dividend of 50 new common shares in August 2018. On December 20, 2018, Lila sold the 50 new shares for $11,000. How much should Lila report in her 2018 return as long-term capital gain?

A. $0
B. $1,000
C. $2,000
D. $11,000

Accounting Methods and Periods—Individuals

assess.AICPA.060824REG-P2-AR

277. Which of the following is correct concerning the LIFO method (as compared to the FIFO method) in a period when prices are rising?

A. Deferred tax and cost of goods sold are lower.
B. Current tax liability and ending inventory are higher.
C. Current tax liability is lower and ending inventory is higher.
D. Current tax liability is lower and cost of goods sold is higher.

assess.AICPA.120742REG

278. In calculating the tax of a corporation for a short period, which of the following processes is correct?

A. Divide current-year income by prior-year income, then multiply the result by prior-year tax.
B. Compute tax on short-period income, then multiply the result by 12 divided by the number of months in the short period.
C. Determine the average taxable income for the past three years, then multiply the result by the number of months in the short period divided by 12.
D. Annualize income and calculate the tax on annualized income, then multiply the computed tax by the number of months in the short period divided by 12.

assess.AICPA.REG.acct.meth-0035

279. Which expense listed below would be subject to the Uniform Capitalization Rules of Code Section 263A?

A. Quality control
B. Research and development
C. Advertising
D. Selling

aq.acct.meth.001_0818

280. An applicable financial statement is a statement that conforms to GAAP and is

A. Reported in a 10 K.
B. Filed with a federal agency (but not for tax purposes).
C. Conforms to International Financial Reporting Standards (IFRS).
D. All of the above.

assess.AICPA.941140REG-AR

281. Under the uniform capitalization rules applicable to property acquired for resale, which of the following costs should be capitalized with respect to inventory if no exceptions are met?

	Marketing Costs	Off-site Storage Costs
A.	Yes	Yes
B.	Yes	No
C.	No	No
D.	No	Yes

testbank.ITAX-0041_2-18

282. Marc Clay was unemployed for the entire year 2017. In January 2018, Clay obtained full-time employment 60 miles away from the city where he had resided during the 10 years preceding 2018. Clay kept his new job for the entire year 2018. In January 2018, Clay paid direct moving expenses of $1,300 in relocating to his new city of residence, but he received no reimbursement for these expenses. In his 2018 income tax return, Clay's direct moving expenses are

A. Not deductible.
B. Fully deductible only if Clay itemizes his deductions.
C. Fully deductible from gross income in arriving at adjusted gross income.
D. Deductible subject to a 2% threshold if Clay itemizes his deductions.

Taxation of Employee Benefits

assess.AICPA.010510REG-AR

283. Darr, an employee of Sorce C corporation, is not a shareholder. Which of the following would be included in a taxpayer's gross income?

A. Employer provided medical insurance coverage under a health plan.
B. A $10,000 gift from the taxpayer's grandparents.
C. The fair market value of land that the taxpayer inherited from an uncle.
D. The dividend income on shares of stock that the taxpayer received for services rendered.

assess.AICPA.101122REG-SIM

284. Easel Co. has elected to reimburse employees for business expenses under a nonaccountable plan. Easel does not require employees to provide proof of expenses and allows employees to keep any amount not spent. Under the plan, Mel, an Easel employee for a full year, gets $400 per month for business

automobile expenses. At the end of the year Mel informs Easel that the only business expense incurred was for business mileage of 12,000 at a rate of 30 cents per mile, the IRS standard mileage rate at the time. Mel encloses a check for $1,200 to refund the overpayment to Easel. What amounts should be reported in Mel's gross income for the year?

A. $0
B. $1,200
C. $3,600
D. $4,800

assess.AICPA.130906REG

285. Johnson worked for ABC Co. and earned a salary of $100,000. Johnson also received, as a fringe benefit, group term-life insurance at twice Johnson's salary. The annual IRS-established uniform cost of insurance is $2.76 per $1,000. What amount must Johnson include in gross income?

A. $100,000
B. $100,276
C. $100,414
D. $100,552

tax.employ_LA_aicpa_1

286. Jensen reported the following items during the current year:

Fair rent value of a condominium owned by Jensen's employer	$1,400
Cash found in a desk purchased for $30 at a flea market	400
Inheritance	11,000

The employer allowed Jensen to use the condominium for free in recognition of outstanding achievement. Based on this information, what is Jensen's gross income for the year?

A. $1,400
B. $1,770
C. $1,800
D. $12,400

Taxation of Retirement Plans

assess.AICPA.060805REG-AR

287. A calendar-year individual is eligible to contribute to a deductible IRA. The taxpayer obtained a six-month extension to file until October 15 but did not file the return until November 1. What is the latest date that an IRA

contribution can be made in order to qualify as a deduction on the prior year's return?

A. October 15
B. April 15
C. August 15
D. November 1

assess.AICPA.090844REG

288. A 33-year-old taxpayer withdrew $30,000 (pretax) from a traditional IRA. The taxpayer has a 33% effective tax rate and a 35% marginal tax rate. What is the total tax liability associated with the withdrawal?

A. $10,000
B. $10,500
C. $13,000
D. $13,500

assess.AICPA.101139REG-SIM

289. John invested $2,000 a year into his retirement plan from his before tax earnings (that is, he received a deduction for these contributions and was not taxed on the income). His employer contributed $3,000 a year to John's retirement fund. After 30 years of contributions, John retires and receives a distribution, which is not tax-free, of $350,000, the balance in his retirement fund. John must include what amount in gross income?

A. $0
B. $200,000
C. $260,000
D. $350,000

tax.retire_LA_aicpa_1

290. Sanderson has made deductible contributions to his traditional IRA for many years. Sanderson recently retired at age 60 and received a distribution of $150,000. In which way, if any, will the distribution be taxed?

A. As a capital gain.
B. As ordinary income.
C. Subject to a 10% penalty.
D. It will **not** be taxed.

Deductions

Deductions—Basic Principles

assess.AICPA.010504REG-AR

291. Mock operates a retail business selling illegal narcotic substances. Which of the following

item(s) may Mock deduct in calculating business income?

I. Cost of merchandise
II. Business expenses other than the cost of merchandise

A. I only.
B. II only.
C. Both I and II.
D. Neither I nor II.

assess.AICPA.101136REG-SIM

292. Tom owns a fast-food restaurant which he reports as a sole proprietorship for tax purposes. Which of the following expenses is allowed as a deduction on Tom's Schedule C for the current year?

A. Wages of $20 per week to his 14-year-old daughter who cleans the restaurant on Saturdays.
B. Speeding ticket of $75 that he incurred while picking up supplies to bring to the restaurant.
C. A bribe of $200 to the city inspector charged with inspecting whether restaurants have met all city health requirements.
D. State income taxes paid during the year of $1,650.

assess.AICPA.941148REG-AR

293. A corporation's penalty for underpaying federal estimated taxes is

A. Not deductible.
B. Fully deductible in the year paid.
C. Fully deductible if reasonable cause can be established for the underpayment.
D. Partially deductible.

Deductions for AGI

assess.AICPA.010507-AR

294. Which of the following conditions must be present for a payment to qualify as deductible alimony?

I. Payments must be in cash.
II. The payments must end no later than the recipient's death.

A. I only.
B. II only.
C. Both I and II.
D. Neither I nor II.

assess.AICPA.120718REG

295. Davidson was transferred from Chicago to Atlanta. In connection with the transfer, Davidson incurred the following moving expenses:

Moving the household goods	$2,000
Temporary living expenses in Atlanta	400
Lodging on the way to Atlanta	100
Meals	40

What amount may Davidson deduct if the employer reimbursed Davidson $2,000 (not included in form W-2) for moving expenses?

A. $100
B. $120
C. $500
D. $520

assess.AICPA.120748REG

296. Cole earned $3,000 in wages, incurred $1,000 in unreimbursed employee business expenses, paid $400 as interest on a student loan, and contributed $100 to a charity. What is Cole's adjusted gross income?

A. $3,000
B. $2,600
C. $2,500
D. $1,600

assess.AICPA.921105REG-P2-AR_2-18

297. Alex and Myra Burg, married and filing joint income tax returns, derive their entire income from the operation of their retail candy shop. Their 2018 adjusted gross income was $50,000. The Burgs itemized their deductions on Schedule A for 2018.

The following unreimbursed cash expenditures were among those made by the Burgs during 2018:

Repair and maintenance of motorized wheelchair for physically handicapped dependent child	$300
Tuition, meals and lodging at special school for physically handicapped dependent child in the institution primarily for the availability of medical care, with meals and lodging furnished as necessary incidents to that care State income tax	1,200
Self-employment tax	7,650

Four tickets to a theater party sponsored by a qualified charitable organization; not considered a business expense; similar tickets would cost $25 each at the box office	160
Repair of glass vase accidentally broken in home by dog; vase cost $500 in 2013; fair value $600 before accident and $200 after accident	90
Fee for breaking lease on prior apartment residence located 20 miles from new residence	500
Security deposit placed on apartment at new location	900

What amount should the Burgs deduct for moving expenses in their itemized deductions on Schedule A for 2018?

A. $0
B. $500
C. $900
D. $1,400

Itemized Deductions—Medical, Taxes, Interest

assess.AICPA.010501REG-AR

298. Carroll, an unmarried taxpayer with an adjusted gross income of $100,000, incurred and paid the following unreimbursed medical expenses for the year:

Doctor bills resulting from a serious fall	$5,000
Cosmetic surgery that was necessary to correct a congenital deformity	15,000

Carroll had no medical insurance and is 60 years old. For regular income tax purposes, what was Carroll's maximum allowable medical expense deduction, after the applicable threshold limitation, for the year?

A. $0
B. $10,000
C. $15,000
D. $20,000

assess.AICPA.120701REG

299. An individual taxpayer earned $10,000 in investment income, $8,000 in noninterest investment expenses, and $5,000 in investment interest expense. How much is the taxpayer allowed to deduct on the current-year's tax return for investment interest expenses?

A. $0
B. $2,000
C. $3,000
D. $5,000

assess.AICPA.120727REG

300. Which of the following statements is correct regarding the deductibility of an individual's medical expenses?

   A. A medical expense paid by credit card is deductible in the year the credit card bill is paid.
   B. A medical expense deduction is allowed for payments made in the current year for medical services received in earlier years.
   C. Medical expenses, net of insurance reimbursements, are disregarded in the alternative minimum tax calculation.
   D. A medical expense deduction is NOT allowed for Medicare insurance premiums.

assess.AICPA.950512REG-AR_2-18

301. Tom and Sally White, married and filing joint income tax returns, derive their entire income from the operation of their retail stationery shop.

   Their 2018 adjusted gross income was $100,000. The Whites itemized their deductions on Schedule A for 2018.

   The following unreimbursed cash expenditures were among those made by the Whites during 2018:

Repair and maintenance of motorized wheelchair for physically handicapped dependent child	$600
Tuition, meals, and lodging at special school for physically handicapped dependent child in an institution primarily for the availability of medical care, with meals and lodging furnished as necessary incidents to that care	8,000

   Without regard to the adjusted gross income percentage threshold, what amount may the Whites claim in their 2018 return as qualifying medical expenses?

   A. $8,600
   B. $8,000
   C. $600
   D. $0

Itemized Deductions—Other

aicpa.aq.item.deduct2.001_17

302. Which of the following would qualify as a deductible charitable contribution in Year 1 for an individual taxpayer?

   A. A $200 contribution to the taxpayer's church charged by credit card on December 31, Year 1.
   B. A $450 contribution to a senator's campaign on December 31, Year 1.
   C. A $1,000 contribution to a foreign charity on December 31, Year 1.
   D. A contribution on December 31, Year 1, of $500 worth of clothing to the Salvation Army for which substantiation was **not** obtained.

aicpa.aq.item.deduct2.002_17

303. Dr. Merry, a self-employed dentist, incurred the following expenses:

Investment expenses	$700
Custodial fees related to Dr. Merry's Keogh plan	40
Work uniforms for Dr. Merry and Dr. Merry's employees	320
Subscriptions for periodicals used in the waiting room	110
Dental education seminar	1,300

   What is the amount of expenses the doctor can deduct as business expenses on Schedule C, *Profit or Loss from Business?*

   A. $1,620
   B. $1,730
   C. $1,770
   D. $2,430

assess.AICPA.120747REG_2-18

304. Carter incurred the following expenses in 2018: $500 for the preparation of a personal income tax return, $100 for custodial fees on an IRA, $150 for professional publications, and $2,000 for union dues. Carter's current year adjusted gross income is $75,000. Carter, who is not self-employed, itemizes deductions. What will Carter's deduction be for miscellaneous itemized deductions after any limitations in 2018?

   A. $0
   B. $750
   C. $1,250
   D. $2,750

assess.AICPA.REG.item.deduct2-0023

305. Robinson's personal residence was partially destroyed by fire. Its fair market value (FMV) before the fire was $500,000, and the FMV after the fire was $300,000. Robinson's adjusted basis in the home was $350,000. Robinson settled the insurance claim on the fire for $175,000. If Robinson's adjusted gross income (AGI) for the year is $120,000, what amount of the casualty loss may Robinson claim after consideration of threshold limitations?

A. $12,900
B. $13,000
C. $24,900
D. $25,000

Business Expenses

assess.AICPA.101120REG-SIM

306. Abe Architect owns his own architectural consulting firm. During the current year he incurred the following expenses related to meetings with clients and potential clients:

Meal expenses	$2,000
Dues to Five-Star Country Club	$5,000
Greens fee for playing golf with clients	$1,500
Tickets to Super Bowl (face value = $1,000)	$3,500

What is the amount of deductible expenses for the current year related to these expenditures?

A. $2,250
B. $4,500
C. $3,500
D. $12,000

assess.AICPA.120717REG

307. Nichol Corp. gave gifts to 15 individuals who were customers of the business. The gifts were not in the nature of advertising. The market values of the gifts were as follows:

5 gifts	@ $15 each
9 gifts	@ $30 each
1 gift	@ $100

What amount is deductible as business gifts?

A. $0
B. $75
C. $325
D. $445

assess.AICPA.941131REG-AR_2-18

308. Banks Corp., a calendar year corporation, reimburses employees for properly substantiated qualifying business meal expenses. The employees are present at the meals, which are neither lavish nor extravagant, and the reimbursement is not treated as wages subject to withholdings.

For 2018, what percentage of the meal expense may Banks deduct?

A. 0%
B. 50%
C. 80%
D. 100%

assess.AICPA.990506REG-AR

309. Baker, a sole proprietor CPA, has several clients that do business in Spain. While on a four-week vacation in Spain, Baker took a five-day seminar on Spanish business practices that cost $700. Baker's round-trip airfare to Spain was $600. While in Spain, Baker spent an average of $100 per day on accommodations, local travel, and other incidental expenses, for total expenses of $2,800.

What amount of educational expense can Baker deduct on Form 1040 Schedule C, *Profit or Loss From Business*?

A. $700
B. $1,200
C. $1,800
D. $4,100

Deductions—Losses and Bad Debts

assess.AICPA.101123REG_2-18

310. Jason Budd, CPA, reports on the cash basis. In April 2017, Budd billed a client $3,500 for the following professional services:

Personal estate planning	$2,000
Personal tax return preparation	1,000
Compilation of business financial statements	500

No part of the $3,500 was ever paid. In April 2018, the client declared bankruptcy, and the $3,500 obligation became totally uncollectible. What loss can Budd deduct on his tax return for this bad debt?

A. $0
B. $500
C. $1,500
D. $3,500

assess.AICPA.101124REG_2-18

311. For the year ended December 31, 2018, Sanchez had a net operating loss of $100,000. Taxable income for the earlier years, computed without reference to the net operating loss, was as follows:

Taxable Income	
2014	$90,000
2015	$80,000
2016	$50,000
2017	$40,000

If Sanchez makes no special election to waive the net operating loss carryback, what amount of net operating loss will be available to Sanchez for 2019?

A. $0
B. $10,000
C. $60,000
D. $100,000

assess.AICPA.990507REG_2-18

312. Destry, a single taxpayer, reported the following on his 2018 U.S. Individual Income Tax Return Form 1040:

Income:

Wages	$5,000
Interest on savings account	1,000
Net rental income	4,000

Deductions:

Personal exemption	$4,150
Standard deduction	6,500
Net business loss	16,000
Net short-term capital loss	2,000

What is Destry's net operating loss that is available for carryback or carryforward?

A. $7,000
B. $9,000
C. $15,100
D. $16,000

Limitations on Business Deductions

aicpa.aq.limit.bus.deduct.001_17

313. Bartlet owns a manufacturing business and participates in the business. Which of the following conditions would cause the business to be considered a nonpassive activity for Bartlet?

A. Bartlet participates in the business for more than 500 hours during a year.
B. The business made a profit in any three of the last five years that preceded the current year.
C. The business has at least 10 employees who, individually or collectively, work for the business more than 1,000 hours in a year.
D. Bartlet files an election with the IRS postponing nonpassive activity classification.

aicpa.aq.limit.bus.deduct.002_17

314. The term active participation for a passive activity loss is relevant in relation to

A. Rental real estate activities.
B. Working interests in oil and gas properties.
C. Passive activities in which the taxpayer materially participates.
D. Passive activities in which the taxpayer **not** materially participate.

assess.AICPA.060808REG-P2-AR

315. Barkley owns a vacation cabin that was rented to unrelated parties for 10 days during the year for $2,500. The cabin was used personally by Barkley for 3 months and left vacant for the rest of the year. Expenses for the cabin were as follows:

Real Estate Taxes	$1,000
Maintenance and Utilities	$2,000

How much rental income (loss) is included in Barkley's adjusted gross income?

A. $0
B. $500
C. $(500)
D. $(1,500)

assess.AICPA.101104REG

316. Lane, a single taxpayer, received $160,000 in salary, $15,000 in income from an S Corporation in which Lane does not materially participate, and a $35,000 passive loss from a real estate rental activity in which Lane materially participated. Lane's modified adjusted gross income was $165,000. What amount of the real estate rental activity loss was deductible?

A. $0
B. $15,000
C. $25,000
D. $35,000

assess.AICPA.130924REG

317. A review of Bearing's year 2 records disclosed the following tax information:

Wages	$18,000
Taxable interest and qualifying dividends	4,000
Schedule C trucking business net income	32,000
Rental (loss) from residential property	(35,000)
Limited partnership (loss)	(5,000)

Bearing actively participated in the rental property and was a limited partner in the partnership. Bearing had sufficient amounts at risk for the rental property and the partnership. What is Bearing's year 2 adjusted gross income?

A. $14,000
B. $19,000
C. $29,000
D. $54,000

Individual Tax Issues

Tax Dependents

aicpa.aq.person.exempt.001_17

318. Anderson, a computer engineer, and spouse, who is unemployed, provide more than half of the support for their child, age 23, who is a full-time student and who earns $7,000. They also provide more than half of the support for their older child, age 33, who earns $2,000 during the year. How many exemptions may the Andersons claim on their joint tax return?

A. One personal and two dependencies.
B. One personal and one dependency.
C. Two personal and one dependency.
D. Two personal and two dependencies.

assess.AICPA.060251REG-V-D

319. Sara Hance, who is single and lives alone in Idaho, has no income of her own and is supported in full by the following persons:

	Amount of Support	Percent of Total
Alma (unrelated friend)	$2,400	48
Ben (Sara's brother)	2,150	43
Carl (Sara's son)	450	9
Total	$5,000	100

Under a multiple support agreement, Sara's dependency exemption can be claimed by:

A. No one
B. Alma
C. Ben
D. Carl

assess.AICPA.101117REG-SIM

320. Which of the following tests does NOT have to be met for Tom to claim a dependency exemption under the qualifying relative rule?

A. Age Test
B. Gross Income Test
C. Support Test (50% support from Tom)
D. Citizenship/Residency Test

assess.AICPA.REG.person.exempt-0031

321. John earned $500,000 in his business during the current year, and his wife received investment income of $15,000. John provides more than half of the support of his widowed sister, who lives with John and earned $45,000 in salary. John also provides full support for his two children, an 18-year-old daughter and a 20-year-old son, who is a full-time college student. The family employs a live-in housekeeper and a live-in butler to assist them with their residence. What is the maximum number of personal and dependency exemptions that John and his wife are eligible to claim?

A. Two exemptions
B. Four exemptions
C. Five exemptions
D. Seven exemptions

Filing Status

assess.AICPA.060319REG-AR

322. Parker, whose spouse died during the preceding year, has not remarried. Parker maintains a home for a dependent child. What is Parker's most advantageous filing status?

A. Single
B. Head of household
C. Married filing separately.
D. Qualifying widow(er) with dependent child.

assess.AICPA.060810REG-AR

323. In which of the following situations may taxpayers file as married filing jointly?

A. Taxpayers who were married but lived apart during the year.
B. Taxpayers who were married but lived under a legal separation agreement at the end of the year.

C. Taxpayers who were divorced during the year.
D. Taxpayers who were legally separated but lived together for the entire year.

assess.AICPA.101106REG

324. A taxpayer's spouse dies in August of the current year. Which of the following is the taxpayer's filing status for the current year?

A. Single.
B. Qualifying widow(er).
C. Head of household.
D. Married filing jointly.

assess.AICPA.921110REG-P2-AR

325. For head of household filing status, which of the following costs are considered in determining whether the taxpayer has contributed more than one-half the cost of maintaining the household?

	Food Consumed in the Home	**Value of Services Rendered in the Home by the Taxpayer**
A.	Yes	Yes
B.	No	No
C.	Yes	No
D.	No	Yes

Alternative Minimum Tax and Other Taxes

aicpa.aq.alt.min.tax.001_17

326. Juan recently started operating a flower shop as a proprietorship. In its first year of operations, the shop had a taxable income of $60,000. Assuming that Juan had **no** other employment-related earnings,

A. the flower shop must withhold FICA taxes from Juan's earnings.
B. Juan must pay self-employment tax on the earnings of the business.
C. Juan will be exempt from self-employment taxes for the first three years of operations.
D. Juan will be exempt from the Medicare tax because the business earnings are below the threshold amount.

assess.AICPA.120735REG

327. Farr, an unmarried taxpayer, had $70,000 of adjusted gross income and the following deductions for regular income tax purposes:

Home mortgage interest on a loan to acquire a principal residence	$11,000
Miscellaneous itemized deductions above the threshold limitation	$2,000

What are Farr's total allowable itemized deductions for computing alternative minimum taxable income?

A. $0
B. $2,000
C. $11,000
D. $13,000

assess.AICPA.130918REG

328. Which of the following may **not** be deducted in the computation of alternative minimum taxable income of an individual?

A. Traditional IRA account contribution
B. One-half of the self-employment tax deduction
C. Personal exemptions
D. Charitable contributions

assess.AICPA.990502REG-AR

329. Baum, an unmarried optometrist and sole proprietor of Optics, buys and maintains a supply of eyeglasses and frames to sell in the ordinary course of business. In 2018, Optics had $350,000 in gross business receipts and its year-end inventory was not subject to the uniform capitalization rules. Baum's 2018 adjusted gross income was $90,000 and Baum qualified to itemize deductions.

During 2018, Baum recorded the following information:

Business expenses:		
Optics cost of goods sold		$35,000
Optics rent expense	$28,000	
Liability insurance premium on Optics		$5,250
Other expenditures:		
Baum's self-employment tax	$29,750	
Baum's self-employment health insurance		$8,750
Insurance premium on personal residence		
In 2018, Baum's home was totally destroyed by fire. The furniture had an adjusted basis of $14,000 and a fair market value of $11,000. During 2018, Baum collected $3,000 in insurance reimbursement and had no casualty gains during the year.	$2,625	

Qualified 2018 mortgage interest on a loan to acquire a personal residence	$52,500
Annual interest on a $70,000, 5-year home equity loan. The loan was secured by Baum's home, obtained January 2, 2018. The fair market value of the home exceeded the mortgage and the home equity loan by a substantial amount. The proceeds were used to purchase a car for personal use.	$3,500
Points prepaid on January 2, 2018 to acquire the home equity loan	$1,400
Real estate taxes on personal residence	$2,200
Estimated payments of 2018 federal income taxes	$13,500
Local property taxes on the car value, used exclusively for personal use	$300

What amount should Baum report as 2018 net earnings from self-employment?

A. $243,250
B. $252,000
C. $273,000
D. $281,750

Tax Planning Strategies for Individuals

assess.AICPA.101086REG-SIM

330. Ms. Planner is in the 25% tax bracket and itemizes on her tax return. She plans to make a charitable contribution of $12,000 to her alma mater this year. The net cost of this contribution to T is:

A. $0
B. $3,000
C. $9,000
D. $12,000

assess.AICPA.101087REG-SIM

331. Chris is in the 50% tax bracket in Year 1 but Congress has decreased his tax bracket to 30% for Year 2. Which of the following would be an appropriate tax planning strategy for Chris?

A. Defer income until Year 2.
B. Accelerate income into Year 1.
C. Defer deductions until Year 2.
D. Increase his estimated tax payments for Year 1.

assess.AICPA.101089REG-SIM

332. Jose has owned stock for eight years that has a basis of $20,000 and fair market value of $100,000. Jose contributes the stock to a qualified charity. Which of the following is a proper tax consequence from this transaction?

A. Jose has recognized gain of $80,000.
B. Jose has a charitable contribution of $100,000.
C. Jose has a charitable contribution of $80,000.
D. Jose has a charitable contribution of $20,000.

assess.AICPA.101090REG-SIM

333. Orleans has owned land as an investment for five years. His basis in the land is $70,000 and the land's current fair market value is $50,000. Which of the following statements is correct with regard to this land?

A. If Orleans sells the land to his father he can deduct the $20,000 loss in the land.
B. If Orleans gives the property to an unrelated friend he can deduct the $20,000 loss in the land.
C. Orleans should sell the land, recognize the $20,000 capital loss, and then gift the $50,000 cash from the sale to his friend.
D. If the land is sold to an unrelated party, the $20,000 loss cannot be recognized since the land is not depreciable.

Tax Credits

Personal Tax Credits

assess.AICPA.101105REG_2-18

334. Which of the following disqualifies an individual from the earned income credit?

A. The taxpayer's qualifying child is a 17-year-old grandchild.
B. The taxpayer has earned income of $5,000.

C. The taxpayer's five-year-old child lived in the taxpayer's home for only eight months.
D. The taxpayer has a filing status of married filing separately.

assess.AICPA.101128REG-SIM_2-18

335. Mr. and Mrs. Alexander have two dependent children, one of whom (Cal) is a freshman in college during 2018. Tuition and fees paid for Cal during 2018 total $15,000. The Alexanders also paid $10,000 in 2018 for their 14-year-old daughter, Kaitlin, to attend a private high school. The Alexanders file a joint tax return for 2018 and report adjusted gross income of $150,000. Cal is a full-time student and enrolled in a degree program. What is the Alexanders' Hope/American Opportunity Tax Credit for 2018?

A. $0
B. $2,500
C. $5,000
D. $15,000

assess.AICPA.101130REG-SIM

336. Which of the following statements is false with regard to the child and dependent care credit?

A. The caregiver cannot be a dependent relative or child of the taxpayer.
B. The credit percentage begins at 35% and phases out once AGI exceeds a certain threshold. As income increases the credit percentage is eventually reduced to zero.
C. The maximum amount of expense eligible for the credit is $3,000 ($6,000 if more than one individual qualifies for care).
D. A qualifying child or dependent under the age of 13 who lives with the taxpayer more than one-half of the tax year is a qualifying individual for purposes of claiming the credit.

assess.AICPA.921111REG-P2-AR_2-18

337. In 2018, to qualify for the child care credit on a joint return, the spouses must

	Have an Adjusted Gross Income of $15,000 or Less	Be gainfully Employed/ Looking for Work or a Student when Related Expenses are Incurred
A.	Yes	Yes
B.	No	No
C.	Yes	No
D.	No	Yes

assess.AICPA.940517REG-AR

338. Which of the following credits can result in a refund, even if the individual had no income tax liability?

A. Credit for prior year minimum tax
B. Elderly and permanently and totally disabled credit
C. Earned income credit
D. Child and dependent care credit

Estate and Gift Taxation

Federal Gift Tax

aicpa.aq.fed.gift.tax.001_17

339. This year, Beck gave $5,000 cash to a nephew, canceled $3,000 of the same nephew's indebtedness, donated $1,500 to a political party, and gave $1,200 of municipal bonds to a parent. What is the amount of Beck's gifts before considering the gift tax annual exclusion?

A. $5,000
B. $8,000
C. $9,200
D. $10,700

assess.AICPA.090842REG_2-18

340. Which of the following payments would require the donor to file a gift tax return?

A. $30,000 to a university for a spouse's tuition
B. $40,000 to a university for a cousin's room and board
C. $50,000 to a hospital for a parent's medical expenses
D. $80,000 to a physician for a friend's surgery

assess.AICPA.090846REG_2-18

341. During the current year, Mann, an unmarried U.S. citizen, made a $5,000 cash gift to an only child and also paid $25,000 in tuition expenses directly to a grandchild's university on the grandchild's behalf. Mann made no other lifetime transfers. Assume that the gift tax annual exclusion is $15,000. For gift tax purposes, what was Mann's taxable gift?

A. $30,000
B. $25,000
C. $15,000
D. $0

assess.AICPA.120705REG

342. The answer to each of the following questions would be relevant in determining whether a tuition payment made on behalf of another individual is excludible for gift tax purposes EXCEPT:

    A. Was the tuition payment made for tuition or for other expenses?

    B. Was the qualifying educational organization located in a foreign country?

    C. Was the tuition payment made directly to the educational organization?

    D. Was the tuition payment made for a family member?

Federal Estate Tax

assess.AICPA.090832REG-SIM

343. Ordinary and necessary administration expenses of an estate are deductible:

    A. Only on the fiduciary income tax return.

    B. Only on the estate tax return.

    C. On the fiduciary income tax return if the estate tax deduction is waived.

    D. On both the fiduciary income tax return and the estate tax return.

assess.AICPA.090833REG

344. Under which of the following circumstances is trust property with an independent trustee includible in the grantor's gross estate?

    A. The trust is revocable.

    B. The trust is established for a minor.

    C. The trustee has the power to distribute trust income.

    D. The income beneficiary disclaims the property, which then passes to the remainderman, the grantor's friend.

assess.AICPA.090882REG-SIM

345. The federal estate tax may not be reduced by a credit of

    A. Foreign death taxes.

    B. Credit for estate tax paid on a prior transfer of the same property within ten years of the death of the decedent.

    C. Gift taxes paid on pre-1977 gifts.

    D. State death taxes paid.

assess.AICPA.941156REG-AR_2-18

346. Bell, a cash-basis calendar-year taxpayer, died on June 1, 2018. In 2018, prior to her death, Bell incurred $2,000 in medical expenses. The executor of the estate paid the medical expenses, which were a claim against the estate, on July 1, 2018.

If the executor files the appropriate waiver, the medical expenses are deductible on

    A. The estate tax return.

    B. Bell's final income tax return.

    C. The estate income tax return.

    D. The executor's income tax return.

Federal Taxation of Entities

Corporate Taxation

Formation of a Corporation

assess.AICPA.090839REG

347. In April, A and B formed X Corp. A contributed $50,000 cash, and B contributed land worth $70,000 (with an adjusted basis of $40,000). B also received $20,000 cash from the corporation. A and B each receives 50% of the corporation's stock. What is the tax basis of the land to X Corp.?

   A. $40,000
   B. $50,000
   C. $60,000
   D. $70,000

assess.AICPA.090851REG

348. Ames and Roth form Homerun, a C corporation. Ames contributes several autographed baseballs to Homerun. Ames purchased the baseballs for $500, and they have a total fair market value of $1,000. Roth contributes several autographed baseball bats to Homerun. Roth purchased the bats for $5,000, and they have a fair market value of $7,000. What is Homerun's basis in the contributed bats and balls?

   A. $0
   B. $5,500
   C. $6,000
   D. $8,000

assess.AICPA.130916REG

349. The sole shareholder of an S corporation contributed equipment with a fair market value of $20,000 and a basis of $6,000 subject to $12,000 liability. What amount is the gain, if any, that the shareholder must recognize?

   A. $0
   B. $6,000
   C. $8,000
   D. $12,000

assess.AICPA.941152REG-AR

350. Adams, Beck, and Carr organized Flexo Corp. with authorized voting common stock of $100,000. Adams received 10% of the capital stock in payment for the organizational services that he rendered for the benefit of the newly formed corporation. Adams did not contribute property to Flexo and was under no obligation to be paid by Beck or Carr.

Beck and Carr transferred property in exchange for stock as follows:

	Adjusted Basis	Fair Market Value	% of Flexo Stock Acquired
Beck	5,000	20,000	20%
Carr	60,000	70,000	70%

What amount of gain did Carr recognize from this transaction?

   A. $40,000
   B. $15,000
   C. $10,000
   D. $0

Corporate Income

assess.AICPA.060813REG-P2-AR

351. Which of the following items should be included on the Schedule M-1, *Reconciliation of Income (Loss) per Books With Income per Return*, of Form 1120, *U.S. Corporation Income Tax Return*, to reconcile book income to taxable income?

   A. Cash distributions to shareholders
   B. Premiums paid on key-person life insurance policy
   C. Corporate bond interest
   D. Ending balance of retained earnings

assess.AICPA.090822REG-SIM

352. On January 2 of this year, Big, an accrual-basis, calendar-year C corporation, purchased all of the assets of a sole proprietorship, including $300,000 of goodwill. Current-year federal income tax expense of $110,100 and $7,500 for goodwill amortization (based upon 40-year amortization period) were deducted to arrive at Big's book income of $239,200. What is Big's current-year taxable income (as reconciled on Schedule M-1)?

   A. $239,200
   B. $329,300
   C. $336,800
   D. $349,300

assess.AICPA.130908REG

353. Azure, a C corporation, reports the following:

    Pretax book income of $543,000.

    Depreciation on the tax return is $20,000 greater than depreciation on the financial statements.

    Rent income reportable on the tax return is $36,000 greater than rent income per the financial statements.

    Fines for pollution appear as a $10,000 expense in the financial statements.

    Interest earned on municipal bonds is $25,000.

    What is Azure's taxable income?

    A. $528,000
    B. $543,000
    C. $544,000
    D. $559,000

assess.AICPA.911149REG-P2-AR

354. Would the following expense items be reported on Schedule M-1 of the corporation income tax return showing the reconciliation of income per books with income per return?

	Interest Incurred on Loan to Carry U.S. Obligations	Provision for State Corporation Income Tax
A.	Yes	Yes
B.	No	No
C.	Yes	No
D.	No	Yes

assess.AICPA.REG.corp.income-0009

355. Filler-Up is an accrual-basis, calendar-year C corporation. Filler-Up uses an allowance method for accounting for bad debts. The allowance for bad debts was $20,000 at the beginning of the year and $30,000 at the end of the year. During the year, Filler-Up wrote off $5,000 of uncollectible receivables and accrued an additional $15,000 of expenses for accounts estimated to be uncollectible. What is the Schedule M-1 adjustment on Filler-Up's federal income tax return?

    A. $10,000 decrease in taxable income.
    B. $10,000 increase in taxable income.
    C. $5,000 decrease in taxable income.
    D. $5,000 increase in taxable income.

assess.AICPA.REG.corp.income-0024

356. Lite-Mart, a C corporation, had a beginning credit balance in its warranty reserve account of $120,000. During the year, Lite-Mart accrued estimated warranty expense of $16,000. At the end of the year, Lite-Mart's warranty reserve had a $90,000 credit balance. What amount of warranty expense should Lite-Mart deduct?

    A. $46,000
    B. $30,000
    C. $16,000
    D. $14,000

Accounting Methods and Periods— Corporations

assess.AICPA.090859REG

357. Dart, a C corporation, distributes software over the Internet and has had average revenues in excess of $20 million dollars per year for the past three years. To purchase software, customers key-in their credit card number to a secure web site and receive a password that allows the customer to immediately download the software. As a result, Dart doesn't record accounts receivable or inventory on its books. Which of the following statements is correct?

    A. Dart may use either the cash or accrual method of accounting as long as Dart elects a calendar year end.
    B. Dart may utilize any method of accounting Dart chooses as long as Dart consistently applies the method it chooses.
    C. Dart must use the accrual method of accounting.
    D. Dart may utilize the cash basis method of accounting until it incurs an additional $10 million to develop additional software.

assess.AICPA.120606REG-SIM

358. Which of the following taxpayers may use the cash basis as its method of accounting for tax purposes?

    A. Partnership that is designated as a tax shelter.
    B. Retail store with $2 million in gross receipts.
    C. An international accounting firm organized as a partnership.
    D. Office cleaning corporation with average annual income of $8 million.

assess.AICPA.120742REG

359. In calculating the tax of a corporation for a short period, which of the following processes is correct?

    A. Divide current-year income by prior-year income, then multiply the result by prior-year tax.

B. Compute tax on short-period income, then multiply the result by 12 divided by the number of months in the short period.

C. Determine the average taxable income for the past three years, then multiply the result by the number of months in the short period divided by 12.

D. Annualize income and calculate the tax on annualized income, then multiply the computed tax by the number of months in the short period divided by 12.

assess.AICPA.130923REG

360. The selection of an accounting method for tax purposes by a newly incorporated C corporation

A. Is made on the initial tax return by using the chosen method.

B. Is made by filing a request for a private letter ruling from the IRS.

C. Must first be approved by the company's board of directors.

D. Must be disclosed in the company's organizing documents.

assess.AICPA.930542REG-P2-AR_2-18

361. Ace Rentals Inc., an accrual-basis taxpayer, reported rent receivable of $35,000 and $25,000 in its 2018 and 2017 balance sheets, respectively. During 2018, Ace received $50,000 in rent payments and $5,000 in nonrefundable rent deposits.

In Ace's 2018 corporate income tax return, what amount should Ace include as rent revenue?

A. $50,000
B. $55,000
C. $60,000
D. $65,000

Special Corporate Deductions

assess.AICPA.060815REG-P2-AR

362. In the current year, Brown, a C corporation has gross income (before dividends) of $900,000 and deductions of $1,100,000 (excluding the dividends-received deduction). Brown received dividends of $100,000 from a Fortune 500 corporation during the current year.

What is Brown's net operating loss?

A. $100,000
B. $130,000
C. $170,000
D. $200,000

assess.AICPA.120736REG

363. Robin, a C corporation, had revenues of $200,000 and operating expenses of $75,000. Robin also received a $20,000 dividend from a domestic corporation and is entitled to a $14,000 dividend-received deduction. Robin donated $15,000 to a qualified charitable organization in the current year. What is Robin's contribution deduction?

A. $15,000
B. $14,500
C. $13,900
D. $13,100

assess.AICPA.130909REG

364. Which of the following **cannot** be amortized for tax purposes?

A. Incorporation costs
B. Temporary directors' fees
C. Stock issuance costs
D. Organizational meeting costs

assess.AICPA.900529REG-P2-AR_2-18

365. John Budd is the sole stockholder of Ral Corp., an accrual basis taxpayer engaged in wholesaling operations.

Ral's retained earnings at January 1, 2018, amounted to $1,000,000.

For the year ended December 31, 2018, Ral's book income, before federal income tax, was $300,000.

Included in the computation of this $300,000 were the following:

Dividends received on 500 shares of stock of a taxable domestic corporation that had 1,000,000 shares of stock outstanding (Ral had no portfolio indebtedness)	$1,000
Loss on sale of investment in stock of unaffiliated corporation (this stock had been held for two years; Ral had no other capital gains or losses)	(5,000)
Keyman insurance premiums paid on Budd's life (Ral is the beneficiary of this policy)	3,000
Group term insurance premiums paid on $10,000 life insurance policies for each of Ral's four employees (the employees' spouses are the beneficiaries)	4,000

		Partial Rate Table	Tax Rate
Amortization of cost of acquiring a perpetual dealer's franchise (Ral paid $48,000 for this franchise on July 1, 2018, and is amortizing it over a 48-month period)	6,000	Up to $50,000	15%
		Over $50,000 but not over $75,000	25%
Contribution to a recognized, qualified charity (this contribution was authorized by Ral's board of directors in December 2018, to be paid on January 31, 2019)	75,000	A. $10,000 B. $10,750 C. $12,500 D. $15,750	

On December 1, 2018, Ral received advance rental of $27,000 from a tenant for a three-year lease commencing January 1, 2018, to cover rents for the years 2019, 2020, and 2021. In conformity with GAAP, Ral did not include any part of this rental in its income statement for the year ended December 31, 2018.

What portion of the dividend revenue should be included in Ral's 2018 taxable income?

A. $150
B. $200
C. $300
D. $900

assess.AICPA.930544BEC-P2-AR_2-18

366. Brown Corp., a calendar-year taxpayer, was organized and actively began operations on July 1, 2018, and incurred the following costs:

Legal fees to obtain corporate charter	$40,000
Commission paid to underwriter	25,000
Other stock issue costs	10,000

Brown wishes to deduct and amortize its organizational costs over the shortest period allowed for tax purposes. In 2018, what amount should Brown deduct (ignoring amortization expenses) for the organizational expenses?

A. $40,000
B. $25,000
C. $10,000
D. $5,000

assess.AICPA.940524REG-AR_2-18

367. Kisco Corp.'s taxable income for 2018 before taking the dividends received deduction was $70,000. This includes $10,000 in dividends from an unrelated taxable domestic corporation.

Given the following tax rates, what would Kisco's income tax be before any credits?

assess.AICPA.951104REG-AR_2-18

368. In 2018, Best Corp., an accrual-basis calendar year C corporation, received $100,000 in dividend income from the common stock that it held in an unrelated domestic corporation.

The stock was not debt-financed and was held for over a year. Best recorded the following information for 2018:

Loss from Best's operations	($10,000)
Dividends received	100,000
Taxable income (before dividends-received deduction)	$90,000

Best's dividends-received deduction on its 2018 tax return was

A. $100,000.
B. $80,000.
C. $70,000.
D. $63,000.

assess.AICPA.951109REG-AR

369. If a corporation's charitable contributions exceed the limitation for deductibility in a particular year, the excess

A. Is not deductible in any future or prior year.
B. May be carried back or forward for one year at the corporation's election.
C. May be carried forward to a maximum of five succeeding years.
D. May be carried back to the third preceding year.

Penalty Taxes

assess.AICPA.910542REG-P2-AR

370. The accumulated earnings tax can be imposed

A. Regardless of the number of stockholders of a corporation.
B. On personal holding companies.
C. On companies that make distributions in excess of accumulated earnings.
D. On both partnerships and corporations.

assess.AICPA.930552REG-P2-AR

371. Acme Corp. has two common stockholders. Acme derives all of its income from investments in stocks and securities, and it regularly distributes 51% of its taxable income as dividends to its stockholders. Acme is a

   A. Corporation subject to tax only on income not distributed to stockholders.
   B. Corporation subject to the accumulated earnings tax.
   C. Regulated investment company.
   D. Personal holding company.

assess.AICPA.930555REG-P2-AR_2-18

372. Kari Corp., a manufacturing company, was organized on January 2, 2018. Its 2018 federal taxable income was $400,000 and its federal income tax was $100,000.

   What is the maximum amount of accumulated taxable income that may be subject to the accumulated earnings tax for 2018 if Kari takes only the minimum accumulated earnings credit?

   A. $300,000
   B. $150,000
   C. $50,000
   D. $0

assess.AICPA.941145REG-AR_2-18

373. Zero Corp. is an investment company authorized to issue only common stock.

   During the last half of 2018, Edwards owned 450 of the 1,000 outstanding shares of stock in Zero. Another 350 shares of stock outstanding were owned, 10 shares each, by 35 shareholders who are neither related to each other nor to Edwards.

   Zero could be a personal holding company if the remaining 200 shares of common stock were owned by

   A. An estate where Edwards is the beneficiary.
   B. Edwards's brother-in-law.
   C. A partnership where Edwards is not a partner.
   D. Edwards's cousin.

assess.AICPA.950523REG-AR

374. Edge Corp. met the stock ownership requirements of a personal holding company. What sources of income must Edge consider to determine if the income requirements for a personal holding company have been met?

   I. Interest earned on tax-exempt obligations.
   II. Dividends received from an unrelated domestic corporation.

   A. I only.
   B. II only.
   C. Both I and II.
   D. Neither I nor II.

assess.AICPA.951112REG-AR_2-18

375. Kane Corp. is a calendar year domestic personal holding company. Which deduction(s) must Kane make from 2018 taxable income to determine undistributed personal holding company income prior to the dividend-paid deduction?

	Federal Income Taxes	Net Long-term Capital Gain Less Related Federal Income Taxes
A.	Yes	Yes
B.	Yes	No
C.	No	Yes
D.	No	No

Taxation of Related Corporations

assess.AICPA.060816REG-AR

376. ParentCo, SubOne, and SubTwo have filed consolidated returns since their inception. The members reported the following taxable incomes (losses) for the year:

ParentCo	$50,000
SubOne	(60,000)
SubTwo	(40,000)

   No member reported a capital gain or loss or charitable contributions. What is the amount of the consolidated net operating loss?

   A. $0
   B. $30,000
   C. $50,000
   D. $100,000

assess.AICPA.060817REG-AR

377. Jans, an individual, owns 80% and 100% of the total value and voting power of A and B Corps., which in turn own the following (both value and voting power):

	Ownership	
Property	**A Corp**	**B Corp**
C Corp	80%	–
D Corp	–	100%

All companies are C corporations except
B Corp., which had elected S status since
inception. Which of the following statements is
correct with respect to the companies' ability to
file a consolidated return?

A. A, C, and D may file as a group.
B. A and C may not file as a group, and B and D
may not file as a group.
C. A and C may file as a group, and B and D
may file as a group.
D. A and C may file as a group, but B and D
may not file as a group.

assess.AICPA.090843REG

378. Which of the following groups may elect to file
a consolidated corporate return?

A. A brother/sister-controlled group
B. A parent corporation and all more-
than-10%-controlled partnerships
C. A parent corporation and all more-
than-50%-controlled subsidiaries
D. Members of an affiliated group

assess.AICPA.900536BEC-P2-AR

379. In the consolidated income tax return of a
corporation and its wholly-owned subsidiary,
what percentage of cash dividends paid by the
subsidiary to the parent is tax-free?

A. 0%
B. 70%
C. 80%
D. 100%

assess.AICPA.930543REG-P2-AR_2-18

380. In 2018, Portal Corp. received $100,000 in
dividends from Sal Corp., its 80%-owned
subsidiary.

What net amount of dividend income should
Portal include in its 2018 consolidated tax return?

A. $100,000
B. $80,000
C. $70,000
D. $0

assess.AICPA.940523REG-AR_2-18

381. Tech Corp. files a consolidated return with its
wholly-owned subsidiary, Dow Corp. During
2018, Dow paid a cash dividend of $20,000 to
Tech.

What amount of this dividend is taxable on the
2018 consolidated return?

A. $20,000
B. $14,000

C. $6,000
D. $0

assess.AICPA.941146REG-AR

382. With regard to consolidated tax returns, which
of the following statements is correct?

A. Operating losses of one group member
may be used to offset operating profits
of the other members included in the
consolidated return.
B. Only corporations that issue their audited
financial statements on a consolidated basis
may file consolidated returns.
C. Of all intercompany dividends paid by
the subsidiaries to the parent, 70% are
excludable from taxable income on the
consolidated return.
D. The common parent must directly own
51% or more of the total voting power of all
corporations included in the consolidated
return.

Distributions from a Corporation

aicpa.aq.distrib.corp.001_17

383. A corporation distributed land with a basis of
$20,000 and a fair market value of $60,000,
but was subject to a non-recourse liability of
$70,000 to its sole shareholder. What amount
represents the corporation's recognized gain?

A. $20,000
B. $50,000
C. $60,000
D. $70,000

asses.AICPA.REG.distrib.corp-0018

384. A distribution from a C corporation to a
shareholder **cannot** be treated by the
shareholder as which of the following
classifications?

A. Dividend income
B. Nontaxable return of capital
C. Capital gain
D. Capital loss

assess.AICPA.090835REG

385. Fox, the sole shareholder in Fall, a C corporation,
has a tax basis of $60,000. Fall has $40,000 of
accumulated positive earnings and profits
at the beginning of the year and $10,000 of
current positive earnings and profits for the
current year. At year end, Fall distributed land
with an adjusted basis of $30,000 and a fair
market value (FMV) of $38,000 to Fox. The land

has an outstanding mortgage of $3,000 that Fox must assume. What is Fox's tax basis in the land?

A. $38,000
B. $35,000
C. $30,000
D. $27,000

assess.AICPA.090850REG

386. Webster, a C corporation, has $70,000 in accumulated and no current earnings and profits. Webster distributed $20,000 cash and property with an adjusted basis and fair market value of $60,000 to its shareholders. What amount should the shareholders report as dividend income?

A. $20,000
B. $60,000
C. $70,000
D. $80,000

assess.AICPA.120714REG

387. On January 1 of the current year, Locke Corp., an accrual-basis calendar-year C corporation, had $30,000 in accumulated earnings and profits. For the current year, Locke had current earnings and profits of $20,000, and made two $40,000 cash distributions to its shareholders, one in April and one in September. What amount of the distributions is classified as dividend income to Locke's shareholders?

A. $0
B. $20,000
C. $50,000
D. $80,000

assess.AICPA.120752REG

388. Simon, a C corporation, had a deficit in accumulated earnings and profits of $50,000 at the beginning of the year and had current earnings and profits of $10,000. At year end, Simon paid a dividend of $15,000 to its sole shareholder. What amount of the dividend is reported as income?

A. $0
B. $5,000
C. $10,000
D. $15,000

assess.AICPA.901126REG-P2-AR_2-18

389. Dahl Corp. was organized and commenced operations in 1930. At December 31, 2018, Dahl had accumulated earnings and profits of $9,000 before dividend declaration and distribution. On December 31, 2018 Dahl distributed

cash of $9,000 and a vacant parcel of land to Green, Dahl's only stockholder. At the date of distribution, the land had a basis of $5,000 and a fair market value of $40,000.

What was Green's taxable dividend income in 2018 from these distributions?

A. $9,000
B. $14,000
C. $44,000
D. $49,000

assess.AICPA.910545REG-P2-AR_2-18

390. Nyle Corp. owned 100 shares of Beta Corp. stock that it bought in 1993 for $9 per share. In 2018, when the fair market value of the Beta stock was $20 per share, Nyle distributed this stock to a noncorporate shareholder.

Nyle's recognized gain on this distribution was

A. $2,000
B. $1,100
C. $900
D. $0

assess.AICPA.940525REG-AR_2-18

391. On January 1, 2018, Kee Corp., a C corporation, had a $50,000 deficit in earnings and profits. For 2018 Kee had current earnings and profits of $10,000 and made a $30,000 cash distribution to its stockholders. What amount of the distribution is taxable as dividend income to Kee's stockholders?

A. $30,000
B. $20,000
C. $10,000
D. $0

assess.AICPA.REG.distrib.corp-0008

392. Which of the following items reported on a C corporation's tax return would **not** require an adjustment to taxable income in computing current earnings and profits (E&P)?

A. Straight-line depreciation
B. Installment sale income
C. Amortization of organizational expenses
D. Meals and entertainment expenses

assess.AICPA.REG.distrib.corp-0016

393. On December 31, a C corporation made a nonliquidating distribution of the following assets to its sole shareholder:

Land	Fair market value	$100,000
	Adjusted basis	50,000
Patent	Fair market value	25,000
	Adjusted basis	0
Building	Fair market value	50,000
	Adjusted basis	150,000

What gain or loss should the corporation recognize as a result of the distribution?

A. $50,000 loss
B. No gain and **no** loss
C. $25,000 gain
D. $75,000 gain

Corporate Redemptions and Liquidations

assess.AICPA.060503REG-SIM

394. S Corporation was a wholly-owned subsidiary of P Corporation. Both corporations were domestic C corporations. P received a liquidating distribution of property (worth $250 and a basis of $135) from S in cancellation of the stock. What amount of gain will P recognize if P had a basis of $100 in the S stock before the receipt of the property?

A. $0
B. $35
C. $150
D. $250

assess.AICPA.090825REG-SIM

395. A corporation was completely liquidated and dissolved this year. The filing fees, professional fees, and other expenditures incurred in connection with the liquidation are:

A. Deducted in full by the dissolved corporation.
B. Deducted in full by the shareholders of the dissolved corporation.
C. Treated as capital losses by the dissolved corporation.
D. Not deductible by the corporation or the shareholders.

assess.AICPA.090826REG-SIM

396. What is the usual result to the shareholders of a distribution in complete liquidation of a corporation?

A. No taxable effect
B. Ordinary gain to the extent of cash received
C. Ordinary gain or loss
D. Capital gain or loss

assess.AICPA.090827REG-SIM

397. How does a noncorporate shareholder treat the gain on a redemption of stock that qualifies as a partial liquidation of the distributing corporation?

A. Entirely as a capital gain
B. Entirely as a dividend
C. Partly as a capital gain and partly as a return of capital
D. Entirely as a tax-free transaction

assess.AICPA.930554BEC-P2-AR

398. What is the usual result to the shareholders of a distribution in complete liquidation of a corporation?

A. No taxable effect
B. Ordinary gain to the extent of cash received
C. Ordinary gain or loss
D. Capital gain or loss

assess.AICPA.931146BEC-P2-AR_2-18

399. A corporation was completely liquidated and dissolved during 2018. The filing fees, professional fees, and other expenditures incurred in connection with the liquidation and dissolution are

A. Deductible in full by the dissolved corporation.
B. Deductible by the shareholders and not by the corporation.
C. Treated as capital losses by the corporation.
D. Not deductible either by the corporation or shareholders.

assess.AICPA.970506BEC-AR_2-18

400. Elm Corp. is an accrual-basis, calendar-year C corporation with 100,000 shares of voting common stock issued and outstanding as of December 28, 2018.

On Friday, December 29, 2018, Hall surrendered 2,000 shares of Elm stock to Elm in exchange for $33,000 cash. Hall had no direct or indirect interest in Elm after the stock surrender. Additional information follows:

Hall's adjusted basis in 2,000 shares of Elm on December 29, 2018 ($8 per share)	$16,000
Elm's accumulated earnings and profits at January 1, 2018	25,000
Elm's 2018 net operating loss	(7,000)

What amount of income did Hall recognize from the stock surrender?

A. $33,000 dividend
B. $25,000 dividend
C. $18,000 capital gain
D. $17,000 capital gain

assess.AICPA.REG.corp.redempt-0017

401. A corporation transferred fully depreciated machinery to an individual shareholder in a liquidating distribution. The original cost of the machinery was $6,000, and the fair market value at the date of the transfer was $5,000. If the shareholder's basis in the corporation's stock was $2,000, then the shareholder reports

A. $3,000 capital gain.
B. $3,000 ordinary income.
C. $5,000 ordinary income and $2,000 capital loss.
D. No gain and **no** loss.

Corporate Reorganizations

assess.AICPA.090824REG-SIM

402. P corporation acquired the assets of its wholly-owned subsidiary, S corporation, under a plan that qualified as a tax-free complete liquidation of S. Which of the following of S's unused carryovers may be transferred to P?

A. Excess charitable contributions.
B. Net operating loss.
C. Both of the above are transferred.
D. None of the above is transferred.

assess.AICPA.090829REG-SIM

403. In a Type B reorganization:

A. The stock of the target corporation is acquired solely for the voting stock of either the acquiring corporation or its parent.
B. The acquiring corporation must have control of the target corporation immediately after the acquisition.
C. Both of the above are correct.
D. None of the above is correct.

assess.AICPA.090830REG-SIM

404. ABC has 200 shares of voting common stock outstanding. XYZ has decided to acquire 90% of the ABC stock solely in exchange for 50% of its voting stock. ABC will become XYZ's subsidiary after the transaction. Which of the following statements is true?

A. XYZ must acquire 100% of ABC for the transaction to qualify as a reorganization.
B. The transaction is a reorganization.
C. XYZ must issue at least 60% of its stock for the transaction to qualify as a reorganization.
D. ABC must surrender assets to XYZ to qualify as a reorganization.

assess.AICPA.910543BEC-P2-AR_2-18

405. Pursuant to a plan of corporate reorganization adopted in July 2018, Gow exchanged 500 shares of Lad Corp. common stock that he had bought in January 2018 at a cost of $5,000 for 100 shares of Rook Corp. common stock having a fair market value of $6,000.

Gow's recognized gain on this exchange was

A. $1,000 long-term capital gain.
B. $1,000 short-term capital gain.
C. $1,000 ordinary income.
D. $0.

assess.AICPA.930556BEC-P2-AR

406. Corporations A and B combine in a qualifying reorganization and form Corporation C, the only surviving corporation.

This reorganization is tax-free to the

	Shareholders	Corporation
A.	Yes	Yes
B.	Yes	No
C.	No	No
D.	No	Yes

assess.AICPA.950525BEC-AR

407. Jaxson Corp. has 200,000 shares of voting common stock issued and outstanding. King Corp. has decided to acquire 90% of Jaxson's voting common stock solely in exchange for 50% of its voting common stock and retain Jaxson as a subsidiary after the transaction.

Which of the following statements is true?

A. King must acquire 100% of Jaxson stock for the transaction to be a tax-free reorganization.
B. The transaction will qualify as a tax-free reorganization.

C. King must issue at least 60% of its voting common stock for the transaction to qualify as a tax-free reorganization.

D. Jaxson must surrender assets for the transaction to qualify as a tax-free reorganization.

assess.AICPA.REG.corp.reorg-0033

408. Which of the following statements correctly represents the tax effect of the liquidation of an 80% or more owned subsidiary?

A. The subsidiary can recognize a loss on depreciated assets transferred to minority shareholders.

B. Assets transferred to the parent of the liquidating corporation generally have a carryover basis.

C. The total basis of assets transferred to the parent of the liquidating corporation must be allocated among the various assets according to their fair market values.

D. The subsidiary recognizes gain on the distribution of appreciated assets to the parent.

Multijurisdictional Tax Issues

State and Local Taxation

assess.AICPA.101074REG-SIM

409. Machine Corporation buys a business van in State V and pays 6% sales tax. The van is used in State W by Machine. State W has a 9% sales tax. Because of this transaction, State W is likely to impose which of the following taxes on Machine?

A. Sales tax.
B. Income tax.
C. Use tax.
D. Franchise tax.

assess.AICPA.101075REG-SIM

410. Woods Corporation's federal taxable income for the current year is $250,000 which includes the following:

$15,000 of deducted state income taxes

$25,000 of interest income on United States Treasury Bonds

Woods also had $10,000 of interest from state and local bonds that it owns. Federal depreciation in excess of that allowed for state purposes was $7,000. Woods operates exclusively in State F, which does not tax income earned on federal obligations, taxes all municipal bond interest, and disallows a deduction for state income taxes. What is Wood's state taxable income?

A. $257,000.
B. $243,000.
C. $307,000.
D. $250,000.

assess.AICPA.101076REG-SIM

411. Which of the following types of income would likely be considered "business income" for state income tax purposes?

A. Dividends from stock held as long term investments.

B. Gain from the sale of land that is not used in the taxpayer's regular business operations.

C. Rent received from corporate office space not used in the taxpayer's regular business operations.

D. Royalties from the licensing of a song that was produced as part of ordinary business operations.

assess.AICPA.101077REG-SIM

412. Callaway Company manufactures its products in State F and sells them in States F and G. Callaway's sales are as follows for the current year:

Sales shipped from State F to customers in State F	$10,000
Sales shipped from State F to customers in State G	40,000

Assume that Callaway has nexus in both states F and G. What is Callaway's State F sales factor for the current year?

A. 0%
B. 20%
C. 50%
D. 100%

assess.AICPA.101078REG-SIM

413. Clock Corporation owns 80%, 90%, and 100%, respectively, of its three subsidiaries, Lamp, Chair, and Table. The corporations have elected to file a consolidated tax return for U.S. federal income tax. The corporations have nexus as follows:

	Nexus
Clock	States M and N
Lamp	States M and N
Chair	State N
Table	States M and N

If a consolidated state income tax return is filed in State M, which corporations will be included in the return?

A. Clock
B. Clock and Table.
C. Clock, Lamp, and Table.
D. Clock, Lamp, Chair, and Table.

Taxation of Foreign Income

assess.AICPA.101069REG-SIM_2-18

414. Mr. Travel is a U.S. citizen who has been a resident of Spain for five years. In 2018, he has the following income from Spanish sources:

	Salary	Interest Income
Gross amount	$90,000	$20,000
Spanish income tax (20%)	(18,000)	(4,000)
Net cash received (80%)	$72,000	$16,000

The interest income was from a Spanish money market account. Mr. Travel also was provided housing from his employer that had a fair market value of $40,000 (not subject to Spanish tax). Total U.S.-source earned income for Mr. Travel was $60,000. What is Mr. Travel's minimum includible United States gross income from these transactions? The housing exclusion is $14,574 and foreign earned income exclusion is $104,100 in 2018.

A. $60,000
B. $105,426
C. $110,000
D. $200,000

assess.AICPA.101070REG-SIM_2-18

415. Mr. Travel is a U.S. citizen who has been a resident of Spain for five years. In 2018, he has the following income from Spanish sources:

	Salary	Interest Income
Gross amount	$90,000	$20,000
Spanish income tax (20%)	(18,000)	(4,000)
Net cash received (80%)	$72,000	$16,000

The interest income was from a Spanish money market account. Mr. Travel also was provided housing from his employer that had a fair market value of $30,000 (not subject to Spanish tax). Total U.S.-source earned income

for Mr. Travel was $60,000. How much of the foreign taxes paid is eligible to be used in the foreign tax credit computation?

A. – $0 –
B. $4,000
C. $18,000
D. $22,000

assess.AICPA.101071REG-SIM

416. ABC, Inc., has $120,000 U.S. source income, $80,000 of foreign source income, and $25,000 foreign taxes deemed paid. Assume that the U.S. income tax liability before the foreign tax credit is $61,250. ABC's foreign tax credit is

A. – $0 –
B. $24,500
C. $25,000
D. $61,250

assess.AICPA.101072REG-SIM

417. Which one of the following types of income is **not** U.S.-source income?

A. Salary earned in the United States
B. Interest income on United States Treasury Bonds
C. Income from the sale of land located in Japan by a Japanese resident to a taxpayer whose residence is in the United States
D. Rents received from property located in the United States

assess.AICPA.101073REG-SIM

418. Which of the following statements is incorrect?

A. Foreign currency exchange gains and losses resulting from the normal course of business operations are ordinary.
B. Foreign currency exchange gains and losses resulting from investment transactions are capital.
C. Foreign currency exchange gains and losses resulting from personal transactions are capital.
D. Foreign currency exchange gains and losses resulting from the normal course of business operations are capital.

Tax-Exempt Entities

Tax-Exempt Organizations

assess.AICPA.101079REG

419. The organizational test to qualify a public service charitable entity as tax exempt requires the articles of organization to

   I. Limit the purpose of the entity to the charitable purpose.
   II. State that an information return should be filed annually with the Internal Revenue Service.

   A. I only.
   B. II only.
   C. Both I and II.
   D. Neither I nor II.

assess.AICPA.101080REG

420. Which of the following exempt organizations must file annual information returns?

   A. Churches.
   B. Internally supported auxiliaries.
   C. Private foundations.
   D. Those with gross receipts of $50,000 or less in each taxable year.

assess.AICPA.101081REG

421. An organization that operates for the prevention of cruelty to animals will fail to meet the operational test to qualify as an exempt organization if

	The Organization Engages in Insubstantial Nonexempt Activities	The Organization Directly Participates in Any Political Campaign
A.	Yes	Yes
B.	Yes	No
C.	No	Yes
D.	No	No

assess.AICPA.101082REG

422. Maple Avenue Assembly, a tax-exempt religious organization, operates an outreach program for the poor in its community. A candidate for the local city council has endorsed Maple's anti-poverty program. Which of the following activities is (are) consistent with Maple's tax-exempt status?

   I. Endorsing the candidate to members.
   II. Collecting contributions from members for the candidate.

   A. I only.
   B. II only.
   C. Both I and II.
   D. Neither I nor II.

assess.AICPA.101083REG

423. Hope is a tax-exempt religious organization. Which of the following activities is (are) consistent with Hope's tax-exempt status?

   I. Conducting weekend retreats for business organizations.
   II. Providing traditional burial services that maintain the religious beliefs of its members.

   A. I only.
   B. II only.
   C. Both I and II.
   D. Neither I nor II.

assess.AICPA.101084REG

424. The private foundation status of an exempt organization will terminate if it

   A. Becomes a public charity.
   B. Is a foreign corporation.
   C. Does not distribute all of its net assets to one or more public charities.
   D. Is governed by a charter that limits the organization's exempt purposes.

assess.AICPA.101085REG

425. Which of the following activities conducted by a tax exempt organization will result in unrelated business income?

   I. Selling articles made by handicapped persons as part of their rehabilitation, when the organization is involved exclusively in their rehabilitation.
   II. Operating a grocery store almost fully staffed by emotionally handicapped persons as part of a therapeutic program.

   A. I only.
   B. II only.
   C. Both I and II.
   D. Neither I nor II.

tax.exempt.org_LA_aicpa_1

426. Which of the following types of business may **not** qualify for a 501(c)(3) exemption from federal income taxes?

   A. A foundation
   B. A fund
   C. A corporation
   D. A partnership

Partnership Taxation

Formation and Basis

aicpa.aq.form.basis.001_17

427. Two partners each own an equal interest in a general partnership. One partner contributes to the partnership a building that has an adjusted basis of $40,000 and a fair market value of $60,000. The asset is subject to a mortgage of $30,000, which is assumed by the partnership. What is the contributing partner's share of liabilities in the partnership?

   A. $0
   B. $15,000
   C. $30,000
   D. $40,000

aicpa.aq.form.basis.002_17

428. A partner received a partnership interest with a fair market value (FMV) of $55,000 in exchange for the following items:

	Basis	FMV
Cash	$20,000	$20,000
Property	10,000	30,000
Services rendered	0	5,000

What is the partner's basis in the partnership interest?

   A. $55,000
   B. $50,000
   C. $35,000
   D. $30,000

assess.AICPA.060226REG

429. Juan contributed land with a basis of $10,000 and a fair market value of $15,000 to the Sounds Partnership. He also contributed services with a value of $25,000. In return, he received a partnership interest in Sounds with a value of $40,000.

What is Juan's basis in his partnership interest?

   A. $0
   B. $10,000
   C. $35,000
   D. $40,000

assess.AICPA.060819REG-P2-AR

430. Kerr and Marcus form KM Partnership with a cash contribution of $80,000 from Kerr and a property contribution of land from Marcus. The land has a fair market value of $80,000 and an adjusted basis of $50,000 at the date of the contribution. Kerr and Marcus are equal partners.

What is Marcus's basis immediately after formation?

   A. $0
   B. $50,000
   C. $65,000
   D. $80,000

assess.AICPA.090853REG

431. A $100,000 increase in partnership liabilities is treated in which of the following ways?

   A. Increases each partner's basis in the partnership by $100,000.
   B. Increases the partners' bases only if the liability is nonrecourse.
   C. Increases each partner's basis in proportion to their ownership.
   D. Does **not** change any partner's basis in the partnership regardless of whether the liabilities are recourse or nonrecourse.

assess.AICPA.120703REG

432. Able and Baker are equal members in Apple, an LLC. Apple has elected not to be treated as a corporation. Able contributes $7,000 cash and Baker contributes a machine with a basis of $5,000 and a fair market value of $10,000, subject to a liability of $3,000. What is Apple's basis for the machine?

   A. $2,000
   B. $5,000
   C. $8,000
   D. $10,000

assess.AICPA.120720REG

433. Turner, Reed, and Sumner are equal partners in TRS partnership. Turner contributed land with an adjusted basis of $20,000 and a fair market value (FMV) of $50,000. Reed contributed equipment with an adjusted basis of $40,000 and an FMV of $50,000. Sumner provided services worth $50,000. What amount of income is recognized as a result of the transfers?

   A. $50,000
   B. $60,000
   C. $90,000
   D. $150,000

assess.AICPA.120738REG

434. George and Martha are equal partners in G&M Partnership. At the beginning of the current tax year, the adjusted basis of George's partnership interest was $32,500, which included his share of $40,000 of partnership liabilities. During the tax year, the following information applied to G&M:

Operating loss	$30,000
Interest and dividend income	8,000
Partnership liabilities at end of year	24,000

What was the basis of George's partnership interest at year end?

A. $13,500
B. $21,500
C. $29,500
D. $43,500

assess.AICPA.120753REG

435. Campbell acquired a 10% interest in Vogue Partnership by contributing a building with an adjusted basis of $40,000 and a fair market value of $90,000. The building was subject to a $60,000 mortgage that was assumed by Vogue. The other partners contributed cash only. The basis of Campbell's partnership interest in Vogue is

A. $84,000s
B. $34,000s
C. $30,000s
D. $0s

assess.AICPA.130907REG

436. In return for a 20% partnership interest, Skinner contributed $5,000 cash and land with a $12,000 basis and a $20,000 fair market value to the partnership. The land was subject to a $10,000 mortgage that the partnership assumed. In addition, the partnership had $20,000 in recourse liabilities that would be shared by partners according to their partnership interests. What amount represents Skinner's basis in the partnership interest?

A. $27,000
B. $21,000
C. $19,000
D. $13,000

assess.AICPA.950526FAR-AR_2-18

437. Dean is a 25 percent partner in Target Partnership. Dean's tax basis in Target on January 1, 2018, was $20,000. At the end of 2018, Dean received a nonliquidating cash distribution of $8,000 from Target. Target's 2018 accounts recorded the following items:

Municipal bond interest income	$12,000
Ordinary income	40,000

What was Dean's tax basis in Target on December 31, 2018?

A. $15,000
B. $23,000
C. $25,000
D. $30,000

assess.AICPA.950527REG-AR

438. Strom acquired a 25 percent interest in Ace Partnership by contributing land having an adjusted basis of $16,000 and a fair market value of $50,000. The land was subject to a $24,000 mortgage, which was assumed by Ace. No other liabilities existed at the time of the contribution.

What was Strom's basis in Ace?

A. $0
B. $16,000
C. $26,000
D. $32,000

Flow-Through of Income and Losses

aicpa.aq.flow.through.inc.001_17

439. Partnership P has an operating loss of $10,000 for the year. Partner A had a 50% interest in the partnership, with a basis of $5,000 at the beginning of the year. P distributed $2,000 to A during the year. What amount of loss is deductible by A?

A. $2,000
B. $3,000
C. $5,000
D. $7,000

assess.AICPA.060823REG-AR

440. A partnership had four partners. Each partner contributed $100,000 cash. The partnership reported income for the year of $80,000 and distributed $10,000 to each partner. What was each partner's basis in the partnership at the end of the current year?

A. $170,000
B. $120,000
C. $117,500
D. $110,000

assess.AICPA.090856REG

441. Dale was a 50% partner in D&P Partnership. Dale contributed $10,000 in cash upon the formation of the partnership. D&P borrowed $10,000 to purchase equipment. During the first year of operations, D&P had $15,000 net taxable income, $2,000 tax-exempt interest income, a $3,000 distribution to each partner, and a $4,000 reduction of debt. At the end of the first year of operation, what amount would be Dale's basis?

    A. $16,500
    B. $17,500
    C. $18,500
    D. $21,500

assess.AICPA.130910REG

442. PDK, LLC had three members with equal ownership percentages. PDK elected to be treated as a partnership. For the tax year ending December 31, year 1, PDK had the following income and expense items:

Revenues	$120,000
Interest income	6,000
Gain on sale of securities	8,000
Salaries	36,000
Guaranteed payments	10,000
Rent expense	21,000
Depreciation expense	18,000
Charitable contributions	3,000

What would PDK report as nonseparately stated income for year 1 tax purposes?

    A. $30,000
    B. $35,000
    C. $43,000
    D. $51,000

assess.AICPA.130925REG

443. What is the tax treatment of net losses in excess of the at-risk amount for an activity?

    A. Any loss in excess of the at-risk amount is suspended and is deductible in the year in which the activity is disposed of in full.
    B. Any losses in excess of the at-risk amount are suspended and carried forward without expiration and are deductible against income in future years from that activity.
    C. Any losses in excess of the at-risk amount are deducted currently against income from other activities; the remaining loss, if any, is carried forward without expiration.
    D. Any losses in excess of the at-risk amount are carried back two years against activities with income and then carried forward for 20 years.

assess.AICPA.REG.flow.through.inc-0006

444. An individual is a 50% partner who materially participates in Stone Partnership. The individual's adjusted basis at the beginning of the year was $0. Stone had a $70,000 loss from its business. Stone borrowed $30,000 from a bank of which $20,000 remained unpaid at year-end. What amount of loss is the individual allowed in the current year from Stone?

    A. $35,000
    B. $15,000
    C. $10,000
    D. $0

assess.AICPA.950528REG-AR_2-18

445. Alt Partnership, a cash basis calendar year entity, began business on October 1, 2018. Alt incurred and paid the following in 2018:

Legal fees to prepare the partnership agreement	$12,000
Accounting fees to prepare the representations in offering materials	15,000

Ignoring amortization, what was the maximum amount that Alt could expense on the 2018 partnership return?

    A. $0
    B. $5,000
    C. $12,000
    D. $15,000

Transactions with Partners

assess.AICPA.101113REG_2-18

446. Evan, a 25% partner in Vista Partnership, received a $20,000 guaranteed payment in 2018 for deductible services rendered to the partnership. Guaranteed payments were not made to any other partner. Vista's 2018 partnership income consisted of:

Net business income before guaranteed payments	$80,000
Net long-term capital gains	10,000

What amount of income should Evan report from Vista Partnership on her 2018 tax return?

    A. $37,500
    B. $27,500
    C. $22,500
    D. $20,000

assess.AICPA.101114REG-SIM

447. Abe, Betsy, and Dan decide to form the equal ABD partnership at the beginning of Year One. Abe contributed depreciable assets that he has owned for five years that have a basis of $15,000 and a value of $20,000. Betsy contributed $20,000 cash. Dan contributed $12,000 in cash and land with a basis of $5,000 and a value of $8,000. How much income is allocated to Abe if the partnership sells the assets contributed by Abe for $18,000?

    A. $0
    B. $1,000
    C. $3,000
    D. $5,000

assess.AICPA.130914REG

448. When the AQR partnership was formed, partner Acre contributed land with a fair market value of $100,000 and a tax basis of $60,000 in exchange for a one-third interest in the partnership. The AQR partnership agreement specifies that each partner will share equally in the partnership's profits and losses. During its first year of operation, AQR sold the land to an unrelated third party for $160,000. What is the proper tax treatment of the sale?

    A. Each partner reports a capital gain of $33,333.
    B. The entire gain of $100,000 must be specifically allocated to Acre.
    C. The first $40,000 of gain is allocated to Acre, and the remaining gain of $60,000 is shared equally by the other two partners.
    D. The first $40,000 of gain is allocated to Acre, and the remaining gain of $60,000 is shared equally by all the partners in the partnership.

assess.AICPA.940529REG-AR

449. Guaranteed payments made by a partnership to partners for services rendered to the partnership, that are deductible business expenses under the Internal Revenue Code, are

    I. Deductible expenses on the *U.S. Partnership Return of Income*, Form 1065, in order to arrive at partnership income (loss).
    II. Included on Schedules K-1 to be taxed as ordinary income to the partners.

    A. I only.
    B. II only.
    C. Both I and II.
    D. Neither I nor II.

assess.AICPA.941157REG-AR_2-18

450. White has a one-third interest in the profits and losses of Rapid Partnership. Rapid's ordinary income for the 2018 calendar year is $30,000, after a $3,000 deduction for a guaranteed payment made to White for services rendered. None of the $30,000 ordinary income was distributed to the partners.

What is the total amount that White must include from Rapid as taxable income in his 2018 tax return?

    A. $3,000
    B. $10,000
    C. $11,000
    D. $13,000

assess.AICPA.950529REG-AR

451. A guaranteed payment by a partnership to a partner for services rendered, may include an agreement to pay
    I. A salary of $5,000 monthly without regard to partnership income.
    II. A 25% interest in partnership profits.

    A. I only.
    B. II only.
    C. Both I and II.
    D. Neither I nor II.

assess.AICPA.990512REG-AR_2-18

452. Peters has a one-third interest in the Spano Partnership. During 2018, Peters received a $16,000 guaranteed payment, which was deductible by the partnership, for services rendered to Spano. Spano reported a 2018 operating loss of $70,000 before the guaranteed payment.

What is(are) the net effect(s) of the guaranteed payment?

    I. The guaranteed payment increases Peters's tax basis in Spano by $16,000.
    II. The guaranteed payment increases Peters's ordinary income by $16,000.

    A. I only.
    B. II only.
    C. Both I and II.
    D. Neither I nor II.

Partnership Distributions

assess.AICPA.020510REG-AR

453. Stone and Frazier decided to terminate the Woodwest Partnership as of December 31. On that date, Woodwest's balance sheet was as follows:

Cash	$2,000
Equipment (adjusted basis)	2,000
Capital—Stone	3,000
Capital—Frazier	1,000

The fair market value of the equipment was $3,000. Frazier's outside basis in the partnership was $1,200. Upon liquidation, Frazier received $1,500 in cash. What gain should Frazier recognize?

A. $0
B. $250
C. $300
D. $500

assess.AICPA.120739REG

454. As a general partner in Greenland Associates, an individual's share of partnership income for the current tax year is $25,000 ordinary business income and a $10,000 guaranteed payment. The individual also received $5,000 in cash distributions from the partnership. What income should the individual report from the interest in Greenland?

A. $5,000
B. $25,000
C. $35,000
D. $40,000

assess.AICPA.120740REG

455. In the current year, when Hoben's tax basis in Lynz Partnership interest was $10,000, Hoben received a *liquidating* distribution as follows:

	Adjusted Tax Basis	Fair Market Value
Marketable securities	$5,000	$5,000
Land	25,000	27,000

Lynz had no appreciated inventory, unrealized receivables, or properties that had been contributed by its partners. What was Hoben's recognized gain on the distribution?

A. $0
B. $15,000
C. $22,000
D. $23,000

assess.AICPA.951131REG-AR

456. Hart's adjusted basis in Best Partnership was $9,000 at the time he received the following nonliquidating distributions of partnership property:

Cash	$5,000
Land	
Adjusted basis	7,000
Fair market value	10,000

What was the amount of Hart's basis in the land?

A. $0
B. $4,000
C. $7,000
D. $10,000

assess.AICPA.951132REG-AR

457. Stone's basis in Ace Partnership was $70,000 at the time he received a nonliquidating distribution of partnership capital assets. These capital assets had an adjusted basis of $65,000 to Ace, and a fair market value of $83,000. Ace had no unrealized receivables, appreciated inventory, or properties which had been contributed by its partners.

What was Stone's recognized gain or loss on the distribution?

A. $18,000 ordinary income.
B. $13,000 capital gain.
C. $5,000 capital loss.
D. $0.

Sales and Terminations

assess.AICPA.120737REG

458. "Hot assets" of a partnership would include which of the following?

A. Cash
B. Unrealized receivables
C. Section 1231 assets
D. Capital assets

assess.AICPA.931159REG-P2-AR_2-18

459. On December 31, 2018, after receipt of his share of partnership income, Clark sold his interest in a limited partnership for $30,000 cash and relief of all liabilities.

On that date, the adjusted basis of Clark's partnership interest was $40,000, consisting of his capital account of $15,000 and his share of the partnership liabilities of $25,000. The partnership has no unrealized receivables or substantially appreciated inventory.

What is Clark's gain or loss on the sale of his partnership interest?

A. Ordinary loss of $10,000
B. Ordinary gain of $15,000
C. Capital loss of $10,000
D. Capital gain of $15,000

assess.AICPA.900523REG-P2-AR_2-18

460. The personal service partnership of Allen, Baker & Carr had the following cash basis balance sheet at December 31, 2017:

Assets	Adjusted Basis per Book	Market Value
Cash	$102,000	$102,000
Unrealized accounts receivable	–	420,000
Totals	$102,000	$522,000
Liability and Capital		
Note payable	$60,000	$60,000
Capital accounts:		
Allen	14,000	154,000
Baker	14,000	154,000
Carr	14,000	154,000
	$102,000	$522,000

Carr, an equal partner, sold his partnership interest to Dole, an outsider, for $154,000 cash on January 1, 2018. In addition, Dole assumed Carr's share of the partnerships liability. What amount of ordinary income should Carr report in his 2018 income tax return on the sale of his partnership interest?

A. $0
B. $20,000
C. $34,000
D. $140,000

assess.AICPA.951134REG-AR

461. Curry's sale of her partnership interest causes a partnership termination. The partnership's business and financial operations are continued by the other members. What is (are) the effect(s) of the termination?

I. There is a deemed distribution of assets to the remaining partners and the purchaser.
II. There is a hypothetical recontribution of assets to a new partnership.

A. I only.
B. II only.
C. Both I and II.
D. Neither I nor II.

S Corporation Taxation

Eligibility, Election, Termination

aicpa.aq.elig.elec.term.001_17

462. A corporation that intends to make an election to become an S corporation seeks advice. An accountant would most appropriately make which of the following recommendations?

A. Limit the number of shareholders to 120 unrelated individuals.
B. Limit the issuance of stock to common and preferred.
C. Ensure that **no** shareholders are resident aliens.
D. Evaluate the eligibility of all shareholders.

assess.AICPA.060255REG-AR

463. Bristol Corp. was formed as a C corporation on January 1, 1980, and elected S corporation status on January 1, 1987. At the time of the election, Bristol had accumulated C corporation earnings and profits which have not been distributed. Bristol has had the same 25 shareholders throughout its existence.

In 2017, Bristol's S election will terminate if it

A. Increases the number of shareholders to 75.
B. Adds a decedent's estate as a shareholder to the existing shareholders.
C. Takes a charitable contribution deduction.
D. Has passive investment income exceeding 90% of gross receipts in each of the three consecutive years ending December 31, 2016.

assess.AICPA.060256REG-AR

464. Which of the following is an eligibility requirement in 2017 to file a valid election to be taxed as an S corporation?

   A. Must have no more than 75 shareholders, and a husband and wife who each own stock are counted as two shareholders.
   B. Must have no more than 100 shareholders, and a husband and wife who each own stock are counted as two shareholders.
   C. Must have no more than 100 shareholders, and a husband and wife who each own stock are counted as one shareholder.
   D. Must have no more 75 shareholders, and a husband and wife who each own stock are counted as one shareholder.

assess.AICPA.120750REG

465. Which of the following statements about qualifying shareholders of an S corporation is correct?

   A. A general partnership may be a shareholder.
   B. Only individuals may be shareholders.
   C. Individuals, estates, and certain trusts may be shareholders.
   D. Nonresident aliens may be shareholders.

assess.AICPA.950521REG-AR

466. Village Corp., a calendar year corporation, began business in 2002. Village made a valid S Corporation election on December 5, 2016, with the unanimous consent of its shareholders. The eligibility requirements for S status continued to be met throughout 2016 and 2017.

   On what date did Village's S status become effective?

   A. January 1, 2016
   B. January 1, 2017
   C. December 5, 2016
   D. December 5, 2017

assess.AICPA.REG.elig.elect.term-0030

467. HDF, a calendar-year corporation, began business in year 1. HDF made a valid S corporation election on December 1, year 2. Assuming the eligibility requirements for S corporation status continued to be met throughout year 3, on which of the following dates did HDF's S corporation status become effective?

   A. January 1, year 2
   B. December 1, year 2
   C. January 1, year 3
   D. December 1, year 3

Income and Basis

aicpa.aq.inc.basis.001_17

468. On January 1 of the first year of operation, an investor paid $10,000 for a 20% interest in Biga, an S corporation. During the same year, Biga earned $10,000 taxable income and $2,000 tax-exempt interest. Biga paid dividends totaling $1,000 to its shareholders during the same year. What is the investor's tax basis in the shares of Biga at the end of the year?

   A. $4,200
   B. $10,000
   C. $12,200
   D. $12,400

aicpa.aq.inc.basis.002_17

469. A taxpayer owns 50% of the stock of an S corporation and materially participated in the corporation's activities. At the beginning of the year, the taxpayer had an adjusted basis in the stock of $25,000 and made a loan to the corporation of $13,000. During the year, $3,000 of the loan was repaid, and the taxpayer's share of the corporation's loss for the year was $40,000. What is the amount of the loss that may be deducted on the taxpayer's tax return?

   A. 25,000
   B. $35,000
   C. $38,000
   D. $40,000

assess.AICPA.020504REG-AR

470. Stahl, an individual, owns 100% of Talon, an S corporation. At the beginning of the year, Stahl's basis in Talon was $65,000. Talon reported the following items from operations during the current year:

Ordinary loss	$10,000
Municipal interest income	6,000
Long-term capital gain	4,000
Short-term capital loss	9,000

What was Stahl's basis in Talon at year-end?

   A. $50,000
   B. $55,000
   C. $56,000
   D. $61,000

assess.AICPA.090858REG

471. An S corporation engaged in manufacturing has a year end of June 30. Revenue consistently has been more than $10 million under both cash and accrual basis of accounting. The stockholders would like to change the tax status of the corporation to a C corporation using the cash basis with the same year end. Which of the following statements is correct if it changes to a C corporation?

A. The year end will be December 31, using the cash basis of accounting.
B. The year end will be December 31, using the accrual basis of accounting.
C. The year end will be June 30, using the accrual basis of accounting.
D. The year end will be June 30, using the cash basis of accounting.

assess.AICPA.120708REG

472. Which of the following items must be separately stated on Form 1120S, *U.S. Income Tax Return for a Corporation, Schedule K-1*?

A. Mark-to-market income
B. Unearned revenue
C. Section 1245 gain
D. Gain or loss from the sale of collectibles

assess.AICPA.130917REG

473. Carson owned 40% of the outstanding stock of a C corporation. During a tax year, the corporation reported $400,000 in taxable income and distributed a total of $70,000 in cash dividends to its shareholders. Carson accurately reported $28,000 in gross income on Carson's individual tax return. If the corporation had been an S corporation and the distributions to the owners had been proportionate, how much income would Carson have reported on Carson's individual return?

A. $28,000
B. $132,000
C. $160,000
D. $188,000

Distributions and Special Taxes

assess.AICPA.020508REG-AR

474. Baker, an individual, owned 100% of Alpha, an S corporation. At the beginning of the year, Baker's basis in Alpha Corp. was $25,000. Alpha realized ordinary income during the year in the amount of $1,000 and a long-term capital loss in the amount of $3,000 for this year. Alpha distributed $30,000 in cash to Baker during the year.

What amount of the $30,000 cash distribution is taxable to Baker?

A. $0
B. $7,000
C. $4,000
D. $30,000

assess.AICPA.060229REG-AR_0318

475. Prail Corporation is a C corporation that on February 1, 2018, elected to be taxed as a calendar-year S corporation. On June 15, 2018, Prail sold land with a basis of $100,000 for $200,000 cash. The fair market value of the land on February 1, 2018, was $150,000. Prail had no other income or loss for the year and no carryovers from prior years.

What is Prail's tax?

A. $7,500
B. $17,500
C. $22,250
D. $35,000

assess.AICPA.090852REG

476. Sandy is the sole shareholder of Swallow, an S corporation. Sandy's adjusted basis in Swallow stock is $60,000 at the beginning of the year. During the year, Swallow reports the following income items:

Ordinary income	$30,000
Tax-exempt income	5,000
Capital gains	10,000

In addition, Swallow makes a nontaxable distribution to Sandy of $20,000 during the year. What is Sandy's adjusted basis in the Swallow stock at the end of the year?

A. $60,000
B. $70,000
C. $80,000
D. $85,000

assess.AICPA.101112REG

477. Beck Corp. has been a calendar year S corporation since its inception on January 2, 2008. On January 1, 2018, Lazur and Lyle each owned 50% of the Beck stock, in which their respective tax bases were $12,000 and $9,000. For the year ended December 31, 2018, Beck had $81,000 in ordinary business income and $10,000 in tax-exempt income. Beck made a $51,000 cash distribution to each shareholder

on December 31, 2018. What was Lazur's tax basis in Beck after the distribution?

A. $1,500
B. $6,500
C. $52,500
D. $57,500

assess.AICPA.120707REG

478. A sole proprietorship incorporated on January 1 and elected S corporation status. The owner contributed the following assets to the S corporation:

	Basis	Fair Market Value
Machinery	$7,000	$8,000
Building	11,000	100,000
Cash	1,000	1,000

Two years later, the corporation sold the machinery for $4,000 and the building for $110,000. The machinery had accumulated depreciation of $2,000, and the building had accumulated depreciation of $1,000. What is the built-in gain recognized on the sale?

A. $100,000
B. $99,000
C. $6,000
D. $0

assess.AICPA.931144REG-P2-AR

479. If an S corporation has no accumulated earnings and profits, the amount distributed to a shareholder

A. Must be returned to the S corporation.
B. Increases the shareholder's basis for the stock.
C. Decreases the shareholder's basis for the stock.
D. Has no effect on the shareholder's basis for the stock.

Fiduciary Taxation

Income Taxation of Fiduciaries

aicpa.aq.income.tax.001_17

480. Which of the following items is **not** normally taken into account in determining distributable net income of a simple trust?

A. Tax-exempt interest
B. Fiduciary fee
C. Taxable interest income
D. Personal exemption.

aicpa.aq.income.tax.002_17

481. A simple trust had $25,000 in capital gains, $10,000 in municipal interest, $5,000 in corporate bond interest, and $2,000 in accounting and trustee fees. According to the trust agreement, capital gains are to be distributed to the beneficiary. What is the distributable net income for this trust?

A. $28,000
B. $30,000
C. $38,000
D. $40,000

aicpa.aq.income.tax.003_17

482. At the close of the prior year, an individual taxpayer transferred assets into an irrevocable trust, retaining the right to the income from the trust for life. During the year, the assets earned ordinary dividends and interest income. The tax liability on the income earned will be paid

A. Entirely by the trust.
B. Entirely by the individual taxpayer.
C. By the trust on the interest income only, and by the individual taxpayer for the dividend income.
D. By the trust on the dividend income only, and by the individual taxpayer for the interest income.

assess.AICPA.090837REG

483. The Simone Trust reported distributable net income of $120,000 for the current year. The trustee is required to distribute $60,000 to Kent and $90,000 to Lind each year. If the trustee distributes these amounts, what amount is includible in Lind's gross income?

A. $0
B. $60,000
C. $72,000
D. $90,000

assess.AICPA.130921REG

484. Pat created a trust, transferred property to this trust, and retained certain interests. For income tax purposes, Pat was treated as the owner of the trust. Pat has created which of the following types of trusts?

A. Simple
B. Grantor
C. Complex
D. Pre-need funeral

assess.AICPA.130926REG

485. A trust has distributable net income of $14,000 and distributes $20,000 to the sole beneficiary. What amounts are taxable to the trust and to the beneficiary?

	Trust	Beneficiary
A.	$14,000	$0
B.	$0	$14,000
C.	$14,000	$20,000
D.	$0	$20,000

assess.AICPA.REG.income.tax-0022

486. Orsen, a U.S. citizen and the sole income beneficiary of a simple trust, is entitled to receive current distributions of the trust income. During the current year, the trust reported:

Dividend income	$8,000
Accounting fees allocable to income	(2,000)
Net short-term capital gain allocable to corpus	3,000

What amount of trust income is includible in Orsen's gross income?

A. $0
B. $6,000
C. $8,000
D. $9,000

Tax Credits

Business Tax Credits

assess.AICPA.101129REG-SIM

487. The following information pertains to Wald Corp.'s operations:

Worldwide taxable income	$300,000
U.S. source taxable income	180,000
U.S. income tax before foreign tax credit	96,000
Foreign source taxable income	120,000
Foreign income taxes paid on foreign source taxable income	39,000

What amount of foreign tax credit may Wald claim?

A. $28,800
B. $36,600
C. $38,400
D. $39,000

assess.AICPA.101131REG-SIM

488. Which of the following statements concerning tax credits is true?

A. The foreign tax credit is available for business entities, such as corporations, but not for individuals.
B. Unused general business credits are carried back two years and forward 20 years.
C. For the rehabilitation credit, expenditures to rehabilitate property placed in service before 1936 are eligible for a 20% credit.
D. The work opportunity tax credit is calculated on the amount of wages paid per eligible employee during the first year of employment. The maximum credit is $2,400 per eligible employee.

assess.AICPA.941149REG-A

489. Which of the following credits is a combination of several tax credits to provide uniform rules for the current and carryback-carryover years?

A. General business credit.
B. Foreign tax credit.
C. Minimum tax credit.
D. Enhanced oil recovery credit.

Other Tax Issues

Tax Planning Strategies for Business Entities

aq.tax.planning.strat.002

490. Which of the following responses is *incorrect* with regard to charitable contributions by corporations?

A. Both corporations and individuals can generally deduct the fair market value of investments given as charitable contributions.
B. Corporations and individuals can never deduct more than the adjusted basis of ordinary income property given to a charitable organization.
C. Corporate and individual charitable contributions that exceed the taxable income limit can be carried forward for five years.
D. The corporation can elect to deduct accrued contributions if the contributions are actually paid in the first three-and-a-half months following the year-end.

aq.tax.planning.strat.003

491. Which of the following statements is the *best* advice for a business that is making a strategic decision?

A. Tax factors should be given more weight than non-tax factors.

B. Non-tax factors should be given substantially all of the weight in the decision.

C. Tax factors and non-tax factors should both be given appropriate consideration in the decision.

D. Tax factors should not be considered at all on the decision making process.

aq.tax.planning.strat.005

492. A business is expecting large losses in the first three years of its life. The owner would like to maximize the benefit from these losses on her personal tax return. Which entity type should the owner choose?

A. Partnership

B. S corporation

C. Limited liability company

D. C corporation

tax.planning.strat_LA_aicpa_1

493. When should a corporate taxpayer elect to forgo carryback of a net operating loss and instead carry the net operating loss forward?

A. When the taxpayer expects net operating losses in the future.

B. When the taxpayer has high marginal tax rates in carryback years and expects to be in lower marginal rates in the future.

C. When the taxpayer expects lower rates in the future.

D. When the taxpayer has low marginal tax rates in carryback years and expects to be in higher marginal rates in the future.

Business Entity Choice

aicpa.aq.bus.ent.choice.001_17

494. Two individuals are planning to start a business and need advice on selecting the appropriate form of entity. Their long-term business plan contemplates receiving future in-kind property distributions. Which of the following is a pair of business entities each of which can make a distribution of appreciated property to its owners that would **not** be taxable to the business entity or to its owners?

A. C corporation and a limited liability company.

B. Limited liability company and an S corporation.

C. S corporation and a general partnership.

D. General partnership and a limited liability partnership.

assess.AICPA.060257REG-AR

495. Which of the following statements concerning S corporations is False?

A. S corporations must be incorporated under state law in the same fashion as C corporations.

B. S corporation shareholders are not liable for the debt of the corporation.

C. An S corporation can issue both voting and non-voting common stock.

D. S corporations are subject to the alternative minimum tax.

assess.AICPA.060504REG-SIM

496. Which one of the following is a difference between an S corporation and a partnership?

A. All owners of an S corporation have limited liability but general partners in a partnership have unlimited liability.

B. Income earned by an S corporation does not flow through to shareholders while income earned by a partnership does flow through.

C. S corporation shareholders can have a negative basis while partners can never have a negative basis.

D. Partnerships can be formed in such a manner that gains or losses to the partners as a result of the formation are deferred, but shareholders forming an S corporation must always recognize formation gains and losses.

assess.AICPA.060814REG-P2-AR

497. Which of the following types of entities is entitled to the net operating loss deduction?

A. Partnerships.

B. S corporations.

C. Trusts and estates.

D. Not-for-profit organizations.

assess.AICPA.060822REG-P2-AR

498. Which of the following is an advantage of forming a limited liability company (LLC) as opposed to a partnership?

A. The entity may avoid taxation.

B. The entity may have any number of owners.

C. The owner may participate in management while limiting personal liability.

D. The entity may make disproportionate allocations and distributions to members.

assess.AICPA.120706REG

499. For which of the following entities is the owner's basis increased by the owner's share of profits and decreased by the owner's share of losses but is NOT affected by the entity's bank loan increases or decreases?

    A. S corporation.
    B. C corporation.
    C. Partnership.
    D. Limited liability company.

assess.AICPA.REG.bus.ent.choice-0032

500. A sole proprietor wants to incorporate and has requested a projection of the first-year tax results as a C corporation and as an S corporation. Taxable income from ordinary operations is projected to be $100,000. The company expects to make a $20,000 charitable contribution and projects a long-term capital loss on stock of $7,000. Which of the following projections is correct?

A. C corporation, $73,000 taxable income; S corporation, $80,000 ordinary business income; long-term capital loss is separately stated.

B. C corporation, $90,000 taxable income; S corporation, $80,000 ordinary business income; long-term capital loss is separately stated.

C. C corporation, $90,000 taxable income; S corporation, $100,000 ordinary business income; remaining items are separately stated.

D. C corporation, $80,000 taxable income; S corporation, $100,000 ordinary business income; remaining items are separately stated.

Answers and Explanations

1. **Answer: D**

   Circular 230 requires that the tax accountant promptly inform the client of this error. The decision regarding how to respond to the error is the client's.

2. **Answer: A**

   Section 10.20 requires prompt compliance with an IRS request for information or records <u>unless</u> the practitioner believes in good faith and on reasonable grounds that they are privileged.

3. **Answer: A**

   Like the AICPA Code of Professional Conduct, Circular 230 requires the tax practitioner to promptly inform a client of such a material error.

4. **Answer: B**

   The IRS allows tax practitioners to retain *copies* of the client's records.

5. **Answer: C**

   Circular 230's section 10.33 recommends these steps as "best practices" for federal tax advisors.

6. **Answer: A**

   A CPA should never give tax advice turning upon the possibility that the IRS might not audit the client's tax return.

7. **Answer: C**

   Both Circular 230 and the Code of Professional Conduct tells CPAs who learn of such errors to inform the client of the error and advise the client of the consequences so that the client can make an informed decision regarding how to proceed.

8. **Answer: A**

   More than one person may be deemed a TRP.

9. **Answer: C**

   This appears to be willful misconduct. At a minimum, it was reckless, so the more severe penalties that go with tax understatement will apply.

10. **Answer: C**

    Under current rules, Sandy must furnish the preparer's identifying number to the IRS but not to her clients.

11. **Answer: A**

    Pak meets the requirements for violating Section 6700 in that he participated in the sale of a tax shelter (in his role as executive vice president of EPS, speaker at its events, etc.) and he made materially false statements because this device is obviously bogus.

12. **Answer: A**

    This is an improper disclosure of the client's confidential information and will violate 6713 (as well as 7216).

13. **Answer: A**

    Monrew clearly willfully aided in the preparation of a tax-related document that was fraudulently backdated.

14. **Answer: C**

    People are TRPs if (a) they are paid, (b) to prepare or retain employees to prepare, (c) a substantial portion, (d) of any federal tax return. Because Louis was not paid specifically to prepare the return, he does not satisfy the first requirement to be a TRP.

15. **Answer: B**

    The I.R.C. contains no penalty for failing to disclose a conflict of interest when preparing a tax return.

16. **Answer: B**

    State boards of accountancy establish CPE requirements.

17. **Answer: C**

    State boards of accountancy both license CPAs and collect the fees for the CPA license.

18. **Answer: D**

    The AICPA handles ethical complaints with national implications.

19. **Answer: C**

    JEEP is the Joint Ethics Enforcement Program that divides ethics complaints and investigations between the AICPA and state societies.

20. **Answer: A**

    If the state agency revokes Smithers' license, s/he will no longer be a CPA, which is requisite to membership in the state society of CPAs.

21. **Answer: A**

    Only state boards of accountancy can grant a CPA license.

22. **Answer: D**

    All three choices represent a requirement to earn a CPA license.

23. **Answer: D**

    All listed acts will likely be cause for serious sanction.

24. **Answer: D**

    While certain types of punishments may be meted out by the SEC, the AICPA, and state CPA societies, only a state board of accountancy truly has the power to revoke a CPA's license to practice public accountancy. Nonetheless, the SEC may, for example, prevent an accountant from appearing before it or doing any attest work for a public company.

    The AICPA may revoke an accountant's membership, as may a state CPA society. But only the state board of accountancy may revoke a license to practice.

25. **Answer: B**

    With disclosure, Clegg can avoid an underpayment penalty even if the position is ultimately rejected because there is a reasonable basis (≥ 20% chance of approval) for it.

26. **Answer: D**

    All choices are needed to establish the good faith defense.

27. **Answer: B**

    This "reasonable basis" standard applies to disclosed positions.

28. **Answer: A**

    These are the two concepts that can avoid liability.

29. **Answer: C**

    Tribble owes 5% of $60,000 ($3,000) times 4 (the number of months late), which multiplies out to $12,000.

30. **Answer: D**

    The late filing penalty is capped at 25% of the amount of taxes owed ($100,000 × 25% = $25,000). Absent the cap, Xina would have owed $50,000.

31. **Answer: A**

    Tera's fine is 0.5% × 4 × $20,000 = $400.

32. **Answer: B**

    This is a substantial understatement, because Omar's $100,000 understatement exceeds both 10% of the tax ($50,000) and the $5,000 level. The penalty is 20% of the underpayment of $100,000, or $20,000.

33. **Answer: A**

    This was a substantial understatement, because the $200,000 amount, while not exceeding $10,000,000, does exceed the lesser amount of 10% of the tax ($100,000) (which, in turn, exceeds $10,000). The penalty will be 20% × $200,000 = $40,000.

34. **Answer: B**

    Because this meets the "reasonable basis" test (≥20%), it can be taken if disclosed without courting an understatement penalty.

35. **Answer: A**

    The Internal Revenue Code is the highest tax authority.

36. **Answer: D**

    Proposed regulations do not have the effect of law, but they do provide an indication of the IRS's view on a tax issue.

37. **Answer: C**

    The United States Court of Appeals hears appeals from the U.S. Tax Court and the U.S. District Court. It is not a court of original jurisdiction.

38. **Answer: D**

    Committee reports are legislative sources of authority which provide insight into the intention of the House Ways & Means Committee, Senate Finance Committee, and Joint Conference Committee.

39. **Answer: B**

    Tax legislation in the Senate begins in the Senate Finance Committee.

40. **Answer: C**

    IRS Publications are a secondary source of the tax law.

41. **Answer: B**

    A notice of proposed rulemaking does not provide information about congressional intent.

42. **Answer: A**

    There are three courts of original jurisdiction: the Tax Court, the U.S. District Court, and the U.S. Court of Federal Claims.

43. **Answer: B**

    The taxpayer is not required to respond to a *30-day letter*, although if there is no response the IRS will follow with a *90-day letter*.

44. **Answer: D**

    IRS Audit Guides provide guidance to revenue agents who are conducting audits but they do not govern the conduct of CPAs engaged in providing tax services.

45. **Answer: B**

    After a "no change" report the IRS cannot reopen the examination unless the corporation has committed fraud.

46. **Answer: B**

    A corporation's tax year may be reopened after the statute of limitations has expired if there is a determination for an open year that an earlier treatment was erroneous. The determination must adopt the position of the successful party and be unfavorable for the inconsistent party. The correction must fall under one of

the following circumstances: double inclusion or exclusion of an item of income; double allowance or disallowance of a deduction or credit; deduction or inclusions for trusts or estates and beneficiaries; or an item involving basis.

The 50 percent nonfraudulent omission from gross income from a tax return could not lead to the reopening of a corporation's tax year after the statute of limitations because it does involve a determination for an open year. However, a corporation prevailing in a determination allowing a deduction in an open tax year that was taken erroneously in a closed tax year would meet the requirements for reopening its tax year after the expiration of the statute of limitations.

47. **Answer: A**

    To avoid an underpayment penalty, the corporation can pay the lower of 100% of the prior year's tax liability ($40,000) or 100% of the current year's tax liability ($48,000).

48. **Answer: B**

    The late filing and late payment penalty is based upon the balance due. $50,000 owed less $45,000 withheld = $5,000 net due.

49. **Answer: C**

    Disclosure or use of the information on a tax return can only be done with the written consent of the taxpayer. Absent the taxpayer's written consent, disclosure or use of the taxpayer's tax return information by a tax preparer makes the preparer subject to a penalty for knowingly or recklessly disclosing tax return information.

    However, there are exceptions to the penalty. Specifically, tax preparers may disclose or use information on a tax return if the disclosure is (1) for quality or peer reviews; (2) for use in preparing state and local taxes and/or in declaring estimated taxes;(3) under code; and (4) under the order of a court of law.

    Thus, disclosing information for a peer review is an allowable exception to the penalty for knowingly or recklessly disclosing tax return information.

50. **Answer: D**

Disclosure or use of the information on a tax return can only be done with the written consent of the taxpayer. Absent the taxpayer's written consent, disclosure or use of the taxpayer's tax return information by a tax preparer makes the preparer subject to a penalty for knowingly or recklessly disclosing corporate tax information. Penalties also may be imposed on income tax preparers that willfully attempt to understate the tax liability on a return or refund claim.

This response indicates penalties may be imposed against preparers that knowingly or recklessly disclose or use tax information obtained in preparing a return or willfully attempt to understate any client's tax liability on a return or claim for refund. Thus, it is correct.

51. **Answer: C**

The accuracy-related penalty applies to any portion of an understatement if tax on a tax return is due to negligence or to substantial income tax understatements, income tax valuation misstatements, estate or gift tax understatements, or pension liability overstatements.

52. **Answer: A**

The required annual amount is usually the lower of 90% of the tax shown on the taxpayer's current year return or 100% of the tax shown on the taxpayer's prior year return. If the taxpayer's adjusted gross income exceeded $150,000 in the prior year and the taxpayer elects to base his/her required annual amount on the prior year, then the taxpayer would have to use 110% of the prior year's return.

Thus, Baker must base his required annual amount on 90% of the current year's tax liability or, since his adjusted gross income exceeded $150,000, 110% of the prior year's liability.

53. **Answer: D**

A civil fraud penalty can be imposed on a taxpayer if the Internal Revenue Service (IRS) is able to show by a preponderance of evidence that the taxpayer had specific intent to evade a tax. After the IRS originally shows that fraudulent actions by the taxpayer have occurred, the taxpayer must prove that any

tax underpayment was not attributable to fraudulent behavior. The civil fraud penalty amounts to 75% of the tax underpayment.

Specific intent to evade taxes could be shown of a corporation that maintained false records and reported fictitious transactions to minimize corporate tax liability.

54. **Answer: B**

Corporations owing $500 or more in income tax for the tax year are required to make estimated tax payments or be subject to an interest penalty. The payments must be equal to the lesser of 100% of the tax liability for the current year (i.e., the annualized income method) or the preceding year (i.e., the preceding-year method). The payments cannot be based on the preceding year if: (1) the corporation did not file a return showing a tax liability for that year (e.g., the corporation experienced a net operating loss); (2) the preceding year was less than 12 months; or (3) the corporation had taxable income of over $1,000,000.

This response correctly indicates that the Edge Corp. could use the annualized income method for calculating its estimated tax payments. Firms can always use the annualized income method to calculate their estimated tax payments because there are no restrictions on the use of the method. In addition, this response correctly indicates that Edge Corp. could not use the preceding year's tax liability as a basis for calculating its current-year estimated tax payments. Edge Corp. cannot use the preceding year's tax liability because the corporation experienced a net operating loss during that year and, as a result, there was no tax liability.

55. **Answer: D**

Tax preparers are subject to civil penalty for each tax return or claim if: (1) any understatement of tax liability is based on an unrealistic position; (2) the preparer was aware of or should have been aware of the unrealistic position; and (3) the unrealistic position was not disclosed as required. Tax preparers are not required to examine or review documents or other evidence to independently verify a taxpayer's information. However, preparers are required to make reasonable inquiries if the taxpayer's information appears to be incorrect or incomplete.

56. **Answer: B**

    Other assessable penalties with respect to the preparation of income tax returns for other persons include:

    (a) Failure to furnish copy to taxpayer;

    (b) Failure to furnish identifying number;

    (c) Failure to retain copy or list;

    (d) Failure to file correct information returns;

    (e) Negotiation of check

57. **Answer: B**

    If we assume that the accounting firm was negligent, as this answer does, then the focus turns to whether or not a third party such as the bank is entitled to sue. It would be helpful to know what the law of this jurisdiction is, what the engagement letter provided, and what the accounting firm knew about the bank.

    Assuming that the AICPA is presuming application of the most common rule—the Restatement "limited class" approach—and assuming further that the accounting firm knew that its client was going to use the report to obtain a loan from a bank—then this is clearly a correct answer.

58. **Answer: B**

    By having to hire a more expensive CPA to do to same job that Fatjo was going to do, Tacko incurred compensatory damages of $300.

59. **Answer: D**

    Because choices A and B are both right, this is the best answer.

60. **Answer: B**

    Arnold must pay for the damage that his error caused. He should recover $17,000 for his fee.

61. **Answer: C**

    Because both A and B are accurate choices, this is the best answer.

62. **Answer: A**

    If a CPA adhered to GAAS, he or she acted according to professional standards and likely was not careless so as to create negligence-based liability.

63. **Answer: C**

    Although the AICPA lists this as the correct answer, it is poorly worded. The majority view is the Restatement "limited class" approach, which generally allows recovery by third parties where the CPA had prior knowledge of the existence of a limited class of potential users (but not necessarily of their individual identities) and of the general purpose of their use of the audit. Prior knowledge is the key, so mere foreseeability is not enough, although this answer implies the contrary.

64. **Answer: A**

    To defend such a case, a CPA must show not that she acted perfectly, but that she acted as a reasonable CPA in the circumstances. By showing that she conformed with GAAS, she makes a strong argument that she acted reasonably.

65. **Answer: A**

    The standard that CPAs are held to is one of due care. They need not perform perfect work in every audit to live up to this standard. They must simply act as a reasonably prudent CPA would in the same circumstances.

66. **Answer: A**

    In a common law negligence suit, the plaintiff attempts to show that the CPA did not use the care of a reasonable accountant in the circumstances. By showing the audit conformed to GAAS, a CPA shows strong evidence of having acted reasonably.

67. **Answer: B**

    Tax accountants owe their clients a duty of confidentiality, but it is only fair that the CPA be able to defend himself or herself in the malpractice lawsuit by the husband. Doing this typically will require disclosure of important documents to the CPA's attorney.

68. **Answer: D**

    Although the state and federal courts have generally refused to recognize any sort of common law statutory privilege for client-accountant communications, Congress (in §7525) and about 15 states have statutorily enacted such privileges.

69. **Answer: C**

Because §7525 applies to neither criminal proceedings nor written advice in connection with tax shelters, this is the best answer.

70. **Answer: C**

State privilege statutes apply only in the state courts in the particular state, not in federal court.

71. **Answer: D**

A, B, and C all list recognized exceptions to the confidentiality obligation.

72. **Answer: D**

Two recognized exceptions to the confidentiality requirement are disclosure to other firm members on a need-to-know basis and disclosure during an ethics examination.

73. **Answer: D**

All of the first three choices are potential consequences of breach of the duty of confidentiality.

74. **Answer: D**

All of the first three choices reflect requirements of GAPP and, therefore, this is the best answer.

75. **Answer: C**

Both of the first two choices are potential consequences of breach of the duty of confidentiality when it involves taxpayer information.

76. **Answer: C**

It is certainly possible that a client would not want it known that s/he was considering filing for bankruptcy. Therefore, members who practice in that area must be sensitive to that fact.

77. **Answer: C**

Generally, the mere name of clients is not confidential information. Therefore, unless the accountant knows (or has reason to know, given the circumstances) that the client wishes to keep its identity as a client confidential, this information may be disclosed. An accountant would have reason to know

there was a problem if disclosure of the client's name informed the world that the client was experiencing financial difficulties.

78. **Answer: B**

Contracts for services are governed by common law.

79. **Answer: D**

Where there are mixed contracts (sale of both goods and services), we look to the price and the intent of the parties. The parts for such a system are small in comparison to the labor required for its installation throughout the construction process. Also, Janice does not just want vacuum parts. She wants the system installed.

80. **Answer: A**

A contract requires consideration, and this is a promise to make a gift, which cannot be consideration because there is love and affection underlying the gift but no detriment on Gwyneth's side.

81. **Answer: B**

Both sides had completed part of the contract, so the contract is partially executed for both Jeff and Jennifer

82. **Answer: A**

A bilateral contract is a promise in exchange for a promise creating a contract. Mary made the offer (promise) to buy Hal's desktop computer, and Hal accepted her offer by the promise to sell. The contract meets the four requirements for a valid contract; offer and acceptance, consideration (computer for $400), nothing to indicate either party lacks legal capacity, and selling and buying of a computer is a legal purpose. An executory contract is one not fully performed. Neither party has performed their part of the contract. Thus, this contract is classified as bilateral, valid, and executory.

83. **Answer: C**

The act of acceptance is not the act of performing the contract, which is what would be a unilateral contract. The act of acceptance is making a promise in exchange for the offer, which is also a promise.

84. **Answer: A**

This is a unilateral contract because it can only be accepted by performing an act. By the terms of the offer, Hammer cannot accept with a promise. Instead, Hammer has to do an act, which results in total performance of the contract. A unilateral contract is formed if the required action is completed. Here, by presenting Kay with the artifacts, Hammer has accepted the offer and formed a valid contract.

85. **Answer: A**

An offer can be withdrawn any time prior to acceptance (unless it is a UCC firm offer or is supported by consideration, as with an option contract). The knowledge of the sale is an effective revocation.

86. **Answer: A**

An offer can provide that acceptance must be received to be effective or that an acceptance must be communicated in a particular manner. Unless so specified in the offer, acceptances can be by any reasonable means.

87. **Answer: B**

Normally, under the mailbox rule acceptances are valid as soon as they are mailed. However, in this case we have an exception, because the offeror specified the method of acceptance (registered or certified mail) AND a time by which offeror had to actually receive the acceptance. By the terms of the offer, the acceptance was not sent as authorized and arrived late. Therefore, it is a counteroffer, which Harris may now accept or reject.

88. **Answer: A**

It is not unusual in a contract setting for "unforeseen difficulties" to arise, making performance more difficult or expensive than anticipated by one of the parties. Parties are nevertheless bound to their promises.

89. **Answer: A**

A real estate contract cannot be modified unless additional or new consideration is given. Only UCC contracts for the sale of goods can be modified without new consideration.

90. **Answer: B**

When the parties agree to accept an alternative means of payment, which they do not have to do, both sides have given detriment and have created an accord. Once the microwave is delivered, there is satisfaction.

91. **Answer: D**

The parol evidence rule does not permit evidence of terms not in a complete, final, and unambiguous contract. If you want terms in your contract, put them in your contract. Oral understandings not part of the contract terms are inadmissible in court.

92. **Answer: A**

This is one of the more difficult questions from the exam. Under the parol evidence rule, one cannot introduce into evidence prior or contemporaneous oral or written statements that add to or modify a final, fully integrated, unambiguous contract. The term "fully refurbish" is ambiguous. We don't know whether chroming is included and how much would have to be rechromed.

93. **Answer: D**

This answer is correct because a contract for the sale of realty falls under the Statute of Frauds requiring a writing signed by both parties or a written memo signed by the party to be charged to be enforceable. Kram signed the letter and the contract is enforceable against Kram.

94. **Answer: A**

A minor can avoid a contract by returning the item, regardless of its condition. If the item has been lost or stolen, the minor can disaffirm even though she or he returns nothing.

95. **Answer: D**

Fresno, as an adult, is bound to a valid contract and must perform even though Bronson as a minor had the right to disaffirm the contract.

96. **Answer: B**

This creates a voidable contract. If someone misrepresents information about the contract subject matter, you are free to go ahead with the contract or rescind it—it is voidable.

97. **Answer: D**

A statute of limitations sets a fixed period (usually four years) that is the maximum amount of time a party has to file a lawsuit. In a breach of contract case, the period begins at the time the contract is breached.

98. **Answer: A**

The rezoning clause is a condition precedent. Alpha has no duty to perform under the contract until and unless the parcel is rezoned by July 31. Essentially, the condition must be met before there are any contractual obligations.

99. **Answer: D**

The statute of limitations sets a limit on the amount of time (usually four years) a party may wait before bringing a lawsuit, and in a breach of contract suit, this time limit does not begin to run until the contract is breached.

100. **Answer: B**

The statute of limitations will begin to run when a cause of action accrues. In this example, that is when the contract is breached.

101. **Answer: A**

The statute of limitations requires that a lawsuit be brought within a specified time after a breach occurs.

102. **Answer: C**

Impossibility of performance will discharge contractual duties. It was impossible for Jackson to repair a boat that no longer existed. Thus, both Jackson and Smith are discharged from their contract obligations.

103. **Answer: A**

Prevention of performance will discharge a party from a contract. With accord and satisfaction, the satisfaction is the performance of the accord and discharges the old contract. Thus, both prevention of performance and accord and satisfaction discharge a party to a contract.

104. **Answer: D**

This is the best answer, as it is always correct. If a service becomes illegal to perform, it is treated as having become objectively impossible, and performance is always excused.

105. **Answer: B**

If the shipment terms require the seller to deliver goods under an F.O.B. destination contract, the seller is required to properly "tender" the goods to the buyer at the specific destination stated in the contract (not a destination specified by the buyer). This place can be other than the buyer's place of business.

106. **Answer: B**

When there is a shipment contract, the obligation of the seller is to place the goods in the hands of a carrier to be delivered to the seller. The risk of loss passes (FOB place of shipment) when the goods are delivered to the carrier.

107. **Answer: C**

When the terms of a sale's contract calls for delivery by a carrier at F.O.B. purchaser's loading dock, "risk of loss" (in absence of express contract) passes from the seller to the buyer upon tender or delivery of the goods at the purchaser's loading dock. Thus, the seller has the risk during shipment.

108. **Answer: A**

The Statute of Frauds does not apply to this contract. Although the sale of goods of $500 or more requires some kind of writing, this is a contract for personal services, not goods (repairing books).

109. **Answer: A**

In suits for breach of contract, a court will award specific performance only where the obligation is to deliver a unique item, such as real estate or a rare artifact. Courts also will force a person to refrain from doing something they have agreed in a contract not to do. But to force a person to perform services would constitute involuntary servitude.

110. **Answer: B**

This answer is correct because specific performance is generally used when money damages will not suffice such as when the subject matter of the contract is unique or rare. A patent sale typically satisfies this rule.

111. **Answer: D**

The formulas for damages require us to compensate for whatever the non-breaching party lost—Dunlap would have been paid $5,000 under the contract. He could only earn $3,000 with a substitute job—compensatory damages are the difference between the two or $2,000.

112. Answer: B

These are rare or unique goods situations, a situation in which specific performance is appropriate.

113. Answer: B

Punitive damages are not usually available in suits for breach of contract and not provided for under the UCC for breach of contract of sales of goods. The goal of contractual damages is to give the wronged party the "benefit of the bargain," not to punish the person who has breached the contract. Punitive damages are usually available only in other types of lawsuits, such as intentional tort suits.

114. Answer: B

The buyer has the following remedies against the seller: upon receipt of nonconforming goods, the buyer may reject the goods, accept the goods, or accept any unit and reject the remainder; the buyer has the right to cover (purchase goods elsewhere upon the seller's breach); the buyer may recover damages (not punitive) for nondelivery of goods or repudiation of the sales contract by the seller; the buyer may recover damages (not punitive) for breach in regard to accepted goods; the buyer may recover goods identified in the contract in possession of the seller upon the seller's insolvency; the buyer may sue for specific performance when the goods are unique; the buyer has the right of replevin (form of legal action to recover specific goods from the seller which are being withheld from the buyer wrongfully); the buyer can cancel the contract; the buyer has a security interest in the goods after the seller's breach; the buyer can recover liquidated damages. Punitive damages, however, are not an available remedy in either the common law or the UCC.

115. Answer: C

Egan has all the rights of West based on the assignment. Thus, Egan can release Barton, discharging the Barton contract, and West has no further liability to Egan. An assignment does not waive or eliminate the contract rights of the original party to the contract. Unless released, the assignor remains liable to the other contracting party. If the assignee fails to perform the obligations under the contract, the assignor is still responsible.

116. Answer: C

Generally, any right can be assigned. One exception is an assignment that materially increases the risks of the obligor (party obligated to perform the contact). For example, if I have a grocery store in Dallas and have a contract with ABC under which they will deliver produce to me, I cannot assign that right to a store in Los Angeles. ABC's shipping costs would rise substantially.

117. Answer: B

All contracts require intent to enter into a contract, including a contract for the assignment of rights under a contract.

118. Answer: D

Assignment of personal services contracts are not permitted because we hire individuals or particular companies for personal services; they are not generic like vehicles, real estate, and businesses.

119. Answer: A

An agency requires an agreement, a meeting of the minds. The principal gives the agent consent to act.

120. Answer: A

The statute of frauds only requires a writing for contracts for sale of goods of $500 or more, real estate, contracts impossible to perform in one year, a promise to answer the debt of another, and an executor's promise to be personally liable for the debt of an estate. An agency to purchase land would require a writing.

121. Answer: A

A power of attorney usually limits an agent's authority to specific transactions.

122. Answer: A

An unincorporated association does not have capacity, because it is not an individual or an entity, and therefore has no contractual capacity.

123. Answer: B

An external auditor is an independent contractor for the audit client.

124. Answer: D

The principal must have the ability to enter into contracts.

125. **Answer: C**

Where the agency is an agency coupled with an interest (i.e., where the agent owns part of the subject matter), the principal does not have the power to terminate the relationship).

126. **Answer: A**

Death or insanity of either the principal or the agent will end an agency immediately. Once Ogden, the principal, was declared insane, the agency relationship between Thorp and Ogden ended. Since the agency was terminated automatically by operation of law, Ogden would not be liable for the contract.

127. **Answer: C**

C is the best answer, as agents have a duty not to commingle their funds with the principal's funds, and should account for the principal's property.

128. **Answer: B**

Bisbee's responsibility as the joint venture's agent is to get the highest value for the joint venture, so this is the right answer. Obviously, Bisbee had an incentive not to pay the highest price if he is part of the buying entity as well. His conflict of interest breached his fiduciary duty to the Bisbees.

129. **Answer: D**

The agent here, Fuller, has allowed him- or herself to be conflicted between loyalty to the principal and to the customer. A payment such as this actually would belong to the principal because the agent was acting on the principal's behalf.

130. **Answer: C**

Rod was an agent for an undisclosed principal. Both the agent and the principal are liable on any contract entered into by the agent as long as it was in the scope of authority. Rod had authority to purchase a home, and in these facts he obtained Andrea's approval prior to entering into the contract.

131. **Answer: B**

This answer is correct because all three parties are potentially liable on the contract. A principal, whether disclosed, undisclosed, or partially disclosed, will be liable for the

contracts of his agent if these agreements are within the scope of the agent's express, implied, or apparent authority. Also, an agent, acting on behalf of an undisclosed principal, remains personally liable for performance of the contract even though the agreement was within the agent's scope of authority.

132. **Answer: B**

The principal is always liable for contracts entered into with authority to do so, but in undisclosed principal situations, the agent is liable under the contract because his/her name is on it. This answer is correct because either Magnus (the undisclosed principal) or Dexter (the agent) may be held liable on the contract for all land entered into by Dexter on Magnus's behalf. Dexter executed the contract within the scope of the agency relationship, and thus Dexter's actions are binding on Magnus. Also, Dexter is liable on each of the contracts because he failed to disclose that he was acting as agent for Magnus Corporation.

133. **Answer: D**

This is the best answer, because corporate presidents certainly have authority to bind the corporation to contracts for normal activities, such as these repairs.

134. **Answer: C**

Because Davis was attempting to advance her employer's interest by maintaining order in the day-care center, even though she did so in a wrongful manner, her employer is liable. Therefore, this is the best answer.

135. **Answer: C**

This question brings in another aspect of law—negligence and the defense of contributory negligence, which is a bar to recovery if established.

136. **Answer: B**

A principal is liable for ALL AUTHORIZED misrepresentations, but not for all UNauthorized misrepresentations. In such a case, the principal is liable only if an employee makes the misrepresentation. For the record, an employee is a worker who tends to be paid wages or salary, has a long-term relationship with the principal, and is supervised by the principal.

137. Answer: C

If a guaranty is made by an express contract with the creditor, to be enforceable against the guarantor the guaranty contract must be in writing and signed by the guarantor. The only exception is the "main purpose" or "leading object" doctrine where the guarantor will benefit financially or economically. Thus, Camp cannot be held liable on the oral guaranty under the Statute of Frauds.

138. Answer: C

Since Edwards released one of the two sureties, the remaining surety is liable for only half of the entire debt. Until the release, Edwards could have collected the entire debt from either surety, and then that surety could have sued the other surety for half of that amount under the right of contribution. However, now Edwards can only collect 50% of the debt from Owen, because it has eliminated Owen's ability to collect anything from Ward.

139. Answer: C

When there are co-sureties, each has a right to a proportionate contribution from the others if a co-surety pays an unfair share of the debt. In this case, Nash's liability is 2/9 of the total liability among all co-sureties ($40,000 out of a total $180,000). She therefore should not pay more than 2/9 of any total settlement. She has a right to recover $7/9 \times \$36,000$ from the others, or $28,000. More specifically, she will get $12,000 from Owen and $16,000 from Polk.

140. Answer: A

Co-sureties have rights against each other in the event that they are forced to pay more than their fair share. Here, Quill and West are equal co-sureties, because they are responsible for the same amount ($100,000). If Quill is initially forced by Ingot to pay the entire amount, it may, in a separate lawsuit, seek 50% of what it paid from West. Since West's release was not consented to by Quill, Quill retains its right of contribution against West.

141. Answer: A

A creditor is required to disclose any known material facts to a surety before the surety signs a loan agreement, if such facts will substantially increase the surety's risks. When a creditor does not make such disclosures, the creditor has committed presumed fraud, and the surety may use this as a defense to repayment.

142. Answer: C

If the loan is repaid in full by any party, the obligations of those liable for repayment are discharged.

143. Answer: D

Tender of full performance will totally release the surety, as in such a case there is no longer a debt to be repaid by anyone.

144. Answer: D

Unless the collateral is in the possession of the secured party, there must be a written or authenticated security agreement (describing the collateral), the secured party must give the debtor something of value, and the debtor must have rights in the collateral. Thus, A, B, and C are requirements to create an enforceable security interest. Perfection (by filing) is merely a means which gives third parties notice of the secured party's priority interest in case of debtor default and not a requirement to create the security interest.

145. Answer: D

For a security interest to attach, the following must be present:

Underlying debt/obligation; Either a security agreement or possession of the collateral by the creditor; and Debtor must have interest in the property.

Until all three are present, the security interest does not attach.

146. Answer: D

These are the exact elements for creation of a security interest.

147. Answer: B

The antiques are classified as inventory (collateral to be held for resell). Thus, although a purchase money security interest was created, being inventory, a filing is required for perfection.

148. Answer: D

There need not be the amount of the debt reflected in the publicly filed financing statement. All that needs to be included is which collateral is subject to the security interest, not the value of the collateral or the debt.

149. **Answer: B**

Filing is not necessary to perfect this security interest, because Grey has a purchase money security interest (PMSI) in the computer to be used for personal use (a consumer good). A PMSI arises when a creditor extends credit that is used to purchase the collateral, as a consumer good, which is the computer in this security agreement. A PMSI is perfected automatically at the time the interest attaches.

150. **Answer: B**

Here, possession as a method of perfection is not practical, and, although it is a purchase money security interest, the collateral equipment is not covered by the automatic perfection rule. Thus, a filing is required.

151. **Answer: B**

Even though the interest is perfected, Cray still gets to keep the refrigerator. A buyer in the ordinary course of business takes goods free from a security interest, even if the buyer has knowledge of the security agreement.

152. **Answer: A**

The debtor may give a security interest in either inventory or equipment that the debtor has rights to and the security agreement can also provide that this security interest applies to any inventory or equipment the debtor acquires in the future.

153. **Answer: C**

All perfected interests take priority over unperfected interests, regardless of when they arose, so II will be last. If more than one perfected interest exists, then the first to be perfected takes priority. Interests I and III are both perfected. The first is obviously perfected on April 15, 2004, and the third is not perfected by filing until April 20, 2004. An exception to the first in time is first in priority rule is when you have a PMSI in collateral other than livestock or inventory (here the collateral is store equipment) where a second in time of perfection takes place before or within twenty (20) days after the debtor takes possession of the collateral.

154. **Answer: D**

Upon the debtor's default, the secured party has the choice to proceed under the Uniform Commercial Code by taking possession of the 70 cows, either peacefully or through judicial process. The secured party can then either sell or, without objection, keep the collateral in full satisfaction of the debt. Alternately, the secured party can proceed to file suit, receive a judgment and levy on the non-exempt property of the debtor.

155. **Answer: A**

The debtor has paid 60% of the PURCHASE PRICE, so BestBuy must sell the TV.

156. **Answer: A**

A secured creditor has a security interest in some collateral. If the debt is not repaid according to the agreement with the debtor, the secured creditor may peacefully repossess the collateral and either keep or sell the collateral to satisfy the debt. In the alternative, the creditor may sue the debtor for amounts owed, just as any other creditor can, and obtain a judgment against the debtor.

157. **Answer: D**

Since Sharp did not sign the Agreement, he is not bound by it. To be an assignment for the benefit of creditors, Green would have to voluntarily transfer certain assets to a trustee or an assignee who, in turn, offers each creditor a pro rata payment. This not only did not happen, but the Agreement assured him that almost all of his debts would be cancelled. Although there may be fraud-in-fact on the sale of the antique car, it will be difficult to prove, since there was a substantial payment (70% of the car's estimated value) to a non-relative. What Sharp can prove is fraud-in-law, whereby, despite the sale, Green was allowed to possess and use the car as if the sale never took place. This gives Sharp the basis for an action of fraud-in-law; a presumption of fraud, which it is doubtful Green can rebut.

158. **Answer: D**

This action, if ordered by a court, will deduct sums directly from a paycheck. State laws generally limit the amount that can be deducted to around 25% of a debtor's after-tax wages.

159. **Answer: B**

Exemption statutes never apply to all personal property. They may exempt selected items, such as a computer, clothes, bibles, trade equipment, and furniture. A creditor cannot seize any and every asset to satisfy a debt. Social Security benefits are exempt from garnishment.

160. **Answer: A**

A mechanic's lien, one based on improvements to real property that have not been paid for, requires the holder to give notice before selling the property. An artisan's lien, one based on amounts unpaid for work done on personal property, also requires notice be given before sale of the property.

161. **Answer: D**

Any action by a debtor that gives a creditor an advantage over other creditors who would have priority in bankruptcy can be set aside as a voidable preference.

162. **Answer: D**

These are all permitted exemptions.

163. **Answer: D**

This answer is correct, because although the trustee can avoid some statutory liens (such as landlord's lien), the trustee cannot avoid all (key word is "any") statutory or common law liens (such as certain warehouse liens).

164. **Answer: A**

A debtor's estate in bankruptcy consists of all tangible and intangible property of the debtor held at the commencement of the bankruptcy proceedings. In addition, the estate consists of any after-acquired income from such property.

Therefore, interest from municipal bonds (held as part of the estate) also becomes part of the estate. Any gifts received within 180 days of the filing the petition also become part of the estate. All other payments received after the filing of the petition are not considered income from the existing debtor's (bankruptcy) estate.

Therefore, B and C are incorrect, because they are payments received after the filing of the petition, and are not considered income from the existing debtor's (bankruptcy) estate.

D is incorrect, because it is a gift received more than 180 days after the filing of the petition.

165. **Answer: C**

This is a contemporary transfer of cash for new goods—and a burglar alarm system may not be needed for a company teetering on bankruptcy, but it is not voidable.

166. **Answer: C**

Fifth Bank is the first in priority because it is a secured creditor—secured creditors are taken care of even before administrative expenses.

167. **Answer: D**

Of the $100,000, the first $70,000 will go to Fracon Bank, as that money was generated by the sale of the house in which they had a security interest. The next $2,000 will similarly go to Decoy as money raised from the sale of their security interest. This leaves $28,000. The next $12,000 will go to the IRS to satisfy their recorded judgment, as all taxes are paid before general creditors are paid.

168. **Answer: C**

Unless the debtor has been denied a discharge decree owing either to an act of the debtor (such as fraud, intentional concealment of assets, and the like), or where, by statute, the debt is not discharged (such as in the case of unpaid taxes), the discharge decree releases the debtor from personal liability for debts owed to his or her creditors.

A judgment creditor's debt is dischargeable and therefore is not on the statutory list of non-dischargeable debts.

169. **Answer: C**

After Chapter 7 liquidation proceedings begin, all non-exempt property at the time of the filing of the petition of the debtor becomes part of the distribution to creditors. In addition, some interests, including inheritances acquired by the debtor within 180 days of filing a voluntary petition, become a part of the debtor's estate for distribution.

170. **Answer: D**

Generally, a bankrupt debtor, at the end of bankruptcy proceedings, will receive a discharge decree. Unless the debtor has committed an act such as fraud, intentional concealment of assets, refusal to explain the loss of assets, and the like, is a partnership or corporation, or the debtor has received a discharge decree within eight years of the current filing petition, the discharge decree will be granted. Here, the debtor has committed an act, has refused satisfactorily to explain a loss of assets, and as such will be denied a discharge decree in bankruptcy.

171. **Answer: B**

All the elements of an investment contract are present. There was an investment of money ($5,000 each) in a common enterprise (all would profit or lose, depending on how the lawsuit came out), with an expectation of profit ($594,000 in this case), to be derived primarily from the efforts of others (Sam and his attorney).

172. **Answer: A**

The court held that these were interests in the form of an investment contract, so this is the correct answer. There was an investment of money (by 1,500 investors) in a common enterprise (all parties would either make or lose money, depending on the outcome), with an expectation of profit (14% return) to be derived primarily by the actions of others (those bundling and administering the leases).

173. **Answer: D**

The 1933 Act applies to sales of securities, including stocks, bonds and notes that are issued for periods over nine months.

174. **Answer: B**

B is the best answer, because the primary purpose of registration is to enable investors to make an informed decision as to whether to invest in a public offering.

175. **Answer: D**

After a prospectus and registration statement have been filed with the SEC, there is a 20-day waiting period before stocks may be issued. During this time, a preliminary, or "red herring," prospectus may be issued to investors.

176. **Answer: D**

During the waiting period of 20 days immediately after registering with the SEC, tombstone ads may be placed. Tombstone ads are heavily restricted and may contain only limited information, such as the type of security and where a potential investor would acquire a now-available prospectus.

177. **Answer: D**

Rule 504 contains no limitation on the number of nonaccredited investors (or accredited investors) who may purchase securities.

178. **Answer: A**

This is the answer that is **not** true. Reg A requires provision of a mini-prospectus to investors.

179. **Answer: A**

Governmental securities are exempt from registration under the 1933 Act.

180. **Answer: A**

Ten-year notes are securities and their public sale requires registration, absent the existence of an applicable exemption (such as under Regulation D).

181. **Answer: C**

Purchasers must hold until Rule 144 allows resale, which for most investors is six months.

182. **Answer: C**

This is the choice where the two rules differ. Only Rule 147 requires that all *offerees* be state residents. Rule 147A requires only that all *purchasers* be state residents.

183. **Answer: B**

Rule 506 will work if all the requirements are met.

184. **Answer: C**

This is a negligence-based statute. If a defendant, such as an auditor, can prove due diligence, that defendant has disproved negligence and can avoid liability.

185. **Answer: C**

With minor exceptions, a plaintiff in a Section 11 suit need not provide reliance in order to prevail.

186. **Answer: D**

Under Section 11 of the 1933 Act, a plaintiff need not show either reliance or fraud (or even negligence) by the defendants. However, defendants can win the day if they can disprove reliance. And the defendants other than the issuer can win if they can establish that they acted with due diligence. The primary things that plaintiffs must show to win their Section 11 claim are that there was a material misstatement in the registration statement on the effective date; that they can trace their shares to that registration statement; and that they suffered damages.

187. **Answer: B**

Section 11 imposes civil liability for untrue statements or omissions made by CPAs who do not use due diligence. Failure to follow GAAP is evidence of a failure to use due diligence; failure to use "generally accepted fraud-detection standards" is not.

188. **Answer: C**

C is the best answer, because public corporations must file 10-Qs with the SEC and negligently false statements therein are remediable under Section 18.

189. **Answer: D**

This answer is correct because it uses the correct statute of limitations (2yr/5yr, rather than 1yr/3yr), and notes properly that the plaintiff must meet both deadlines.

190. **Answer: C**

Section 18(a) establishes a presumption of liability for false statements in filed documents, but allows defendants to escape liability if they prove that they "acted in good faith and had no knowledge that such statement was false or misleading."

191. **Answer: B**

Section 10(b)/Rule 10b-5 are fraud provisions; they do not remedy mere negligence.

192. **Answer: A**

Any intentional violation of any provision of the 1934 Act is a crime. It should also be noted that potential criminal penalties include jail time, as well as fines. In addition, such a violation certainly opens an accountant up to potential civil liability, because the courts have implied a private right to sue on behalf of investors injured by Section 10(b)/Rule 10b-5 violations.

193. **Answer: A**

The SEC may bring civil charges against Seimone.

194. **Answer: B**

It is common for the SEC to bring civil charges and then the DOJ to bring criminal charges in insider-trading cases.

195. **Answer: C**

Because both A and B are accurate, this is the best answer.

196. **Answer: B**

As a sole proprietor, Juan is self-employed and must pay self-employment taxes on the earnings of the business, which are, in essence, also his earnings.

197. **Answer: C**

Telford has the discretion to decide which bills are paid and which are not. That is the key to determining who is a responsible person. As CFO, Telford is an officer, probably owns stock, probably takes an active role in daily management, and probably exercises control over daily bank accounts and records. He is the best choice here.

198. **Answer: A**

Toddrick was involuntarily separated because of business reverses and is definitely entitled to recover unemployment compensation benefits.

199. **Answer: B**

Businesses pay into a fund that is used to pay unemployment benefits. The monies put into this fund are tax deductible.

200. **Answer: D**

Payments for such things as over-the-counter drugs, funeral expenses, toiletries, most cosmetic surgery, nicotine patches and nicotine gum, maternity clothes, and health club dues are *not* typically deductible.

201. **Answer: C**

Under the ACA, Tessa could deduct all expenses over $7,500 (the 10% threshold), which means a $2,500 deduction.

202. **Answer: D**

And here's why. Tran first pays for the surgery–$1,200 for the deductible and then the co-pay which is 20% × $3800 ($5,000 cost – $1,200 deductible) which is $760. So far, he has paid $1,960 ($1,200 + $760), which is less that the maximum. Then Tran turns to the hospital bill. His deductible has been exhausted, so he would pay, absent the ceiling, coinsurance of 20% of $40,000, or $8,000. However, this puts him well over the maximum. He would pay only $6,850 (the maximum) minus $1,960 (the amount he has already paid), which comes to $4,890. The health insurer will pay the other $35,110 ($40,000 – $4,890). And it will pay the entire cost of the home health care ($4,000) and all of the rest of Tran's essential medical care expenses for the rest of the year.

203. **Answer: C**

The factors we know about (same work as employees, regular hours, required to work overtime, paid on an hourly basis) all point toward Tim being an employee.

204. **Answer: C**

Although it would be helpful to have more facts, Shanline appears to be an employee of ARC, going where ARC tells him to go, doing the tasks ARC tells him to do.

205. **Answer: D**

Among those other factors: lack of attempt to exert control, QWW is paid by the task, QWW uses its own equipment; this is not what QWW does for a living—it is a one-off.

206. **Answer: C**

If XYZ can fit itself within the safe harbor by proving that it had a reasonable basis for its classification, perhaps one based on an IRS letter ruling, it will probably not be punished.

207. **Answer: D**

Because there are so many restrictions on types of shareholders for a Subchapter S corporation (no more than 100, no nonresident aliens, all must be individuals—though exceptions are made for certain tax exempt organizations, estates and trusts)

208. **Answer: D**

No form of business organization excuses an accountant from liability for his or her own malpractice.

209. **Answer: B**

Owners of LLCs are typically known as "members."

210. **Answer: B**

If the requirements of a Subchapter S corporation are met, the corporate entity pays no federal income tax. All income is passed through to the shareholders. Although the shareholders enjoy limited liability, they do pay personal income tax on dividends received.

211. **Answer: B**

The general rule is that promoters are liable on pre-incorporation contracts that they negotiate on the corporation's behalf.

When the corporation comes into existence and adopts the contracts, the general rule is that both the promoter and the corporation are now liable under them.

However, if the other party agrees to release the agent from liability and to look only to the corporation for satisfaction, then a novation has taken place.

212. **Answer: A**

The articles of incorporation must include (1) the name of the corporation; (2) the number of shares it is authorized to issue; (3) the street address of its registered office and the name of its agent at that address; and (4) the name and address of each incorporator.

213. **Answer: A**

While limited partners may consult with the general partners, work for the partnership in a non-management capacity, guaranty its obligations and do a number of other things without forfeiting limited liability, they may not participate in management. They are granted limited liability and in exchange are expected to remain passive investors.

214. Answer: D

The articles of incorporation must include (1) the name of the corporation; (2) the number of shares it is authorized to issue; (3) the street address of its registered office and the name of its agent at that address; and (4) the name and address of each incorporator.

215. Answer: C

There is no evidence of commingling of funds, diversion of corporate assets, failure to maintain formalities, or any of the other factors that can induce a court to pierce the corporate veil. The mere fact that a business fails does not indicate that it was originally undercapitalized.

216. Answer: B

A partnership requires at least one other person or entity to be Sal's partner in ownership and management of the firm, so this is not a good choice.

217. Answer: C

This is the purpose of an LLC operating agreement, which is why it is a good idea that these be in writing and filed with the state (although this is not required).

218. Answer: B

B is the best answer, as distributions to owners reduce the corporate treasury and thereby decrease stockholder equity.

219. Answer: D

Because both I and II are false, this answer is the best choice.

220. Answer: D

A stock dividend is a pro rata distribution of additional shares of a corporation's stock to shareholders. For example, shareholders may receive two additional shares of stock for each ten they already own. Because the corporation essentially created new stock, giving stock dividends to shareholders is not considered a distribution for these purposes.

221. Answer: A

In the absence of agreement to the contrary, profits are to be shared equally among the partners.

222. Answer: D

Creditors may seek an involuntary judicial dissolution of a corporation in this situation (corporation admits in writing that the claim is due and it is insolvent) or if the creditor has a claim that has been reduced to judgment, is unsatisfied, and the corporation is proved to be insolvent).

223. Answer: C

The Revised Uniform Limited Liability Company Act (RULLCA) provides for dissolution via court order if a member sues and shows that those in control are behaving illegally, fraudulently, or oppressively.

224. Answer: C

Simply deciding to dissolve a partnership does not dissolve liability. If money is owed on contracts, tort judgments, or otherwise, the partners are still responsible for them. Apparent authority does continue after partners have decided to dissolve the partnership. Notice must be given to others (by contact for those with which the partnership has actually done business and by publication for everyone else) before apparent authority stops.

225. Answer: A

Shareholders have the right to vote on many important corporate changes, including amendments to the articles of incorporation, dissolution, sale of all or substantially all of the corporation's assets, and mergers & consolidations. Choices B, C, and D are all on this list. Choice A is, therefore, the correct answer. Often, one corporation can buy all or substantially all of the assets of another company without there being any large qualitative change in the life of the purchasing corporation. Therefore, when a large corporation gobbles up the assets of a smaller corporation, the shareholders of the large buyer do not have the right to vote on the transaction. There would be a much greater impact on the life of the selling corporation and its shareholders would therefore have the right to vote on the transaction.

226. Answer: B

This was an opportunity that the partnership knowingly passed on. Therefore, it would have been fine for Hurl to purchase it, except for the fact that, given the circumstances, it put Hurl in competition with the partnership and, therefore, breached his fiduciary duty to it.

227. Answer: D

Because a partnership creditor must proceed against the assets of the partnership first, this answer is correct.

228. Answer: C

This provision would be improper, because it is manifestly unreasonable to eliminate a manager's liability for intentional violation of criminal law, intentional infliction of harm on the firm, or intentional violation of criminal law.

229. Answer: C

The core of the directors' relationship to the company is that they owe it a fiduciary duty— the duty of highest loyalty.

230. Answer: C

The shareholder franchise allows owners of a corporation to vote for the election and removal of the board of directors (but not of the officers, who are chosen by and serve at the pleasure of the board).

231. Answer: B

This answer is the answer recommended by the AICPA, and although it is not perfect, it is probably the best of the four.

It is not ideal because it represents one way that such a contract may be validated, but not the only way. A contract between a company and a director may also be valid if

(a) it is approved by shareholders after full disclosure, or

(b) it is determined to be "fair" to the corporation, even if knowing approval of directors or shareholders was not obtained.

232. Answer: D

Under the business-judgment rule, courts refuse to second guess the decisions of corporate directors (and officers) in most situations, because the judges realize that they themselves are not business experts. There are some recognized exceptions to the business-judgment rule, particularly where the corporate managers were in a conflict-of-interest situation when they acted.

233. Answer: A

General partners are jointly and severally liable, or potentially liable, for an entire tort judgment against their firm. Their liability extends beyond acts they authorized. Even unauthorized acts can create liability for the general partners.

234. Answer: C

Choice I is correct, because partnership law is simply an application of agency law in this area. Every partner, acting to advance partnership business, is an agent acting on behalf of his or her principals, which consist of the partnership and the other partners. Choice II is also correct, because under the now majority RUPA view, partners are jointly and severally liable for both partnership tort judgments and contractual obligations. (In some states, partners remain only jointly liable for contractual obligations).

235. Answer: A

Directors breach their fiduciary duty to their corporation when they put themselves in a conflict-of-interest situation (as they would by serving on the Board of a competing company) or profit from inside information. So, Choices B and D are not accurate. Although a majority of directors may propose to sell control of the corporation, an individual director could not do so and even the entire Board would have to obtain shareholder approval.

So, Choice C is also incorrect.

Choice A is correct. In the absence of "red flags," indicating that the information provided is inaccurate, corporate directors are allowed to reasonably rely on information provided by corporate officers, by other directors, and by the company's auditor. The Board need not hire private detectives to follow officers around to ensure that they are telling the truth. However, recent case law indicates that directors should take some steps to ensure the relative reliability of financial information they receive from officers.

236. Answer: A

Losses on the sale or disposition of assets utilized for personal use are not deductible. The realized loss is $350,000 but it is not recognized.

237. **Answer: B**

Losses from the sale of personal use assets are not deductible so the loss for the television is not deducted. There is a realized loss of $500 ($1,000 amount realized − $1,500 adjusted basis) for the laptop. Since this is a business asset, the $500 loss can be recognized and deducted.

238. **Answer: A**

When the shares are bequeathed to Boone, his basis in the shares is the fair market value at the date of death, which is $100 per share. When the stock splits 2 for 1, Boone then owns 200 shares of stock with a basis of $50 each. When the shares are gifted to Dixon, she takes the basis in the stock that Boone had, or $50. Therefore, Boone's total basis is $5,000 (100 shares × $50 per share).

239. **Answer: A**

Bluff's adjusted basis in the equipment before the gift is $31,000 (cost basis of $35,000 + $1,000 capital improvement − $5,000 cost recovery). When property is gifted, the donee has two bases in the gifted property: the gain basis is the donor's adjusted basis of $31,000 and the loss basis (also $31,000) is the lower of the adjusted basis ($31,000) and fair market value ($32,000). Therefore, Russett's gain and loss bases are both $31,000.

240. **Answer: A**

Property bequeathed due to the death of the owner has a fair market value basis to the beneficiary, and a long term holding period. Jordan's gain on the sale of the inherited stock is:

Amount Realized	$7,500
Adjusted Basis	(5,000)
Recognized Gain	$2,500

Even though Jordan has owned the stock for only four months her holding period is long term since the stock was inherited.

241. **Answer: B**

Marketable securities are an investment that qualifies as a capital asset.

242. **Answer: D**

An individual can deduct only $3,000 of net capital losses each year. Excess capital losses are carried over indefinitely. In Year 1, $3,000 of the losses are deducted and the other $2,000 is carried forward. In Year 2, the $2,000 carryforward capital loss offsets the $1,000 capital gain to produce a $1,000 net capital loss. There is no carryforward loss to Year 3 so the entire $4,000 capital gain is recognized.

243. **Answer: A**

To quality for ordinary treatment, 1244 stock must be issued to the taxpayer for money or other property transferred by the taxpayer to the corporation.

244. **Answer: B**

The taxpayer has a loss of $50,000 on the option since it lapsed. The character is capital since the underlying asset, the XYZ stock, is a capital asset. The loss is short term since the option was owned for only six months.

245. **Answer: C**

Even though the NOL includes $15,000 ($20,000 × 3/4) of Section 1244 loss that can be combined with the current Section 1244 loss of $50,000, the maximum deduction for a given tax year is $50,000 for a Section 1244 loss ($100,000 if married filing jointly).

246. **Answer: C**

May 12 Sale		
Amount realized	(500 × $23)	$11,500
Adjusted basis	(500 × $25)	(12,500)
Realized loss		$(1,000)

Since 250 shares of the Jackey stock was repurchased within 60 days of the sale date (30 days before/30 days after), 50% of the realized loss is not recognized. So the recognized loss is $500.

The basis in the 250 shares purchased on May 28 is $6,000 (cost of $5,500 + the deferred loss of $500). The cost per share is $24 ($6,000/250 shares).

October 15 Sale		
Amount realized	(100 × $18)	$1,800
Adjusted basis	(100 × $24)	(2,400)
Realized loss and recognized loss		$(600)

The total capital loss is $1,100 ($500 + $600).

247. **Answer: C**

Tangible assets that are used in a trade or business and owned for one year or less are ordinary assets. Since the computer was owned for slightly more than four months, the gain is classified as ordinary income.

248. **Answer: D**

The lookback provision states that the net Section 1231 gains must be offset by net Section 1231 losses from the five preceding tax years that have not previously been recaptured. To the extent of these losses, the net Section 1231 gain is treated as ordinary income. The $75,000 gain in Year 3 was recaptured as ordinary income by $50,000 of the Year 1 loss and $25,000 of the Year 2 loss. Note that $5,000 of the Year 2 loss remains unrecaptured. The $80,000 gain is recaptured as ordinary income to the extent of the $5,000 remaining Year 2 loss, $20,000 Year 4 loss, and $30,000 Year 5 loss for a total of $55,000. The remaining $25,000 gain is treated as a Sec. 1231 gain.

249. **Answer: C**

The gain recognized from the sale is:

Amount realized	$200,000
Adjusted basis ($160,000 − $60,000)	100,000
Recognized gain	$100,000

Personalty is subject to the Section 1245 depreciation recapture rules which indicate that gain will be taxed as ordinary income up to the amount of depreciation claimed on the property. Since there was $60,000 of depreciation on the equipment, $60,000 of the gain is taxed as ordinary income and the remaining $40,000 is taxed as Section 1231 gain.

250. **Answer: D**

All of the assets sold are assets that have been used in a business and are therefore Section 1231 losses. Thus, all of the losses are Section 1231 losses and total $290,000.

251. **Answer: A**

The computer desks ($22,000) and office furniture ($4,000) are MACRS seven-year property.

252. **Answer: C**

Customer lists, trade names, and goodwill are intangible assets that are amortized over 180 months. For the current year the assets are amortized for six months since the business began July 1. ($240,000/180 months × 6 months = $8,000).

253. **Answer: D**

Under MACRS, the office building is considered nonresidential real property. Land cannot be depreciated. Its class life is 39 years. MACRS requires that the straight-ine method be used to compute the depreciation of 39-year class life property. Therefore, the office building would be depreciated at a rate of $6,000 per year ([$264,000 building cost, less $30,000 cost of land]/39 years). However, the mid-month convention applies to 39-year class life property. This convention requires that, regardless of when realty is placed into service, it is considered to be placed into service at mid-month. Therefore, for August 2018 (the first month of service), Graham could deduct $250 (= $6,000/12 months × one-half of a month). For the period of September 2018 to December 2018 (the remainder of the tax year), Graham could deduct $2,000 (= $6,000 × 4/12 months). Hence, Graham's MACRS deduction for the office building in 2018 would be $2,250, the sum of the two periods.

254. **Answer: C**

The statutory amortization period for a covenant not to compete that is related to a business acquisition is 15 years.

255. **Answer: D**

An exchange will be non-taxable if it qualifies under the like-kind exchange rules. All realty is considered like-kind property. Since the building and the land are both realty, this qualifies as a non-taxable like-kind exchange.

256. **Answer: B**

This is a qualified like-kind exchange because a machine was exchanged for equipment and Hogan's use for each is for business purposes.

Amount Realized:		
Equipment received	$80,000	
Cash	1,000	
Debt relief	2,000	
Total		$83,000
Adjusted Basis:		
Cost	$100,000	
Depreciation	(30,000)	
		(70,000)
Realized Gain		$13,000

Debt relief and the cash received are both considered to be boot received, which is a total of $3,000. The recognized gain is the lower of the realized gain, $13,000, or boot received, $3,000.

257. Answer: B

A fire qualifies as an involuntary conversion, and realized gain can be deferred since the old warehouse is replaced with a new warehouse.

Amount realized from conversion	$195,000
Adjusted basis of old property	(75,000)
Realized gain	$120,000
Amount realized from conversion	$195,000
Cost of replacement property	(167,000)
	$28,000

The recognized gain is $28,000, the lower of the realized gain or the amount realized that was not reinvested in the new warehouse. The deferred gain is $92,000 ($120,000 – $28,000).

The adjusted basis of the new property is its cost reduced by any deferred gain: $167,000 – $92,000 = $75,000.

258. Answer: C

Sand's basis per share is $180 ($18,000/100 shares). Sand's realized loss on the 50 shares sold is $2,000 ($7,000 amount realized – $9,000 basis ($180 × 50 shares). This loss is not recognized under the wash sale rule if the same stock is repurchased within 30 days. Since only 25 shares were repurchased during the 30 day period, 50% (25 shares/50 shares) of the loss is not recognized. Therefore, $1,000 of the realized loss is recognized.

259. Answer: A

A taxpayer may exclude realized gains up to $250,000 ($500,000 if filing joint) on the sale of a residence if the residence has been owned and used by the taxpayer as a principal residence for at least two of the preceding five years. (Note that for the $500,000 exclusion both spouses must meet the use test, but only one must meet the ownership test). Wynn's realized gain is $200,000 ($450,000 amount realized – $250,000 adjusted basis), so all of this gain can be excluded.

260. Answer: D

The total recognized gain from the sale is $20,000 ($100,000 selling price – $80,000 basis). Under the installment method, recognized income = cash collected × (gross profit/contract price). Therefore, $25,000 × ($20,000/$100,000) = $25,000 × 20% = $5,000.

261. Answer: A

A taxpayer acquiring property through purchase or exchange from a person who sustained a loss on the transaction that was disallowed owing to related taxpayer rules realizes a gain on the sale or other disposition of the property only to the extent that the gain exceeds the amount of the disallowed loss. Alice acquired the Zinco stock from her father, who sustained a disallowed loss of $10,000 ($20,000 selling price, less $30,000 purchase price). Hence, Alice would have to realize a gain of more than $10,000 for her to recognize a gain, since she now has a right of offset of $10,000.

Alice purchased the stock from her father for $20,000 and sold the stock for $25,000 – realizing a gain of $5,000. Since Alice's realized gain is less than her father's right of offset, Alice does not recognize any gain on the sale of the stock.

262. Answer: C

Generally, interest-free loans are subject to the imputed interest rules if they exceed $10,000. The interest that is not being paid by the child to the parents is considered a gift from the parents each year that the loan is outstanding.

263. Answer: A

Under the tax benefit rule, recoveries of taxes previously deducted by a taxpayer that were overpaid should be reported as income by the taxpayer in the year of recovery. The taxes subject to the tax benefit rule are: state income taxes; personal property taxes; real property taxes; state sales and use taxes; state corporation franchise taxes; stamp taxes; federal excise taxes; customs duties; and farmland preservation credits.

Farb's overstatement arose from personal property taxes, a tax subject to the tax benefit rule. Thus, Farb should deduct $8,000 in his 2017 income tax return and should report the $5,000 refund as income in his 2018 income tax return when the case is settled.

264. Answer: B

Under the accrual method of accounting, income is reported once all events to establish a taxpayer's right to receive the income have occurred and the amount can be determined with reasonable accuracy.

If an amount of income has been accrued on the basis of a reasonable estimate with the exact amount to be determined at a later date, any difference between the estimate and exact amount is to be included in income or deducted in the year when the exact amount can be determined.

265. Answer: D

Wages are included in gross income for the year in which they are received. Unemployment compensation is also included in gross income since it replaces income that would have been received if working. Therefore, the total amount included in gross income is $41,000.

266. Answer: C

Alimony is included in the recipient's income, but child support payments and property settlements are not.

267. Answer: C

All of the items received are included in gross income except for the state income tax refund. Since Randolph always uses the standard deduction, no tax benefit is received when the state income taxes are paid. Therefore, the refund is not taxable.

268. Answer: B

Alimony received by a taxpayer is included in that taxpayer's gross income and alimony paid by a taxpayer is deductible from that taxpayer's gross income. To be considered alimony, the payments must be made under a divorce or separation agreement. Payments to third parties (such as tuition, rent and mortgage) by the spouse paying alimony for the spouse receiving alimony receive the same treatment as cash payments.

John and Mary have a divorce decree stipulating $10,000 per year payments from John to Mary, but the amount decreases to $8,000 when their child reaches the age of 18 years. Due to this decrease, $2,000 of the $10,000 payment would be considered child support and, as a result, would not be reported by Mary as income. The remaining $8,000 would be considered alimony and, therefore, reported as income by Mary.

269. Answer: A

Alimony must be received in cash so the painting and beach house do not qualify.

270. Answer: B

Decker's cost basis is the $25,000 he paid for the policy plus the $40,000 he paid in premiums. $200,000 less $65,000 = $135,000.

271. Answer: D

Joan meets all of the requirements to exclude the gift from income, except that she accepted the award and received payment. Therefore, the FMV of the award, $10,000, is included in her income.

272. Answer: B

Since the scholarship was used to pay tuition and fees, none of it is taxable. For purposes of this section, a qualified scholarship is any amount received by an individual as a scholarship or fellowship grant (as defined in paragraph (c)(3) of this section), to the extent the individual establishes that, in accordance with the conditions of the grant, such amount was used for qualified tuition and related expenses

Amounts receive for teaching are taxable. Inclusion of qualified scholarships and qualified tuition reductions representing payment for services are taxable.

273. Answer: B

The $100 dividend on Gail's life insurance policy is treated as a reduction of the cost of insurance (because total dividends have not yet exceeded accumulated premiums paid) and is excluded from gross income. Thus, Gail will report the $300 dividend on common stock and the $500 dividend on preferred stock, a total of $800 as dividend income.

274. Answer: B

Dividends are included in income at earlier of actual or constructive receipt. When corporate dividends are paid by mail, they are included in income for the year in which received. Thus, the $875 dividend received 1/2/18 is included in income for 2018. The $500 dividend on a life insurance policy from a mutual insurance company is treated as a reduction of the cost of insurance and is excluded from gross income.

275. Answer: A

Since the tax basis of the preferred stock is determined in part by the basis of the common stock, the holding period of the preferred stock includes the holding period of the common stock (i.e., the holding period of the common stock tacks on to the preferred stock). Thus, the holding period of the preferred stock starts when the common stock was acquired, January 2018.

276. Answer: C

After the stock dividend, the basis of each share would be determined as follows:

$$\frac{\$90,000}{450 + 50} = \$180 \text{ per share}$$

Since the holding period of the new shares includes the holding period of the old shares, the sale of the 50 new shares for $11,000 results in a LTCG of $2,000 [$11,000 − (50 shares × $180)].

277. Answer: D

If prices are rising and LIFO is used then the cost of inventory, and therefore the total for costs of goods sold, will be higher. If costs of good sold is higher then taxable income will be lower, which also means that the current tax liability will be lower.

278. Answer: D

If a corporation filed a short-year return for 3 month, the income for that period is first multiplied by 4 (12 months/3 months) to annualize the income for 12 months. The corporate tax liability is then computed on this amount for the full 12 months. That amount is the multiplied by 3/12 to prorate for the short tax year.

279. Answer: A

Quality control expenses are directly related to the manufacturing process so the costs are included in the basis of the inventory per the uniform capitalization rules.

280. Answer: D

An applicable financial statement is a statement that conforms to GAAP and is

1. Reported in a 10-K
2. An audited financial statement used for a nontax purpose, or
3. Filed with a federal agency (but not for tax purposes).

An applicable financial statement also includes a financial statement that conforms to IFRS.

281. Answer: D

Manufacturers and certain retailers and wholesalers are required to use the uniform capitalization rules to capitalize direct and indirect costs allocable to property they produce and for property they purchase for resale. Marketing, selling, advertising, and distribution expenses are not required to be capitalized. Storage costs are required to be capitalized to the extent that they can be traced to an off-site storage or warehouse facility. Those storage costs attributed to an on-site facility are not required to be capitalized.

This response correctly indicates that marketing costs are not required to be capitalized and that costs attributable to off-site storage facilities are required to be capitalized.

282. Answer: D

Moving expenses are deductible if closely related to the start of work at a new location and a distance test (i.e., distance from new job to former residence is at least 50 miles further than distance from old job to former residence) and a time test (i.e., employed at least 39 weeks out of 12 months following move) are met. Since the two tests are met, Clay's unreimbursed direct moving expenses are fully deductible from gross income in arriving at adjusted gross income.

283. **Answer: D**

Dividend income is taxable income.

284. **Answer: D**

Since this is not an accountable plan, all reimbursements are included in the employee's income ($400 × 12 months = $4,800) and all employee deductions will be 2% miscellaneous itemized deductions.

285. **Answer: C**

The first $50,000 of group-term life insurance provided by an employer is a tax-free fringe benefit. Johnson receives $200,000 of group-term life insurance, so $150,000 of this coverage is taxable. There are 150 units of $1,000 each of excess coverage, included in income at $2.76 for each unit. The income from the insurance coverage is $414 ($2.76 × $150). When the $414 is included with the $100,000 salary, gross income is $100,414.

286. **Answer: C**

The fair value of the condominium is included in income since this was received in return for services rendered to her employer. The $400 cash is also included in income under the treasure trove principle. The $400 is not offset by the $30 used to purchase the desk, but she does have a basis of $30 for the desk. Inheritances are never included in gross income.

287. **Answer: B**

IRA contributions must be made by the original due date of the return (April 15) even if the return is extended.

288. **Answer: D**

The $30,000 distribution from the traditional IRA is taxable at the taxpayer's marginal tax rate for federal income tax purposes. In addition, since this is an early distribution (before age 59½) and none of the exceptions for early distributions are met, the distribution is also subject to a 10% penalty tax. Therefore, the $30,000 distribution will be taxed at a 45% rate (35% marginal tax rate + 10% penalty tax). Total tax liability is $13,500 ($30,000 × 45%).

289. **Answer: D**

John does not have any basis in his retirement account. He did not receive basis for his contributions because they were made from earnings that were not taxed. He did not receive basis for his employer's contributions since they were made from employer funds. Therefore, the entire $350,000 distribution is included in John's gross income.

290. **Answer: B**

Distributions from traditional IRAs are taxed as ordinary income.

291. **Answer: A**

No deduction or credit shall be allowed for any amount paid or incurred during the taxable year in carrying on any trade or business if such trade or business (or the activities which comprise such trade or business) consists of trafficking in controlled substances (within the meaning of schedule I and II of the Controlled Substances Act) which is prohibited by federal law or the law of any state in which such trade or business is conducted. However, a deduction is allowed for the cost of merchandise purchased.

292. **Answer: A**

It is an ordinary and necessary expense to have the restaurant cleaned, and the $20 is reasonable.

293. **Answer: A**

Fines and penalties generally may not be deducted as a business expense, including those paid to the federal government. Hence, a corporation's penalty for underpaying federal estimated taxes is not deductible.

294. **Answer: C**

Alimony payments you make under a divorce or separation instrument, such as a divorce decree or a written agreement incident thereto, are deductible if all of the following requirements are met:

- You and your spouse or former spouse do not file a joint return with each other;
- You pay in cash (including checks or money orders);
- The divorce or separation instrument does not say that the payment is not alimony;
- If legally separated under a decree of divorce or separate maintenance, you and your former spouse are not members of the same household when you make the payment;

- You have no liability to make any payment (in cash or property) after the death of your spouse or former spouse; *and*
- Your payment is not treated as child support.

295. Answer: A

Qualified moving expenses are limited to the expenses for moving the household goods ($2,000) and lodging ($100). Meals are not deductible during a move and temporary living expenses are never deductible. The $2,100 of qualified expenses is reduced by the $2,000 reimbursement from the employer.

296. Answer: B

The unreimbursed employee business expenses and charitable contribution are itemized deductions, so these do not affect the computation of adjusted gross income. AGI equals the $3,000 of wages less student loan interest of $400, or $2,600.

297. Answer: A

If an employee or a self-employed individual moves his/her residence due to a change of his/her principal place of work, reasonable expenses resulting from moving household goods and personal effects from the old residence to the new residence and from traveling from the old residence to the new residence may be deducted. To qualify for the deduction, the new job site must be at least 50 miles further away from the old residence than was the old principal job.

If the taxpayer was unemployed before the move, the job site must be at least 50 miles away from his/her old residence. In addition, the taxpayer must be employed full-time in the area of the new principal place of work for at least 39 weeks during the 12-month period following the move, or if self-employed, for at least 78 weeks in the 24-month period following the move with at least 39 of the 78 weeks in the 12-month period following the move.

Neither the $500 fee for breaking the lease on the prior apartment residence nor the $900 for the security deposit placed on the apartment at the new location may be deducted as moving expenses. They are not qualified expenses nor was the move work related or more than 50 miles.

Also note that the question asks to determine the moving expenses that are deducted on Schedule A. Moving expenses are deducted on Form 1040; they are not itemized deductions.

298. Answer: B

Total allowable medical expenses is $20,000. Only medical expenses in excess of 10% of AGI are allowable as a deduction. Carrol's AGI is $100,000 × .010 = $10,000. Total expenses of $20,000 − $10,000 = $10,000 deductible expenses.

299. Answer: B

Investment interest expense is deductible to the extent of net investment income. Net investment income is defined as investment income ($10,000) less noninterest investment expenses ($8,000), or $2,000. So, $2,000 of the $5,000 of investment interest expense is deductible as an itemized deduction. The remaining $3,000 is carried over, indefinitely, and deducted in a year that has sufficient net investment income.

300. Answer: B

Medical expenses paid by an individual are deductible in the year paid.

301. Answer: A

In addition to their own expenditures, taxpayers are allowed to deduct the qualified medical expenditures of their spouse and dependents. Qualified medical expenditures include those incurred for diagnosis, cure, mitigation, treatment or prevention of disease, or for the purpose of affecting any structure or function of the body. The cost of inpatient care (including meals and lodging) also is a qualified medical expenditure. If the institution furnishes medical care but is not a hospital, the expenditures are qualified medical expenditures as long as the individual is at the institution primarily for the medical care, and the meals and lodging costs are necessary incidents of the care.

All of the Whites' medical expenditures were for their dependent child, so they may claim a deduction for any qualified medical expenditures. Since special equipment, such as wheelchairs, help mitigate a person's disease, the cost of such equipment is considered a qualified medical expenditure. Therefore, the Whites may claim a deduction for the $600 spent on the repair and maintenance of their child's motorized wheelchair.

The Whites also may deduct the $8,000 spent on tuition, meals, and lodging at the special school for their child because their child attends the institution primarily for the availability of medical care, with meals and lodging furnished as necessary incidents to that care.

Thus, without regard to the 10% of adjusted gross income floor applicable to medical expenditures, the Whites may claim $8,600 on their 2018 return as qualifying medical expenses.

5 × $15 =	$ 75
9 × $25 =	$225
1 × $25 =	$ 25
Total	$325

308. Answer: B

Meals and entertainment expenses are limited to 50% of their total amount. For meals and entertainment expenses that an employee is reimbursed by his/her employer, the percentage limit applies to the employer. However, if the reimbursement is included in the employee's income, the percentage limits apply to the employee and not the employer. Food and beverage expenses are only deductible, if: (1) the expenses are not lavish or extravagant; (2) the taxpayer (or one of his employees) is present when the food or beverages were provided; and (3) the expense relates directly to the conducting of business.

Assuming that a Banks Corp.'s employee was present when the meals were provided and that the expenses were for a bona fide business purpose, the meals expense can be deducted because they were not lavish or extravagant. Since the corporation reimbursed its employees, Banks Corp. may deduct 50% of the meals expense.

302. Answer: A

A church is a qualified charity and charges to credit cards are deemed as cash payments on the date of the charge.

303. Answer: B

The deductible business expenses are the uniforms ($320), subscriptions ($110), and seminar ($1,300). The investment expenses and custodial fees are deductible but not on Schedule C. They are investment expenses deductible as 2% miscellaneous itemized deductions on Schedule A.

304. Answer: C

All of the expenses listed are allowed as 2% miscellaneous itemized deductions, which total $2,750. This amount is reduced by 2% of AGI ($75,000), which is $1,500. Thus, Carter's deduction is $1,250.

309. Answer: B

When traveling outside the U.S. primarily for vacation (4 weeks total versus 1 week seminar), the cost of the trip is a nondeductible personal expense. Baker can deduct the registration fees for the business seminar and deduct the out of pocket expenses for the time that was directly related to the business seminar (1 week). 5 days × $100 per day plus $700 registration = $1200 of deductible education expense.

305. Answer: A

Lower of decline in FMV ($200,000) or AB of property ($350,000)	$200,000
Insurance Reimbursements	(175,000)
− $100 per casualty	(100)
− 10% × AGI	(12,000)
Casualty loss deduction	$12,900

306. Answer: A

Dues are not deductible. All of the other expenses are deductible but subject to the 50% limitation for meals and entertainment. Note that the deduction for the Super Bowl tickets is limited to the face value of the tickets, before the 50% limitation. The allowable deduction is $2,250 (($2,000 + $1,500 + $1,000) × 50%).

310. Answer: A

Since Budd reports on the cash basis he did not recognize income when the client was billed. Therefore, he has no basis in the receivable to deduct when it becomes uncollectible.

311. Answer: B

The $100,000 NOL would first be carried back to 2016 and offset $50,000 of income. It would then be carried to 2017 and offset $40,000 of income. This would leave $10,000 of NOL ($100,000 − $50,000 − $40,000) to carryforward to 2019.

307. Answer: C

The deduction for business gifts is limited to $25 per individual/customer who receives a gift. The total deduction is computed as follows:

312. **Answer: A**

$7,000 is correct.

Wages	$5,000
Interest on savings account	1,000
Net rental income	4,000
Net business loss	(16,000)
Net short-term capital loss	(2,000)
AGI	(8,000)
Deductions:	
Personal exemption	$4,150
Standard deduction	6,550
Taxable Loss	(18,650)

Adjustments to arrive at NOL carry back or carry forward (Use Form 1045, Schedule A for calculation purposes.)

$18,400	TAXABLE LOSS
Plus $4,150	Personal exemption, Destry cannot deduct his personal exemption.
Plus $5,500	Adjustment for deductions that are not connected to a trade or business or employment, such as the standard deduction of $6,500 reduced by the non-business income of $1,000 interests from savings.
Plus $2,000	Short term capital loss as adjusted by business capital gains and losses (–0–).
($7,000)	Correct carry back or forward

313. **Answer: A**

For the business to be nonpassive Barltet must materially participate in the business. One method to materially participate is to work in the business more than 500 hours for a year.

314. **Answer: A**

An owner of rental real estate can deduct up to $25,000 of rental real estate losses against other income if he actively participates in managing the real estate.

315. **Answer: A**

Special rules apply to realty that is used for both personal and rental purposes. If the number of rental days is less than 14 then the property is treated as if it was used 100% for personal use. In that case, the rental revenue is ignored (i.e., does not have to be recognized).

The only items that can be deducted are real estate taxes and mortgage and these items must be reported on Schedule A.

Therefore, there is no rental income and no rental expenses.

316. **Answer: B**

Lane has $160,000 in active income, $15,000 of passive income, and $35,000 of passive losses. Note that the exception that allows deduction for up to $25,000 of rental real estate losses does not apply since Lane's modified AGI exceeds $150,000. The passive losses can only be deducted to the extent of passive income, so $15,000 is correct.

317. **Answer: C**

Wages, interest, dividends, and Schedule C income are all taxable for a total of $54,000. $25,000 of the rental loss is allowed since Bearing actively participates in the rental real estate activity and his modified AGI does not exceed $100,000. However, the $5,000 passive loss from the partnership cannot reduce other income. Therefore, AGI is $29,000.

318. **Answer: D**

Personal exemptions are allowed for Anderson and spouse. The 23-year old child is a qualifying child because she is less than 24 and a full-time student, so the age test is met, and she does not provide more than 50% of her own support. The 33-year old child is a qualifying relative because the parents provide more than 50% of his support and the gross income test is met (his earned income does not exceed the exemption amount). Thus, two dependency exemptions are also allowed.

319. **Answer: C**

Ben has provided over 10% of Sara's support and all of the qualifying relative tests are met (gross income, joint return, citizen) except for the support test, but it is met through the multiple support agreement. The individuals as a group have provided over 50% of Sara's support.

320. **Answer: A**

The Age Test applies to the qualifying child rule but not the qualifying relative rule. The gross income, support, and citizenship/residency tests must all be met for the qualifying relative rule to be met.

321. **Answer: B**

There are two personal exemptions for John and his wife. Dependency exemptions are as follows:

Widowed sister: Fails the gross income test
Daughter: Meets age test so is a qualifying child
Son: Meets age test since is a full-time college student and less than 24, so is a qualifying child
Housekeeper: Facts do not indicate that John and wife provide more than 50% of support
Butler: Facts do not indicate that John and wife provide more than 50% of support

322. **Answer: D**

In the year that an individual's spouse dies, the spouse's filing status is married filing jointly. For the two years after the year of death, the qualifying widow(er) can continue to use the married filing joint rates if the taxpayer provides more than half of the cost of maintaining the household (rent, mortgage interest, taxes, home insurance, repairs, food, utilities, etc.) for a **dependent child** (step and adopted also).

323. **Answer: A**

Whether taxpayers live together does not impact filing status. Marital status is determined on the last day of the tax year. Since the taxpayers were married as of the end of the tax year they may file married filing joint (note that they could also file married filing separately).

324. **Answer: D**

In the year of death, the surviving spouse may always file as married filing jointly.

325. **Answer: C**

For head of household filing status, the following costs are considered in determining whether the taxpayer has contributed more than one-half the cost of maintaining the household: rent; mortgage interest; taxes; insurance on the home; repairs; utilities; and food eaten in the home. The following costs may not be considered: clothing; education; medical treatment; vacations; life insurance;

transportation; rental value of home owned by taxpayer; and the value of services provided by the taxpayer or a member of the taxpayer's household.

This response correctly indicates that the food consumed may be considered in determining whether the taxpayer has contributed more than one-half the cost of maintaining the household and that value of services provided by the taxpayer may not be considered.

326. **Answer: B**

Juan's net income from his sole proprietorship is subject to self-employment tax.

327. **Answer: C**

2% miscellaneous itemized deductions are not allowed for AMT purposes. Home mortgage interest is allowed as long as the loan proceeds were used to acquire or make capital improvements to a principal residence. Thus, the correct answer is $11,000.

328. **Answer: C**

Personal exemptions cannot decrease AMT income.

329. **Answer: D**

D is correct because	$350,000 less
Optics cost of goods sold	$35,000 less
Optics rent expense	$28,000 less
Liability insurance premium on Optics	$5,250 equals
New income from self-employment of	$281,750

330. **Answer: C**

Her tax savings is $3,000 ($12,000 × 25%) since the contribution is deductible. Therefore, her net cost is $9,000 ($12,000 − $9,000).

331. **Answer: A**

Since his income tax rate is declining, he will save 20% on any income deferred from the 50% tax rate in Year 1 to the 30% tax rate in Year 2.

332. **Answer: B**

When long-term capital gain property is contributed to a qualified charity, the fair market value of the property can be deducted as a charitable contribution.

333. Answer: C

If Orleans gives the property to his friend, the $20,000 loss disappears since the friend's loss basis in the land will be its fair market value of $50,000. Therefore, Orleans should sell the land so he can recognize the loss. He can then contribute the cash from the sale to his friend.

334. Answer: D

A married taxpayer must file as married filing jointly to qualify for the earned income credit.

335. Answer: B

The credit is computed as 100% of the first $2,000 and 25% of the next $2,000 of qualified educational expenses, for a total of $2,500. This credit does not begin phasing out in 2018 for married filing joint returns until AGI reaches $160,000. The credit applies only to postsecondary expenses so the tuition for Kaitlin does not qualify.

336. Answer: B

The credit percentage begins at 35% if AGI is less than $15,000, and is reduced by 1% for each $2,000 increment (or part) in AGI above $15,000. The minimum dependent care credit is 20%. Therefore, this statement is false.

337. Answer: D

Individual taxpayers with adjusted gross income of $15,000 or less may claim a child care credit for 35% of employment related expenses. The credit is reduced by 1% of the expenses for each $2,000 of adjusted gross income over $15,000, but is not reduced to less than 20% of the expenses.

This response correctly indicates at least one spouse does not need to earn $15,000 or less to claim the credit. Earning more than $15,000 does not make a taxpayer ineligible for the credit, it reduces the amount of the credit by decreasing the percentage of the expenses that may be claimed.

This response also correctly indicates that at least one spouse must be gainfully employed or looking for work to claim the credit.

338. Answer: C

Certain tax credits can result in a refund, even if the individual had no income tax liability. Tax credits resulting in a refund are credits for earned income, tax withheld, excess Social Security tax withheld, and excise tax for certain nontaxable uses of fuels and lightweight diesel vehicles.

339. Answer: C

The $5,000 cash, $3,000 debt cancellation, and $1,200 municipal bonds are all subject to the gift tax. Donations to political parties are not subject to the gift tax.

340. Answer: B

There is an unlimited exclusion for education gifts if the tuition is paid directly to the educational institution. However, this exclusion is limited to tuition and does not apply to room and board. For 2018, $15,000 of the gifts to the cousin can be excluded from the gift tax, so the remaining $25,000 is subject to the gift tax. A gift tax return must be filed to reflect this transaction.

341. Answer: D

Mann can give up to $15,000 to any individual and pay no gift tax since the annual exclusion for the given year is $15,000. There is an unlimited exclusion from the gift tax for education gifts as long as the gift is made directly to the educational institution, as is the case here. Therefore, the $25,000 gift is also not subject to the gift tax.

342. Answer: D

Tuition payments can potentially be excluded from the gift tax if made for any individual. The exclusion is not limited to just family members so this information is not relevant.

343. Answer: C

Ordinary and necessary administration expenses of an estate are deductible on the fiduciary income tax return if the administrator of the estate waives the deduction on the estate tax return.

344. Answer: A

In general, once a trust is established and the taxpayer has transferred property to the trust, this property will not be included in the taxpayer's gross estate at death unless the taxpayer maintains ownership or control of the property. Since this trust can be revoked, the taxpayer still controls the property so at death the property will be included in his gross estate. Other conditions listed in the problem (trust for a minor, independent trustee can distribute income, disclaimer) do not cause the taxpayer to retain ownership in the property.

345. Answer: D

An estate tax credit is not allowed for death taxes paid to states.

346. Answer: B

A decedent's medical expenses paid by the decedent's estate are deductible on the decedent's tax return in the year incurred if:

(1) the expenses were paid within a year of the decedent's death;
(2) the expenses are not deducted for federal estate tax purposes; and
(3) a waiver stating that no estate tax deduction for the expenses was taken by the estate and that the estate waives its right to the deduction.

Bell's estate paid the medical expenses a month after Bell's death, easily within a year. In addition, the appropriate waiver was filed. Thus, assuming that the estate not deducted the expenses for federal estate tax purposes, the medical expenses may be deducted on Bell's final income tax return.

347. Answer: C

X Corp's basis in the land is B's basis in the land ($40,000) plus any gain recognized by B. B's recognized gain is the lower of (1) the realized gain, or (2) the boot received. The realized gain is $30,000 ($70,000 − $40,000). The boot received is the cash of $20,000. Thus, the gain recognized is $20,000. X Corp's basis in the land is $60,000 ($40,000 + $20,000).

B's amount realized is computed as follows: The corporation received cash of $50,000 and land of $70,000 for a total of $120,000. But it also gave $20,000 cash back to B as part of the formation. This is subtracted from above, so the net value of what the corporation received is $100,000. $100,000 × 50% = $50,000, so that is the value of the stock received by B. His amount realized is $50,000 + cash received of $20,000 = $70,000.

348. Answer: B

When property is contributed to a corporation in exchange for stock, the corporation takes the same basis in the property that the shareholder had, increased by any gain recognized by the shareholder. Ames had a cost basis in the balls of $500 and Roth had a basis of $5,000 in the bats, so the total basis for Homerun is $5,500.

349. Answer: B

On a corporate formation, gain is recognized to the extent that the liabilities assumed by the corporation exceed the basis in the assets contributed by the shareholder. The gain for this shareholder is $6,000 ($12,000 debt less $6,000 basis).

350. Answer: D

The transaction would qualify as a tax-free event for Carr because it would be considered to be a Section 351 transfer. Under Section 351, no gain or loss is recognized if the property is transferred solely for the exchange of stock of the corporation, if immediately after the transfer the transferring taxpayer or taxpayers have control over the corporation. Control is defined as owning at least 80% of corporation's voting stock and at least 80% of the corporation's other classes of stock.

Since Beck and Carr together own 90% of the corporation immediately after the transfer, the transaction would be a tax-free event for both taxpayers.

351. Answer: B

Premiums paid on key-person life insurance policies reduce book income but not taxable income, so this is a reconciling item for Schedule M-1.

352. Answer: C

The purpose of Schedule M-11 of Form 1120 *U.S. Corporation Income Tax Return* is to reconcile book income (loss) with income per the return. Federal income tax is not deductible for tax purposes so it must be added back to book income, giving $349,300 ($239,200 + $110,100). The goodwill is amortized over 15 years for tax purposes, or $20,000 per year ($300,000/15 years). Thus, the book goodwill amortization is added back and the tax goodwill is deducted. This results in taxable income of $336,800 ($349,300 + $7,500 − $20,000).

353. Answer: C

Taxable income is computed as follows:

Pretax book income	$543,000
Excess depreciation	(20,000)
Prepaid rental income	36,000
Fines	10,000
Municipal interest income	(25,000)
Taxable income	$544,000

354. Answer: B

The purpose of Schedule M-1 of Form 1120, *U.S. Corporation Income Tax Return* is to reconcile book income (loss) with income per the return. Certain items need to be added to and subtracted from book income to reconcile with income per the tax return. Federal income taxes; excess capital losses over capital gains; income subject to tax not recorded on the books; and expenses recorded on the books not deducted on the return must be added to book income. Income recorded on the books but not included on the return, including tax-exempt interest, and deductions on the return not charged against the books must be subtracted from book income.

Both the interest incurred on loan to carry U.S. obligations and the provision for state corporation income tax are deductible for GAAP. and for income tax purposes. Hence, since both of the expenses would be included in book income and in income per the return, there is no difference to reconcile and, as a result, neither expense would appear on the Schedule M-1 of Form 1120, *U.S. Corporation Income Tax Return*.

355. Answer: B

The allowance method for bad debts is not allowed for tax purposes, so the direct write-off method is used. Bad debts actually expensed during the current year are computed as follows:

Written off in current year	$5,000
Change in allowance account during year:	
Beginning balance	$20,000
Accrued bad debts	15,000
	$35,000
Less: Ending balance	(30,000)
	5,000
Bad debts written off during year	$10,000

356. Answer: A

For tax purposes, businesses cannot deduct estimated warranty expense. Warranty expense can be deducted only when it is actually incurred with respect to a specific product. This is similar to the rule that does not permit the "allowance for bad debts" method for tax purposes. The actual warranty expense is computed as:

Warranty reserve, beginning of year	$120,000
Estimated warranty expense during the year	16,000
Less warranty expense incurred during year	(?)
Warranty reserve, end of year	$90,000

Warranty expense = $136,000 − $90,000 = $46,000.

357. Answer: C

C corporations cannot use the cash method of accounting unless their average annual gross receipts for the previous three years do not exceed $5,000,000. Once the $5,000,000 test is failed the accrual method must be used for all future tax years. Since Dart has had revenues of more than $20 million for the last three years it must use the accrual method of accounting.

358. Answer: C

Partnerships can use the cash method regardless of the amount of gross receipts as long as none of the partners are C corporations.

359. Answer: D

If a corporation filed a short-year return for 3 month, the income for that period is first multiplied by 4 (12 months/3 months) to annualize the income for 12 months. The corporate tax liability is then computed on this amount for the full 12 months. That amount is the multiplied by 3/12 to prorate for the short tax year.

360. Answer: A

Accounting methods for a new corporation are made on the initial tax return.

361. Answer: D

Ace Corp. would report rent revenue of $65,000. Of this amount, $55,000 (the sum of $50,000 in rental payments and $5,000 in nonrefundable rent deposits) would be cash receipts. Ace Corp. is an accrual based taxpayer. Therefore, for tax purposes, income is earned when (1) all the events have occurred to attach the taxpayer's right to receive the income and (2) the amount of income can be determined with reasonable accuracy. With respect to rent receivable, the income must have been earned to record it as a receivable.

Hence, in calculating rent revenue, the $10,000 increase in rent receivable from 2017 to 2018 would have to be added to the corporation's cash receipts.

362. **Answer: C**

Ignoring the dividend, Brown has a net operating loss (NOL) of $200,000. Brown must also include the $100,000 of dividends in income, reducing the NOL to $100,000. Brown also is permitted to take the dividends received deduction.

Since the dividend is received from a Fortune 500 corporation it is reasonable to assume that Brown owns less than 20% of the corporation, so the dividends received deduction is 70% of the dividends received, or $70,000. This increases the NOL to $170,000.

Note that the dividends received deduction is not limited to the taxable income of Brown since Brown has a loss before the dividends received deduction.

363. **Answer: B**

Taxable income before dividends and contributions is $125,000 ($200,000 − $75,000). The 10% of taxable income limitation for C corporations uses taxable income BEFORE the dividends received deduction, which is $145,000. Thus, the charitable contribution limitation is $14,500 ($145,000 × 10%).

Taxable income before dividends	$125,000
Dividends	20,000
Taxable income before special deductions	$145,000
Charitable contributions	(14,500)
Taxable income after charitable deduction	$130.500
Dividends-received deduction	(14,000)
Taxable income	$116,500

364. **Answer: C**

Stock issuance costs are a syndication cost. Therefore, they are not deductible.

365. **Answer: C**

Since Ral Corp. owns less than 20% of the domestic corporation that paid the dividends (500 shares of 1,000,000 total shares), it may take a 70% dividend received deduction for the dividends.

Hence, Ral Corp. would include $300 of its dividend revenue in its taxable income. If Ral Corp. owned 20 or more but less than 80% of the domestic corporation, it could have deducted 80% of the dividends. Similarly, if 80% or more of the corporation was owned, 100% of the dividends would be deductible. Thus, this response is correct.

366. **Answer: D**

$5,000 of organizational expenses may be deducted, but the $5,000 is reduced by the amount of expenditures incurred that exceed $50,000. Expenses not deducted must be capitalized and amortized over 180 months, beginning with the month that the corporation begins its business operations. Organizational expenditures qualifying for the election are:

1. Legal expenditures incurred by the corporation;
2. necessary accounting services;
3. expenditures of temporary directors and of organizational meeting directors and shareholders; and
4. fees paid to the state of incorporation. Expenditures for issuing or selling shares of stock and for transferring the assets to the corporation do not qualify for the election.

Hence, only the $40,000 in legal fees expended to obtain the corporate charter qualified as an organizational expense. Commission paid to an underwriter and other stock issue costs do not qualify for the election as they are syndication costs. Ignoring amortization, $5,000 of the costs may be deducted this year.

367. **Answer: B**

If a C corporation owns less than 20% of a domestic corporation, 70% of dividends received or accrued from corporation may be deducted. A C corporation owning 20% or more but less than 80% of a domestic corporation may deduct 80% of the dividends received or accrued from the corporation. Similarly, C corporation owning 80% or more of a domestic corporation may deduct 100% of the dividends received or accrued from the corporation. However, the dividend received deduction is limited to a percentage of the taxable income of the corporation, unless the corporation sustains a net operating loss. If the corporation has a net operating loss, the dividend received deduction may be taken without limiting the deduction to a percentage of the corporation's taxable income.

Since it is not otherwise noted, it is assumed that Kisco Corp. owns less than 20% of the domestic corporation. Hence, Kisco may deduct 70% (or $7,000) of the dividends received, giving taxable income of $63,000. Kisco's income tax on that amount of income is $10,750 – the sum of multiplying the first $50,000 of income by the tax rate of 15% and the remaining $13,000 of income by 25 percent.

368. **Answer: D**

If a C corporation owns less than 20% of a domestic corporation, 70% of dividends received or accrued from the corporation may be deducted.

A C corporation owning 20% or more but less than 80% of a domestic corporation may deduct 80% of the dividends received or accrued from the corporation. Similarly, C corporation owning 80% or more of a domestic corporation may deduct 100% of the dividends received or accrued from the corporation. However, the dividend received deduction is limited to a percentage of the taxable income of the corporation, unless the corporation sustains a net operating loss.

For this question, the taxable income limitation rule comes into effect:

When ownership is less than 80%, the dividends received deduction (DRD) equals the lesser of 70% or 80% of the dividends received (whichever applies), or 70% or 80% of taxable income computed (whichever applies) without regard to the DRD, any net operating loss (NOL) deduction, or capital loss carry back. The taxable income limitation rule does not apply however if the DRD creates or adds to a NOL.

If the corporation has a net operating loss, the dividend received deduction may be taken without limiting the deduction to a percentage of the corporation's taxable income.

This response uses the correct deduction percentage for Best Corp.'s ownership percentage and correctly limits the dividend received deduction to a percentage of the corporation's taxable income. The limit is calculated by multiplying taxable income (before the dividend received deduction), i.e., $90,000, by the correct dividend received deduction percentage, i.e., 70 percent.

369. **Answer: C**

When a corporation's charitable contributions exceed the limitation for deductibility in a particular year (i.e., 10% of taxable income for the year), the excess may be carried over and deducted for five years. This response states the correct carryover period and is, therefore, correct.

370. **Answer: A**

The accumulated earnings tax is a tax imposed on corporations that accumulate earnings beyond reasonable amount. This tax was imposed to prevent corporations from accumulating earnings and profits with the purpose of avoiding income tax on its shareholders.

Any corporation accumulating earnings beyond the point of reasonable needs of the business is considered to have accumulated the earnings for the tax benefit of its shareholders, unless a preponderance of the evidence indicates otherwise. Only the shareholders of closely-held corporations would tend to have the power to retain corporate earnings for their benefit. As a result, the accumulated earnings tax tends to be applied more often to closely-held corporations.

However, the number of shareholders in a corporation is not a determining factor in imposing the tax. Hence, the accumulated earnings tax may be applied regardless of the number of shareholders in a corporation.

371. **Answer: D**

Domestic and foreign corporations satisfying the personal holding company stock ownership and income tests are personal holding companies. The stock ownership test is satisfied if, at some time during the corporation's tax year, 50% or more of the corporation's stock was directly or indirectly owned by five or fewer individuals. Acme Corp. only has two shareholders, satisfying the stock ownership test.

The income test is satisfied if 60% or more of the corporation's adjusted ordinary gross income is personal holding company income. Personal holding company income consists of: dividends; interest; annuities; rents; mineral, oil and gas royalties; copyright and patent royalties; produced film rents; compensation for more than 25% use of corporate property by shareholders; amounts received under personal services contracts; and amounts received from estates and trusts.

Since all of Acme Corp.'s income comes from investments, all of the corporation's income is considered personal holding company income and, as a result, the corporation satisfies the income test.

Since Acme Corp. satisfies the stock ownership and income tests, it is a personal holding company.

372. **Answer: C**

The accumulated earnings tax is a penalty tax imposed on corporations that accumulates earnings and profits for the purpose of avoiding income tax for its shareholders. The accumulated earnings tax is equivalent to 20% of the corporation's accumulated taxable income.

Accumulated taxable income is composed of taxable income adjusted downward for federal income and excess profits taxes, charitable deduction in excess of the ceiling, net capital gains and losses, and taxes of foreign countries and U.S. possessions and upward for certain corporate deductions, net operating loss deduction and capital loss carryback or carryover.

When calculating the accumulated earnings tax, corporations are given a credit, the accumulated earnings credit, of $250,000 ($150,000 for certain service corporations) plus dividends paid within the first 3 1/2 months of the corporation's tax year less accumulated earnings and profits at the end of the preceding tax year.

Hence, the maximum amount of accumulated taxable income that may be subject to the accumulated earnings tax for 2018 if Kari Corp. takes only the minimum accumulated earnings credit is $50,000. This amount is composed of $400,000 in taxable income less both a downward adjustment of $100,000 for federal income taxes and the $250,000 accumulated earnings credit.

373. **Answer: A**

Domestic and foreign corporations satisfying the personal holding company stock ownership and income tests are personal holding companies. As such, the corporation will be subject to a 15% penalty tax on undistributed personal holding company income. The stock ownership test is satisfied if, at some time during the corporation's tax year, 50% or more of the corporation's stock was directly or indirectly owned by five or fewer individuals.

An individual indirectly owns stock if it is owned by the individual's family or partner. Family includes the individual's brothers, sisters, spouse and lineal descendants and ancestors. An individual will not be considered to be the constructive owner of the stock owned by nephews, cousins, uncles, aunts, and any of his/hers spouses relatives. Constructive ownership also may exist if the individual is a partner in a partnership or the beneficiary of an estate that is a shareholder. The income test is satisfied if 60% or more of the corporation's adjusted ordinary gross income is personal holding company income.

With 450 shares, Edwards already directly owns 45% of Zero Corp.'s outstanding stock. If an estate where Edwards is the beneficiary owns the remainder of the corporation's 200 shares of stock, Edwards would directly or indirectly own 5% of the corporation. An ownership exceeding the 50% direct or indirect ownership percentage is needed to satisfy the stock ownership test.

Hence, Zero Corp. could be a personal holding company if the remaining 200 shares were owned by an estate where Edwards is the beneficiary. Each response given to this question satisfies the stock ownership test for a personal holding company because, in each response, five or fewer individuals would own more than 50% of the corporation's stock. However, this response is the best as it concentrates over 50% ownership under the control of one individual.

374. **Answer: B**

For the personal holding company (PHC) tests, interest earned on tax-exempt obligations is excluded from PHC income. PHC income consists of: dividends; interest; annuities; rents; mineral, oil and gas royalties; copyright and patent royalties; produced film rents; compensation for more than 25% use of corporate property by shareholders; amounts received under personal services contracts; and amounts received from estates and trusts.

Since only the dividends should be included, this response is correct.

375. **Answer: A**

Personal holding companies are required to pay taxes on their undistributed personal holding company income. Personal holding company income and undistributed personal holding company income differ. Undistributed personal holding company income is computed by adjusting taxable income, then subtracting the dividends paid deduction. Deductions are made from taxable income for federal and foreign taxes; charitable contributions (based on a higher percentage limitation than the 10% of income limitation imposed on corporations); and excess capital gains (i.e., any excess net long-term capital gain over net short-term capital loss for the tax year).

Corporate deductions for dividends received and any net operating loss deduction must be added back, and business expenses and depreciation exceeding rental income may have to be added back. Hence, both the federal income taxes and the net long-term capital gain should be deducted from taxable income by Kane in determining undistributed personal holding company income prior to the dividend-paid deduction.

376. **Answer: C**

On the consolidated tax return the income and losses of all the corporations are netted. Therefore, the net loss for the year is $50,000 ($100,000 of losses less $50,000 of income from ParentCo).

377. **Answer: D**

A and C are an affiliated group because A owns at least 80% of C and A is the parent company. B and D may not file a consolidated return because S corporations are not eligible to be in an affiliated group.

378. **Answer: D**

By definition, members of an affiliated group are eligible to elect to file a consolidated tax return. In general, an affiliated group contains a parent corporation and other corporations that are owned at least 80% by other members of the affiliated group.

379. **Answer: D**

When filing a consolidated return, the intercompany dividends between the parent and its subsidiaries are not taxable. To be permitted to file a consolidated return, the parent and its subsidiaries must be members of an affiliated group. Corporations qualify as members of an affiliated group by having a common parent that directly owns at least 80% of the total voting stock and at least 80% of the total value of the stock in at least one other

includible corporation. In addition, a minimum of one of the other includible corporations must own at least 80% in each of the remaining includible corporations. The primary advantages of filing a consolidated return are that: (1) intercompany dividends are excludable from taxable income; (2) losses of one affiliated member offset gains of another member; and (3) intercompany profits are deferred until realized. Hence, the dividends are fully deductible and this response is, therefore, correct.

380. **Answer: D**

A C corporation owning 80% or more of a domestic corporation may deduct 100% of the dividends received or accrued from the corporation. Owning 20% but less than 80% of a domestic corporation allows for an 80% deduction of dividends received or accrued from the corporation. An ownership percentage of less than 20% leads to a deduction of 70% of the dividends—received. However, the dividend received deduction is limited to a percentage of the corporation's taxable income, unless the corporation sustains a net operating loss. If the corporation has a net operating loss, the dividend—received deduction may be taken without limiting the deduction to a percentage of the corporation's taxable income.

Since Portal Corp. owns 80% of Sal Corp., Portal Corp. may deduct all of the dividends received from Sal Corp. and, as a result, have no dividend income.

381. **Answer: D**

When filing a consolidated return, the intercompany dividends between the parent and its subsidiaries are not taxable. To be permitted to file a consolidated return, the parent and its subsidiaries must be members of an affiliated group.

Corporations qualify as members of an affiliated group by having a common parent that directly owns at least 80% of the total voting stock and at least 80% of the total value of the stock in at least one other includible corporation. In addition, a minimum of one of the other includible corporations must own at least 80% in each of the remaining includible corporations. The primary advantages of filing a consolidated return are that: (1) intercompany dividends are excludable from taxable income; (2) losses of one affiliated member offset gains of another member; and (3) intercompany profits are deferred until realized.

382. **Answer: A**

The primary advantages of filing a consolidated return are that: (1) losses of one affiliated member offset gains of another member; (2) intercompany dividends are excludable from taxable income; and (3) intercompany profits are deferred until realized.

Since this response indicates that the operating losses of one group member may be used to offset operating profits of the other members, it is correct.

383. **Answer: B**

If the non-recourse liability attached to property exceeds the property's fair market value, the fair market value is deemed to be equal to the amount of the liability ($70,000). When the corporation distributes appreciated property, it must recognize gain equal to the liability ($70,000) over the property's basis ($20,000).

384. **Answer: D**

A distribution to a C corporation is:

1. Taxable as dividend income to extent of the shareholder's pro rata share of earnings and profits.
2. Excess is tax-free to extent of shareholder's basis in stock (and reduces the basis).
3. Remaining distribution amount is taxed as a capital gain.

Capital losses are not included as an option.

385. **Answer: A**

For dividends, the amount distributed is the fair market value of the property received less any liabilities assumed by the shareholder, or $35,000 ($38,000 − $3,000). Fox would have $35,000 of dividend income since earnings and profits is at least this amount. However, the basis in the property received as a taxable dividend is always the fair market value of the property, or $38,000.

386. **Answer: C**

Dividend income must be reported for the distribution to the extent of Webster's current and accumulated earnings and profits ($70,000). The amount of the distribution is the cash of $20,000 plus the fair market value ($60,000) of the property distributed, or $80,000. This distribution is taxed as $70,000 of dividend income with the remaining $10,000 treated as a return of the shareholders' bases in their stock.

387. **Answer: C**

When both accumulated and current E&P are positive, distributions are taxed as dividends to the extent of the sum of these amounts, or $50,000 ($30,000 + $20,000). The remaining $30,000 of the $80,000 distributions is treated as a return of capital.

388. **Answer: C**

When accumulated E&P is negative and current E&P is positive, distributions are treated as dividends to the extent of current E&P. Thus, $10,000 is reported as dividend income and the other $5,000 is a return of capital.

389. **Answer: C**

Corporate distributions to shareholders are taxed to shareholders as dividend income to the extent that the distribution does not exceed current and accumulated earnings and profits. Distributions in excess of current and accumulated earnings and profits are treated as returns of capital. The distribution of appreciated property increases a corporation's earnings and profits increase by the amount of the difference between the distributed property's fair market value and the corporation's adjusted basis in the distributed property.

Thus, while Dahl Corp. had earnings and profits totaling $9,000 before the dividend declaration and distribution, the corporation's earnings and profits increased by $35,000, the land's $40,000 fair market value less its adjusted basis of $5,000, to $44,000 due to the distribution of the land.

Green received $49,000 of property in the distribution −$9,000 in cash and land with a fair market value of $40,000. The amount of the distribution classified as dividend income is limited to the corporation's earnings and profits. Thus, Green would report $44,000 of dividend income from the distribution.

390. **Answer: B**

Corporations recognize taxable gains but not losses from nonliquidating distribution of appreciable property to their shareholders. The transaction is viewed as if the corporation sold the property to its shareholders at its fair market value on the day of the distribution.

Hence, Nyle Corp. would recognize a gain of $1,100, the fair market value of the Beta stock (100 shares multiplied by $20 per share) less its basis in the stock (100 shares multiplied by $9 per share).

391. Answer: C

Corporate distributions to shareholders are taxable to the shareholder as dividend income to the extent earnings and profits, current and accumulated. Distributions in excess of earnings and profits are treated as returns of capital that are nontaxable except to the extent that the distribution exceeds the shareholders basis in the property.

Since Kee Corp. had current earnings of $10,000, the shareholders would be viewed as receiving $10,000 in dividend income. The remaining $20,000 of the distribution would be treated as a return of capital. Distributions are deemed to be paid from current earnings and profits and then from accumulated earnings and profits.

392. Answer: A

Depreciation for E&P purposes is straight line, so if the tax depreciation is straight line, then no adjustment is necessary.

393. Answer: D

When a corporation distributes property to a shareholder in a nonliquidating distribution, gains are recognized to the corporation, but not losses. A $50,000 gain is recognized for the land ($100,000 – $50,000) and a $25,000 gain for the patent ($25,000 – 0) for a total gain of $75,000. The loss on the building is not recognized.

394. Answer: A

If stock of a subsidiary is liquidated by its parent company, any realized gain on the transaction is, in general, not recognized. The realized gain to parent is $150 ($250 property received – $100 basis). The recognized gain is zero.

395. Answer: A

Expenses related to a liquidation are deductible by the liquidating corporation.

396. Answer: D

Shareholders of a distribution in complete liquidation of a corporation receive capital gain or loss treatment just as if they hold their stock.

397. Answer: A

Noncorporate shareholders treat the gain on a redemption of stock that qualifies as a partial liquidation of the distributing corporation as a capital gain, just as if they had sold their stock. Corporate shareholders receive dividend treatment on a partial liquidation.

398. Answer: D

In a complete liquidation, shareholders generally recognize capital gains and losses from corporate distributions. The amount of assets received by a shareholder is treated as full payment in exchange for the stock.

The capital gain or loss recognized by a shareholder equals the total distribution less the shareholder's basis.

399. Answer: A

Filing, professional fees (accounting and legal), and other expenditures incurred in connection with liquidations and dissolutions are fully deductible for the dissolving corporation.

400. Answer: D

This answer is correctly calculated as follows: Cash received $33,000 less adjusted basis of $16,000 = $17,000 capital gain. Amounts received by a shareholder in a distribution in complete liquidation of a corporation shall be treated as in full payment in exchange for the stock. If property is received in a distribution in complete liquidation, and if gain or loss is recognized on receipt of such property, then the basis of the property in the hands of the distributee shall be the fair market value of such property at the time of the distribution.

401. Answer: A

Shareholder's gain is computed as the fair market value received ($5,000) less basis in stock ($2,000) = $3,000. The gain is capital since stock is a capital asset.

402. Answer: C

Tax attributes of the subsidiary transfer to the parent after a tax-free liquidation of the subsidiary into the parent.

403. **Answer: C**

A Type B reorganization must be stock for stock, and only voting stock of the acquiring firm, or its parent, is permitted. Acquiring must also control target after the acquisition.

404. **Answer: B**

The 80% control test is met since 90% of ABC's voting stock is being acquired. XYZ is using its voting stock as required for B reorganizations.

405. **Answer: D**

If taxpayer receives stocks or securities under a plan of reorganization from a corporation included in the reorganization, the taxpayer does not recognize a gain or loss from the transaction. However, if the taxpayer receives boot, the transaction is taxable up to the amount of the boot.

Since Gow received the Rook Corp. stock solely in exchange for his Lad Corp. stock under a plan of reorganization and did not receive any boot, the transaction would be tax-free for Gow.

406. **Answer: A**

Corporate reorganizations generally are tax-free for both shareholders and the corporation.

In this case, the reorganization would be viewed as a Type A: Merger or Consolidation, which qualifies for tax-free treatment for both shareholders and the corporation.

This response correctly indicates that the transaction would be tax-free for both shareholders and the corporation and, therefore, it is correct.

407. **Answer: B**

No gain or loss is recognized by a corporation that is a party to a qualified reorganization in which stock is exchanged solely for stock or securities of another corporation that is also a party to the reorganization.

As this reorganization is a Type B: Stock for Stock transaction, the reorganization is tax-free.

408. **Answer: B**

Assets transferred to the parent of the liquidating corporation generally have a carryover basis.

409. **Answer: C**

If property is purchased in one state but used in a different state, the state of use is likely to impose a use tax for the use of the property in its jurisdiction.

410. **Answer: A**

The starting point for computing state taxable income is $250,000. Adjustments are:

State income taxes	+$15,000
Municipal interest income	+$10,000
Excess federal depreciation	+$7,000
U.S. Treasury interest income	−$25,000
State taxable income	$257,000

411. **Answer: D**

Business income is generated from the business's regular operations, or from the sale of property that is an integral part of the business. Therefore, the royalty income could be business income

412. **Answer: B**

$10,000/($10,000 + $40,000) = 20%.

413. **Answer: C**

Only affiliated corporations that have Nexus with State M will be included in the state consolidated income tax return for State M.

414. **Answer: B**

The $90,000 of salary is completely excluded. Foreign-earned income from personal services is excluded up to 104,100 in 2018. The housing is excludable to the extent it exceeds 16% × $104,100, or $16,656. This excess is $23,344 ($40,000 − $16,656). However, the housing exclusion may never exceed $14,574 in 2018, so the includible housing income is $25,426 ($40,000 − $14,574). The interest income is fully includible as is the U.S. source earned income of $60,000. Therefore, includible income is $25,426 + $20,000 + $60,000, or $105,426.

415. **Answer: B**

Since the $90,000 earned income was excludable from U.S. income the $18,000 in Spanish taxes is not eligible for the foreign tax credit. The $4,000 related to the interest income is eligible.

416. Answer: B

$25,000, but not to exceed the foreign tax credit limitation of $80,000/($120,000 + $80,000) × $61,250 = $24,500.

417. Answer: C

Income from the sale of personalty is determined based on the location of the property.

418. Answer: D

Foreign currency exchange gains and losses resulting from the normal course of business operations are ordinary, not capital, so this is the incorrect statement.

419. Answer: A

The charitable entity must affirm that its activities will be limited to its charitable purposes.

420. Answer: C

Private foundations must file Form 990-PF annually.

421. Answer: C

Engaging in insubstantial nonexempt activities will not cause an exempt organization to lose its exempt status. However, exempt organizations are strictly prohibited from engaging in political campaigns and activities.

422. Answer: D

Exempt organizations cannot endorse political candidates or provide support to them. Therefore, both of these statements are incorrect.

423. Answer: B

Conducting retreats for business organizations would not be considered an activity related to the tax-exempt purpose of a religious organization so this response is not correct. Providing burial services consistent with its religious beliefs would be related and therefore permissible.

424. Answer: A

A *private foundation* is a tax-exempt organization which receives less than one-third of its annual support from its members and the general public. Therefore, public charities that solicit broad public support do not meet this definition.

425. Answer: D

Neither activity produces unrelated business income because the activities generating the revenue relate to the tax-exempt purpose of the organization. (Articles were made as part of the rehabilitation process and the store was being operated for the purpose of creating a therapeutic process for the participants.)

426. Answer: D

Corporations, community chests, funds, or foundations having religious, charitable, scientific, testing for public safety, literary, or educational purposes or organized for prevention of cruelty to children or animals, or to foster national or international amateur sports competition are tax-exempt. Partnerships are not included on this list.

427. Answer: B

After the contribution, the partnership has $30,000 of liabilities. Each of the general partners share in 50% of the liabilities, or $15,000.

428. Answer: C

The partner received a partnership interest in return for property and services. His basis in his partnership for the property contributed is equal to the basis of the property he contributed, or $30,000 ($20,000 + $10,000). For the services rendered he must recognize $5,000 of income for the interest received, so he has a $5,000 basis in that portion of his partnership interest. His total basis in the partnership interest is $35,000 ($30,000 + $5,000).

429. Answer: C

Juan receives basis in his partnership interest equal to the basis of the property contributed. He also must recognize $25,000 of wage income for receiving a portion of the partnership interest in return for services rendered. Therefore, he also receives $25,000 of basis for this income recognition. Thus, his total basis is $10,000 + $25,000, or $35,000.

430. Answer: B

Marcus's basis in his partnership interest is equal to the basis of the property contributed, or $50,000.

431. **Answer: C**

Partners increase their bases in their partnership interests by their respective share of the partnership's debt, both recourse and nonrecourse.

432. **Answer: B**

Upon a partnership formation the partnership's basis in the assets received from the contributing partners is the basis in the hands of the partner. Thus, Apple's basis is $5,000.

433. **Answer: A**

Turner and Reed do not recognize gain on the formation since they contributed property in return for their partnership interests. Sumner received her interest in return for services, so she must recognize $50,000 of wage income.

434. **Answer: A**

50% of the loss and income impacts George's basis. Partnership debt decreased by $16,000 ($40,000 – $24,000) during the year, so George's basis is decreased by 50% of the reduction, or $8,000. Ending basis is computed as follows:

Beginning basis	$32,500
Operating loss	(15,000)
Interest and dividend income	4,000
Partnership debt change	(8,000)
Ending basis	$13,500

435. **Answer: D**

Basis in the partnership is computed as follows:

Adjusted basis of building contributed	$40,000
Less: Debt assumed by partnership	(60,000)
Plus: Campbell's 10% share of debt	6,000
	($14,000)
Gain recognized	14,000
Ending basis	–

The computation above reflects that Campbell transferred 90% of the debt to other partners. The $14,000 of gain is recognized because basis cannot be negative. Therefore, ending basis is zero.

436. **Answer: D**

Basis is determined as follows:

Cash	$ 5,000
Basis of land	12,000
Mortgage assumed by partnership	(10,000)
Skinner's share of mortgage (20%)	2,000
	4,000
	$13,000

437. **Answer: C**

A partner's basis in the partnership interest is increased by:

1. additional contributions;
2. additional interest's purchased or inherited;
3. the partner's share of the partnership's income (including tax-exempt income); and
4. any increases in the partner's share of partnership liabilities. A partner's basis in the partnership interest is decreased by:

   1. cash and the partnership's adjusted basis of property received by the partner in a nonliquidating distribution;
   2. the adjusted basis allocable to any part of the partner's interest sold or transferred;
   3. the partner's share of the partnership's losses; and
   4. any decreases in the partner's share of partnership liabilities.

Thus, Dean's basis in the partner's interest would be increased by Dean's share of the partnership's income (including tax-exempt income) and decreased by the nonliquidating cash distribution. The partnership's income is $52,000, ordinary income of $40,000 plus municipal bond interest income of $12,000. Dean's 25 percent share is $13,000. Hence, adding the $13,000 in income and subtracting the $8,000 distribution to Dean's beginning tax basis in the partnership of $20,000, puts Dean's ending tax basis in the partnership at $25,000.

This response correctly added Dean's share of the tax-exempt income to and subtracts the nonliquidating distribution from the basis.

438. Answer: A

A partner's initial basis in a partnership is equal to the amount of cash that the partner contributed plus the partner's adjusted basis for property when contributed. If the partnership assumes indebtedness from the contributed property, the contributing partner's basis is reduced by the amount of indebtedness assumed by the other partners. Strom's basis in the contributed property was $16,000.

However, the property was subject to a $24,000 mortgage. Strom's partners assumed $18,000 of the mortgage, $24,000 multiplied by 75% (the percentage of the partnership not owned by Strom). Subtracting the $16,000 in liabilities assumed by the other partners, gives Strom a negative basis.

However, a partner's basis in the partnership's interest cannot be negative. Thus, Strom's basis in the partnership is zero.

439. Answer: B

A's share of the partnership loss is $5,000 ($10,000 × 50%). The ordering rules for computing partnership basis provide that distributions reduce basis before losses. The $2,000 distribution reduces the basis to $3,000 ($5,000 basis − $2,000). Thus, only $3,000 of the loss can be used to reduce the basis to zero. The remaining $2,000 loss is carried forward to future tax years.

440. Answer: D

Basis is computed as follows:

Contribution	$100,000
25% of income	20,000
Distribution	(10,000)
	$110,000

441. Answer: C

Dale's basis is computed as follows:

Cash contributed	$10,000
Equipment debt (50%)	5,000
Taxable income (50%)	7,500
Tax-exempt income (50%)	1,000
Debt reduction (50%)	(2,000)
Distribution	(3,000)
Ending basis	$18,500

442. Answer: B

Non-separately stated income is the ordinary business income of the LLC, computed as follows:

Revenues	$120,000
Salaries	(36,000)
Guaranteed payments	(10,000)
Rent expense	(21,000)
Depreciation expense	(18,000)
Ordinary income	$35,000

443. Answer: B

This is a true statement.

444. Answer: C

Beginning basis jn partnership interest	$0
Share of partnership debt ($20,000 × 50%)	10,000
Basis before loss flow-through	$10,000
Portion of $35,000 ($70,000 × 50%) loss allowed	(10,000)
Ending basis in partnership interest	$0

Loss allowed to be deducted on Form 1040 is limited to basis in partnership interest.

445. Answer: B

$5,000 of organizational expenses may be deducted, but the $5,000 is reduced by the amount of expenditures incurred that exceed $50,000. Expenses not deducted must be capitalized and amortized over 180 months, beginning with the month that the corporation begins its business operations. Deductions are not allowed to the partnership or any partner for expenses incurred to sell partnership interests. Hence, $5,000 of the legal fees to prepare the partnership agreement may be deducted.

However, the accounting fees to prepare the representations in offering materials may not be expensed or amortized because these expenses are related to selling partnership interests.

446. **Answer: A**

Guaranteed payments from a partnership for the services of a partner are treated as salary payments and, as a result, are made without regard to the partner's share of the partnership's income. Thus, Evan would treat the $20,000 payment from the partnership for services rendered as income on her 2018 tax return. She also must report her share of the partnership's net income. Since the guaranteed payments qualify as a deductible expense, Vista's partnership income may be reduced by the amount of the expense. Hence, the partnership's income would be $70,000; $80,000 in net business income before guaranteed payments plus the $10,000 net long-term capital gain less the $20,000 guaranteed payment. Evan's 25% share of the partnership's income would be $17,500 (25% × $70,000). Thus, Evan would report $37,500 in income from the Vista Partnership on her 2018 tax return—the sum of the guaranteed payment ($20,000) and her share of the partnership's income ($17,500).

447. **Answer: C**

The realized gain on the sale of the assets is $3,000 ($18,000 − $15,000 basis in assets). Abe's built in gain on the contribution is $5,000. The amount of gain allocated to Abe is the lower of the realized gain or built-in gain, so $3,000 is the allocation.

448. **Answer: D**

This is a true statement.

449. **Answer: C**

Guaranteed payments from a partnership for the services of a partner are treated as salary payments and, as a result, receive similar treatment under the Internal Revenue Code. Therefore, in contrast to provisions applying to other withdrawals of assets from partnerships by partners, guaranteed payments are deductible by the partnership. The deduction for guaranteed payments may create an ordinary loss for the partnership. Guaranteed payments are required to be reported separately from the partner's share of the partnership's income on the partner's K-1.

Thus, guaranteed payments made by a partnership to partners for services rendered to the partnership, that are deductible business expenses under the Internal Revenue Code, are deductible expenses on the *U.S. Partnership*

Return of Income, Form 1065, in order to arrive at partnership income (loss) and included on Schedules K-1 to be taxed as ordinary income to the partners.

450. **Answer: D**

Guaranteed payments to partners from their partnership for partnership services or capital are not treated as partnership distributions. Instead, the payments are treated as salary payments to employees or interest payments.

Hence, White would have to include the $3,000 guaranteed payment on his 2018 tax return. In addition, since partnerships are pass-through for tax purposes, White must include his share of the partnership's income on his tax return. White share of the partnership's income would be $10,000 (= $30,000 in partnership income multiplied by White's 1/3 share in profits and losses).

Therefore, the total amount that White must include from Rapid Partnership as taxable income in his 2018 tax return is $13,000, the sum of the $3,000 in guaranteed payments made to White and White's share of the partnership's income.

451. **Answer: A**

Guaranteed payments from a partnership for the services of a partner are treated as salary payments and, as a result, are made without regard to the partner's share of the partnership's income.

Thus, a guaranteed payment by a partnership to a partner for services rendered may include an agreement to pay a salary of $5,000 monthly without regard to partnership income and may not include an agreement to pay 25% interest in partnership profits.

452. **Answer: B**

Guaranteed payments are those made by a partnership to a partner that are determined without regard to the partnership's income. A partnership treats guaranteed payments for services, or for the use of capital, as if they were made to a person who is not a partner. This treatment is for purposes of determining gross income and deductible business expenses only.

453. **Answer: C**

Fraizer received cash of $1,500 less his basis in the partnership of $1,200 = gain of $300.

454. Answer: C

The partner must report $25,000 of ordinary income and the $10,000 guaranteed payment. The distribution does not generate additional income since the partner has sufficient basis to absorb it.

455. Answer: A

Gain is recognized on a partnership distribution ONLY if the cash distributed exceeds the basis in the partnership interest. In this case there was no cash distributed, so no gain is recognized.

456. Answer: B

A partner's basis in property received in a nonliquidating distribution is the same as the partnership's basis immediately before the distribution. However, the partner's basis in the property may not exceed his/her basis in the partnership less any cash received in the distribution.

Hart received property with a basis of $12,000 ($5,000 in cash plus the partnership's basis in the land of $7,000). However, his basis in the partnership interest is $9,000, so the basis in the property distributed must be limited to this amount. Since the distribution included $5,000 in cash, Hart's basis in the land is $4,000 ($9,000 − 5,000).

457. Answer: D

A partner receiving a distribution from a partnership usually does not recognize a gain or loss. Gains are recognized only to the extent the partner receives an amount of cash exceeding his/her adjusted basis in the partnership interest. Gains from property distributions other than cash are not recognized until the partner sells or disposes of the property. Therefore, Stone does not recognize any gain or loss from the distribution.

458. Answer: B

"Hot assets" for a partnership include ONLY inventory and unrealized receivables.

459. Answer: D

If a partner sells his/her interest in the partnership, the partner recognizes a capital gain equal to the amount that the payment exceeds the partner's adjusted basis in the partnership.

Clark's adjusted basis in the partnership is $40,000 immediately before the sale. His amount realized is $55,000 ($30,000 cash received + $25,000 debt relief). Hence, Clark must recognize a capital gain of $15,000 ($55,000 − $40,000).

460. Answer: D

If a partner sells or exchanges his/her partnership interest and the partnership has either unrealized receivables or substantially appreciated inventory, the partner recognizes an ordinary gain to the extent that the amount realized by the partner due to the unrealized receivables or substantially appreciated inventory is greater than the partner's basis in the items.

When Carr sold his partnership interest in Allen, Baker and Carr, the partnership had unrealized receivables. The amount realized by Carr due to the unrealized receivables was $140,000, the partnership's total unrealized receivables of $420,000 multiplied by Carr's one-third ownership interest.

Carr does not have any basis in the unrealized receivables (indicating that none of the receivables have been collected). Hence, Carr must report an ordinary gain of $140,000, the $140,000 realized by Carr due to the unrealized receivables less Carr's basis in the receivables, which is zero.

461. Answer: C

For tax purposes, a partnership terminates when it stops doing business as a partnership or 50% or more interest in partnership capital and profits is exchanged within 12 months.

When the partnership's business and financial operations are continued by other members, there is a deemed distribution of assets to the remaining partners and the purchaser and a hypothetical recontribution of assets to a new partnership.

462. Answer: D

Since all shareholders must meet the eligibility requirements the accountant would pursue this recommendation.

463. Answer: D

This is correct.

464. Answer: C

The shareholder limit is 100 and members of the same family count as one shareholder.

465. Answer: C

Individuals, estates, and certain trusts may be shareholders in an S corporation.

466. Answer: B

An S Corporation election is effective for the current tax year, if made by the 15th day of the third month of the tax year. Since the election is after March 15, 2016, it is effective for 2017.

467. Answer: C

S corporation elections made after two and one-half months into the current tax year are effective at the beginning of the next tax year (January 1, year 3).

468. Answer: C

Basis is computed as follows:

Initial investment	$10,000
Taxable income ($10,000 × 20%)	2,000
Tax-exempt income ($2,000 × 20%)	400
Cash distribution ($1,000 × 20%)	(200)
Ending basis	$12,200

469. Answer: B

An S corporation shareholder can deduct losses ($40,000) up to her stock basis ($25,000) plus loan basis ($13,000 − $3,000 = $10,000). $35,000 is deducted this year and her stock basis and loan basis are reduced to zero. The other $5,000 of the loss is carried forward to future tax years.

470. Answer: C

65,000 − 10,000 + 6,000 + 4,000 − 9,000 = 56,000. The question is asking how the municipal interest income effects basis as well as the effect of the net capital losses.

1. 1. Stock purchases
   2. Capital contributions
   3. Nonseparately stated income items
   4. Separately stated income items
2. Decreases
3. 1. Nonseparately stated computed loss
   2. Separately stated loss and deduction items
   3. Distributions not reported as income by shareholder
   4. Nondeductible expenses of corporation

4. Separately stated items.
   - Tax-exempt income
   - Capital gains and losses
   - Section 1231 gains and losses
   - Charitable contributions
   - Passive gains, losses, and credits
   - Portfolio income
   - Foreign income
   - Investment income and expense
   - Depletion
   - Section 179 expense

471. Answer: C

Once the S corporation completes the steps necessary to become a C corporation, it will be allowed to retain its June 30 year-end since C corporations are not subject to the tax-year limitations to which partnerships and S corporations are. However, C corporations cannot use the cash method of accounting unless their average annual gross receipts for the previous three years do not exceed $5,000,000. Once the $5,000,000 test is failed the accrual method must be used for all future tax years. Since this corporation has had revenues of more than $10 million it must use the accrual method of accounting.

472. Answer: D

Collectible gain is taxed at a maximum rate of 28% and can be offset with collectible losses, so it needs to be separately stated.

473. Answer: C

The distributive share to Carson would be $400,000 × 40% = $160,000.

474. Answer: C

Calculate basis in an S corporation as follows: The current basis of $25,000 is increased by the $1,000 of income to $26,000, then reduced for the distribution of $30,000 which would reduce the basis to $0 and produce a $4,000 gain. The $3,000 loss is suspended until there is more basis in the future.

If the amount of the distribution exceeds the adjusted basis of the stock, such excess shall be treated as gain from the sale or exchange of property.

475. Answer: B

A C corporation that makes an S election and has unrealized built-in gains in its assets as of the election day must pay a built-in gains tax on this appreciation if it is recognized within the next 10 years.

When Prail makes the S election it has appreciation in the land of $50,000 ($150,000 – $100,000). Since the land was sold within 5 years of the election day, the first $50,000 of gain is taxed to the corporation at the rate of 35%.

Therefore, Prail must pay a tax of $17,500 ($50,000 × 35%).

476. **Answer: D**

An S corporation shareholder increases/decreases her basis in the S corporation stock by her share of the corporation's income (taxable and nontaxable) and expenses (deductible and nondeductible). Distributions also reduce the stock basis. Sandy's basis is reduced to $40,000 for the distribution ($60,000 – $20,000) and is increased for all three income items for an ending basis of $85,000 ($40,000 + $30,000 + $5,000 + $10,000).

477. **Answer: B**

$6,500 is correct. His/her portion of income items of the corporation that are separately computed and passed through to shareholder, including tax-exempt income, increases the stock basis of each S corporation shareholder. Basis is calculated as follows:

Beginning Basis	$12,000
Plus 50% profits	40.500 (81,000 × 50%)
Plus 50% exempt	5,000 (10,000 × 50%)
Less distributions	(51,000)
Ending Basis	$6,500

478. **Answer: D**

The built in gains tax applies only when an existing C corporation makes an S corporation election. The built in gains tax does not apply when a sole proprietorship makes an S election, so the correct answer is $0.

479. **Answer: C**

A distribution from an S corporation that has no accumulated earnings and profits reduces the basis of a shareholder's stock. If the payment exceeds the shareholder's basis in the stock, it is viewed as a payment in exchange for stock.

480. **Answer: D**

The personal exemption for a trust is not included in distributable net income.

481. **Answer: C**

Municipal interest income ($10,000), taxable interest ($5,000), and accounting and trustee fees ($2,000) are included in distributable net income. Capital gains ($25,000) are included only if they can be distributed to the beneficiary. $25,000 + $5,000 + $10,000 – $2,000 = $38,000.

482. **Answer: B**

Income earned by a trust that is distributed to the income beneficiary, such as the dividends and interest, is taxed to the income beneficiary. If the income is retained by the trust, it is taxed to the trust.

483. **Answer: C**

The amount of income recognized by the beneficiaries is the lower of the amount distributed ($150,000) or distributable net income ($120,000). Thus, Kent and Lind will recognize income of $120,000. Since they received total distributions of $150,000, the income recognized is 80% ($120,000/$150,000) of the amount received. Thus, Lind's income is 80% × $90,000, or $72,000.

484. **Answer: B**

When the individual creating a trust retains certain interests in the trust, the trust is known as a grantor trust and the income from the trust is taxed to the grantor.

485. **Answer: B**

DNI is the maximum amount of income taxable to the beneficiaries. Since all of the income was distributed, the beneficiary is taxed on $14,000 and the trust has no taxable income.

486. **Answer: B**

The net short-term capital gain is not included in the trust income since it is allocable to corpus. So the trust income is the $8,000 dividend income less the $2,000 accounting fees.

487. **Answer: C**

The foreign tax credit is the lower of:

1) foreign tax paid ($39,000), or

2) U.S. tax x foreign taxable income / worldwide taxable income

$96,000 × $120,000 / $300,000 = $38,400

488. Answer: D

The work opportunity tax credit is 40% of the first $6,000 of wages per employee, so the maximum credit is $2,400.

489. Answer: A

The general business credit is a combination of several tax credits that are computed separately under each under its own set of rules. The purpose of the general business credit is to combine these credits into a single amount to provide uniform rules for the current credits that may be taken to offset a taxpayer's tax liability.

In addition, the credit provides uniform rules for carryback-carryover years. The general business credit may be carried back for 1 year, then forward for 20 years. The general business credits are composed of the: investment credit; work opportunity credit; alcohol fuel credit; incremental research credit; low-income housing credit; disabled access credit; credit for producing electricity from specified renewable resources; enhanced oil recovery credit; Indian employment credit; employer Social Security credit; empowerment zone employment credit; orphan drug credit; and excise tax payments to the Trans-Alaska Pipeline Liability Fund credit.

490. Answer: B

This statement is false since corporations can deduct more than the adjusted basis for inventory that is contributed to a charity that uses it for the care of ill, needy, or infants.

491. Answer: C

Tax factors and non-tax factors should both be given appropriate consideration in the decision. The goal is to maximize after-tax income, not minimize taxes.

492. Answer: A

Partners can increase basis in partnership interest with partnership debt so that additional losses can be used by partners on their tax returns.

493. Answer: D

The NOL provides more benefit to the taxpayer when it is used in the years that have the highest marginal tax rates.

494. Answer: D

When appreciated property is distributed to a partner, no gain is recognized by the partnership. However, if a C corporation or S corporation distributes appreciated property, gain must be recognized by the corporation.

Property distributions never create gain for a partner. Gain is recognized by the partner only if cash distributed exceeds the basis in the partnership interest. C corporation and S corporation shareholders may have to recognize income when receiving property distributions.

495. Answer: D

This statement is false. Since S corporation income flows directly to the shareholders, the corporation is not subject to the AMT.

496. Answer: A

Owners of an S corporation have limited liability but general partners in a partnership have unlimited liability.

497. Answer: C

Trusts and estates can carryback or carryforward a net operating loss.

498. Answer: C

In an LLC, a member can participate in management and have limited liability. In a partnership, if a partner participates in management she must be a general partner, and general partners have unlimited liability.

499. Answer: A

The owner's basis is increased for her distributive share of profits and losses for S corporations, partnerships, and limited liability companies. However, owner's basis is not affected by the debt of S corporations, while it is for partnerships and limited liability companies.

500. Answer: C

C corporations can deduct $10,000 of charitable contributions (limited to 10% of taxable income) and none of the capital losses since net capital losses are not deductible. Net income is $100,000 ordinary income less $10,000 equals $90,000. For S corporation, the charitable contribution and capital loss are separately stated. The ordinary income is reported on page 1 of form 1120S.

Task-Based Simulations

Ethics, Professional Responsibilities, and Federal Tax Procedures

Federal Tax Practice and Procedures

Tax Practice and Procedure

Task-Based Simulation 1

tbs.tax.practice.001_1808

Document Review		
	Authoritative Literature	
		Help

Bea N. Happy and Bob N. Happy have been married since 1998 and have two children, Bobby and Betsy. Both Bea and Bob work for the University of Tampa in Florida. Bea N. Happy filed for divorce from Bob N. Happy in 2017. The divorce was final in January 2018. Bea has custody of both children, and she paid more than 50% of maintaining her household. Bea and Bob have been audited by the IRS for their 2015 Form 1040. They have received a preliminary notice of deficiency from the IRS and 90 day letter from the IRS. (These documents only need to be skimmed for useful information.)

Bea prepared her own 2018 tax return. You can assume the amounts given in the attached Form 1040 for 2018 are correct unless different information is provided elsewhere.

To revise the document, click on each segment of underlined text below and select the needed correction, if any, from the list provided. If the underlined text is already correct in the context of the document, select [Original text] from the list.

IN THE CIRCUIT COURT OF THE THIRTEENTH JUDICIAL CIRCUIT,
IN AND FOR HILLSBOROUGH COUNTY, FLORIDA

Case No.:_____
Division:_____

Bea N. Happy,
      Petitioner

   and

Bob N. Happy
      Respondent

MARITAL SETTLEMENT AGREEMENT

Bea N. Happy of 99 Argument Lane, Tampa Florida 33602, born April 15, 1975, and Bob N. Happy of 516 Dreary Road, Tampa Florida 33602, born June 12, 1972, being sworn do hereby slate the following statements are true and correct and that except as otherwise specifically stated in this agreement, this agreement serves as a full and final settlement all matters arising from the dissolution of their marriage, including division of all property rights, debts, spousal support, child custody, visitation, and child support. The parties agree this Agreement contains a fair, just, and equitable division of property, and subject to court approval agree as follows:

1.   JURISDICTION. Bea N. Happy and Bob N. Happy have resided in Hillsborough for at least six (6 months) before the petition in the above-entitled action was filed which satisfies Florida's residency requirements.

2.   ARMED FORCES. Neither party is a member of the armed forces.

3.   MARRIAGE DATE. The parties were married to each other on May 05, 1997 in Tampa, Florida and 2 children were born to this marriage.

The remaining minor children of the marriage are as follows:

Bobby N. Happy
son, who was born January 02, 1998.

Betsy N. Happy
daughter,
Who was born November 15, 1999.

The parties are not currently expecting any children.

4.   SEPARATION DATE. The parties' date of physical separation is August 17, 2016.

5.   CAUSE OF DISSOLUTION. The parties acknowledge that the marriage has been irretrievably broken due to irreconcilable differences and they are beyond reconciliation.

6.   DISCLOSURE. The parties acknowledge that each has made a full disclosure of all assets and debts owned jointly or individually. Nothing has been withheld and each party believes that other has been truthful in their disclosure.

The parties waive the requirement to file a Financial Affidavit as each party has voluntarily made a full disclosure to the other of all assets and debts. The parties further waive any additional disclosure required under 12.285, Florida Family Law Rules of Procedure.

7.   INCOME. Bea N. Happy has a total gross monthly income of $4,000.00 which includes income from the following sources:

University of Tampa
Teacher
$4,000.000 per month.

Bob N. Happy has a total gross monthly income of $5,000.00 which includes income from the following sources:

University of Tampa
Teacher
$5,000.000 per month.

8.   CUSTODY. The parties acknowledge that this is the home state of the children pursuant to the state's Uniform Child custody Jurisdiction and Enforcement Act. The children have resided in this state for more than six months before this action began and no other court has made a child custody determination.

9.   CHILD CUSTODY & VISITATION. The parties acknowledge that issues of child custody or visitation relative to the parties' minor children have been determined by the Hillsborough Judicial Court of Hillsborough in the state of Florida under docket/case number 1276. That court maintains continuing and exclusive jurisdiction over issues relating to the minor children of this marriage. A copy of all orders entered relative to custody or visitation is attached to this agreement and shall be incorporated into any Judgment or Decree of Divorce subsequently entered.

10.   CHILD SUPPORT. The parties acknowledge that the issue of child support has been determined by the Hillsborough Judicial Court of Hillsborough in the state of Florida under docket/case number 12356. Under this court order Bob N. Happy is responsible for

paying child support in the amount of $500.00 monthly. That court maintains continuing and exclusive jurisdiction over issues relating to the minor children of the marriage. A copy of all orders entered relative to child support is attached to this agreement and shall be incorporated into any Judgment or Decree of Divorce subsequently entered.

11. COOPERATION. The parties agree to cooperate with one another in signing any papers or legal documents needed to finalize this agreement or any provision contained in this agreement, including deeds, title certificates, etc. Within 10 days of notification of Entry of Judgment, the parties shall execute any document, transfer papers, titles or other documents to affect the provisions of this Agreement and any resulting Decree of Divorce. In the event a party fails to sign transfer documents, the final Decree of Divorce shall operate to transfer title.

12. DIVISION OF ASSETS. Each party shall receive any and all, tangible and intangible, property, in his/her possession including personal items and household goods, unless otherwise stated in this agreement.

13. FUTURE EARNINGS AND ACQUISITIONS. All income, earnings, or other property received or acquired by either party to this Agreement on or after the date of execution of this Agreement shall be the sole and separate property of the receiving or acquiring party. Each party, as of the effective dates of this Agreement, does hereby and forever waive, release, and relinquish all the right, title, and interest in all such income, earnings, and other property except as necessary to collect any sums due hereunder in the event of default.

14. DEBTS. Each spouse will be responsible for any indebtedness incurred in his or her individual name prior to the date of marriage unless otherwise specifically stated in this agreement. Each spouse will be responsible for any indebtedness incurred in his or her individual name subsequent to the date of separation August 17, 2015 unless otherwise specifically stated in this agreement. Each spouse will be responsible for any indebtedness incurred in his or her individual name during the course of the marriage unless otherwise specifically stated in this agreement.

15. SPOUSAL SUPPORT/ALIMONY. Bea N. Happy is 41 years of age, has been married for 19 years, has a total monthly income of $4,000.000, and has total monthly expenses of $5,000.000. Bob N. Happy has a gross monthly income of $5,000.000 from all sources and has the ability to pay support. Bob N. Happy agrees to pay Bea N. Happy spousal support in the amount of $400.00 per month until ex-spouse remarries or dies.

APPENDIX – IRS LETTERS AND NOTICES

Letter 915(DO) – 30-Day Letter from District Office

Internal Revenue Service
District Director

Department of the Treasurey

Date: 5/8/18

Taxpayer Identification Number: 200-89-4 55
From: 1040
Tax Period(s) Ended: 12/31/15
Person to Contact: Susan Hope
Contact Telephone Number: 888-444-1040
Employee Identification Number: 123
Refer Reply to:
Last Date to Respond to this letter: 6/7/18

Dear Bob N. and Bea N. Happy

We have enclosed two copies of our examination report showing the changes we made to your tax for the period(s) shown above. Please read the report and let us know whether you agree or disagree with the changes. (Our report may not reflect the results of later examinations of partnerships, S Corporations, trusts, etc., in which you have an interest. Changes made to their tax returns could affcct your tax.

IF YOU AGREE with the changes in the report, please sign, date, and return one copy to us by the response date shown above. If you filed a joint return, both taxpayers must sign the report. If you owe more tax, please include payment for the full amount to limit penalty and interest charges.

IF YOU CAN'T PAY the full amount you owe now, pay as much as you can. If you want us to consider an installment agreement, please complete and return the enclosed Form 9465, *Installement Agreement Request*. If we approve your request, we will charge a $43 fee to help offset the cost of providing this service. We will continue to charge penalties and interest until you pay the full amount you owe.

IF YOU DON'T AGREE with the changes shown in the report, you should do one of the following by the response date shown above:

- Mail us any additional information you'd like us to consider
- Discuss the report with the examiner
- Discuss your position with the examiner's supervisor
- Request a conference with an Appeals Officer, as explained in the enclosed Publication 5, *Your Appeal Rights and How to Prepare a Protest If you Don't Agree*

Letter 915(DO) (Rev. 4-2000)
Catalog Number 82712V

Chapter 6 – Administratively Appealing Adverse IRS Determinations

Appendix IRS Letters and Notices-Letter 915(DO) – 30-Day Letter From District Office

APPENDIX – IRS FORMS, LETTERS AND NOTICES
Letter 915(DO) – 30-Day Letter from District Office

IF YOU DON'T TAKE ANY ACTION by the response date shown above, we will process your case based on the information shown in the report, We will send you a statutory notice of deficiency that allows you 90 days to petition the United States Tax Court. If you allow the 90-day period to expire without petitioning the tax court, we will bill you for any additional tax, interest, and penalties.

We have enclosed Publication 1, *Your Rights as a Taxpayer*. If additional tax is due, we have also enclosed Publication 594. *The IRS Collection Process*, for your information.

If you have any questions, please contact thhe person whose name and telephone number are shown in the heading of this letter. If you write, please include your telephone number and the best time for us to call in case we need more information. We have enclosed an envelope for your convenience.

Thank you for your cooperation.

Sincerely yours,

Disctict Director

Enclosures:
Examination Reprt (2)
☐ Form 9465
Publication 1
Publication 5
☐ Publication 594
Envelope

Letter 915 (DO) (Rev. 4-2000)
Catalog Number 62712V

Chapter 6 – Administratively Appealing Adverse IRS Determination
Appendix IRS Letters and Notices-Letter 915(DO) – 30-Day Letter From Disctict Office

APPENDIX—IRS LETTERS AND NOTICES

Letter 894 (RO) - Notice of Deficiency from Appeals Office (with Waive Form 4089-A)

Department of Treasury
Internal Revenue Service

Date: 5/8/18

Letter Number: 884 (RO)	
Letter Date:	6/30/18
Taxpayer Identification Number:	200-89-4455
Form:	1040
Person to Contact:	Alan Space
Contact Telephone Number:	888-444-1040
Contact Person Identification Number:	
Refer Reply to:	
In Re:	
Last Day to File a Petition With the United States Tax Court	9/28/18

NOTICE OF DEFICIENCY

<u>Tax year(s) Ended: 12/31/15</u>

Tax

Dear Bob N. and Bea N. Happy:

We have determined that you owe additional tax or other amounts, or both, for the tax year(s) identified above. This letter is your NOTICE OF DEFICIENCY as requested by law. The enclosed statement shows how we figure the deficiency.

- If you want to contest the determination in court before making any payment, you have 90 days from the date of this letter (150 days if this letter is addressed to you outside of the United States) to file a petition with the United States (U.S.) Tax Court for a redetermination of the deficiency. You can get a copy of the rules for filing a petition and a petition form you can use by writing to the address below:

United States Tax Court
400 Second Street, N.W.
Washington, DC 20217

The Tax Court has a simplified procedure for small cases when the amount in dispute is $50,000 or less for any one tax year. You also can get information about this procedure by writing to the Tax Court. You should write promptly if you intend to file a petition with the Tax Court.

(over)

Letter 894 (RO) (Rev. 3-1990)
Catalog Number 40356H

Chapter 6—Adminstratively Appealing Adverse IRS Determinations
Appendix IRS Letters and Notices—Letter 894 (RO)—Notice of Deficiency from Appeals

APPENDIX—IRS LETTERS AND NOTICES

Letter 8984 (RO)—Notice of Deficiency from Appeals Office (with Waiver Form 4089-A) (p. 2)

Send the completed petition form, a copy of this letter, and copies of all statements and/or schedules you have received with this letter to the Tax Court at the above address. The court cannot consider your case if you file the petition late. The petition is considered timely filed if the postmark date falls within the prescribed 90- or 150-day period and the envelope containing the petition is properly addressed with the correct postage.

The time you have to file a petition with the court is set by law and cannot be extended or suspended. Thus, contacting the Internal Revenue Service (IRS) for more information or receiving correspondence from the IRS won't change the allowable period for filing a petition with the Tax Court.

As required by law, separate notices are sent to husbands and wives. If this letter is addressed to both husband and wife and both want to petition the Tax Court, both must sign and file the petition or each must file a separate signed petition. If only one spouse petitions the Tax Court, the full amount of the deficiency will be assessed against the non-petitioning spouse. If more than one tax year is shown above, you may file one petition form showing all of the years you are contesting.

You may represent yourself before the Tax Court, or you may be represented by anyone admitted to practice before the Tax Court.

If you decide not to file a petition with the Tax Court, please sign the enclosed waiver form and return it to us at the IRS address on the top of the front of this letter. This will permit us to assess the deficiency quickly and can help limit the accumulation of interest. The enclosed envelope is for your convenience.

If you decide not to sign and return the waiver, and you don't file a petition with the Tax Court within the time limit, the law requires us to assess and bill you for the deficiency after 90 days from the date of this letter (150 days if this letter is addressed to you outside the United States).

If you are a C corporation, under Internal Revenue Code Section 6621, large corporate underpayments may be subject to a higher rate of interest than the normal rate of interest for underpayments.

If you have any questions about this letter, you may write or call the contact the person whose name, telephone number, and IRS address are shown on the front of this letter. If you write, please include your telephone number and the best time for us to call you if we need more information, and a copy of this letter to help us identify your account. Keep the original letter for your records. If you prefer to call and the telephone number is outside your local calling area, there will be a long distance charge to you.

Thank you for your cooperation.

Sincerely,

Commissioner
By

Enclosures:

Letter 894 (RO) (Rev. 3-1999)
Catalog Number 48356H

Chapter 6—Adminstratively Appealing Adverse IRS Determinations
Appendix IRS Letters and Notices—Letter 894 (RO)—Notice of Deficiency from Appeals

APPENDIX—IRS LETTERS AND NOTICES

Letter 8984 (RO)—Notice of Deficiency from Appeals Office (with Waiver Form 4089–A) (p. 2)

Form 4089-A (Rev. April 1982)	Department of the Treasury - Internal Revenue Service **Notice of Deficiency Statement**	Symbols

Balance due plus penalty of $382 and interest of $176.

Kind of Tax	Individual Form 1040

Tax year Ended 12/31/15	Deficiency (Increase in Tax and Penalties)

☐ Copy to Authorized Representative

Cat No = 413350

Form 4089-A (Rev.-1982)

Chapter 6—Adminstratively Appealing Adverse IRS Determinations
Appendix IRS Letters and Notices—Letter 894 (RO)—Notice of Deficiency from Appeals

Form 1040 Department of the Treasury—Internal Revenue Service (99)
U.S. Individual Income Tax Return **2018** OMB No. 1545-0074 | IRS Use Only—Do not write or staple in this space.

For the year Jan. 1–Dec. 31, 2017, or other tax year beginning ____ , 2017, ending ____ , 20 ____ See separate instructions.

Your first name and initial	Last name	Your social security number
Bea N.	Happy	199 88 4433

If a joint return, spouse's first name and initial | Last name | Spouse's social security number

Home address (number and street). If you have a P.O. box, see instructions. | Apt. no.
99 Argument Lane

▲ Make sure the SSN(s) above and on line 6c are correct.

City, town or post office, state, and ZIP code. If you have a foreign address, also complete spaces below (see instructions).
Tampa, FL 33602

Presidential Election Campaign
Check here if you, or your spouse if filing jointly, want $3 to go to this fund. Checking a box below will not change your tax or refund. ☐ You ☐ Spouse

Foreign country name | Foreign province/state/county | Foreign postal code

Filing Status

Check only one box.

1 ☐ Single
2 ☐ Married filing jointly (even if only one had income)
3 ☐ Married filing separately. Enter spouse's SSN above and full name here. ▶
4 ☐ Head of household (with qualifying person). (See instructions.) If the qualifying person is a child but not your dependent, enter this child's name here. ▶
5 ☐ Qualifying widow(er) with dependent child

Exemptions

6a ☒ Yourself. If someone can claim you as a dependent, do not check box 6a
b ☐ Spouse

Boxes checked on 6a and 6b **1**

c Dependents:	(2) Dependent's social security number	(3) Dependent's relationship to you	(4) ✓ if child under age 17 qualifying for child tax credit (see instructions)
(1) First name Last name			
Bobby N. Happy	962 11 4237		☐
Betsy N. Happy	369 22 7411		☒
			☐
			☐

If more than four dependents, see instructions and check here ▶ ☐

No. of children on 6c who:
• lived with you **2**
• did not live with you due to divorce or separation (see instructions) ____
Dependents on 6c not entered above ____

d Total number of exemptions claimed

Add numbers on lines above ▶ **3**

Income

Attach Form(s) W-2 here. Also attach Forms W-2G and 1099-R if tax was withheld.

If you did not get a W-2, see instructions.

7	Wages, salaries, tips, etc. Attach Form(s) W-2	7	48,000
8a	Taxable interest. Attach Schedule B if required	8a	120
b	Tax-exempt interest. Do not include on line 8a	8b	
9a	Ordinary dividends. Attach Schedule B if required	9a	1,000
b	Qualified dividends	9b	
10	Taxable refunds, credits, or offsets of state and local income taxes	10	
11	Alimony received	11	10,800
12	Business income or (loss). Attach Schedule C or C-EZ	12	
13	Capital gain or (loss). Attach Schedule D if required. If not required, check here ▶ ☐	13	
14	Other gains or (losses). Attach Form 4797	14	
15a	IRA distributions 15a ____ b Taxable amount	15b	
16a	Pensions and annuities 16a ____ b Taxable amount	16b	
17	Rental real estate, royalties, partnerships, S corporations, trusts, etc. Attach Schedule E	17	
18	Farm income or (loss). Attach Schedule F	18	
19	Unemployment compensation	19	
20a	Social security benefits 20a ____ b Taxable amount	20b	
21	Other income. List type and amount	21	
22	Combine the amounts in the far right column for lines 7 through 21. This is your total income ▶	22	59,920

Adjusted Gross Income

23	Educator expenses	23	
24	Certain business expenses of reservists, performing artists, and fee-basis government officials. Attach Form 2106 or 2106-EZ	24	
25	Health savings account deduction. Attach Form 8889	25	
26	Moving expenses. Attach Form 3903	26	
27	Deductible part of self-employment tax. Attach Schedule SE	27	
28	Self-employed SEP, SIMPLE, and qualified plans	28	
29	Self-employed health insurance deduction	29	
30	Penalty on early withdrawal of savings	30	
31a	Alimony paid b Recipient's SSN ▶	31a	
32	IRA deduction	32	
33	Student loan interest deduction	33	
34	Tuition and fees. Attach Form 8917	34	
35	Domestic production activities deduction. Attach Form 8903	35	
36	Add lines 23 through 35	36	
37	Subtract line 36 from line 22. This is your **adjusted gross income** ▶	37	59,920

For Disclosure, Privacy Act, and Paperwork Reduction Act Notice, see separate instructions. Cat. No. 11320B Form **1040** (2017)

	(A)	(B)	(C)	(D)	(E)
1. Divorce Decree A. Bea should file her 2018 Form 1040 as Head of Household. B. Bea should file her 2018 Form 1040 as Married Filing Jointly. C. Bea should file her 2018 Form 1040 as Married Filing Separately. D. Bea should file her 2018 Form 1040 as Single. E. Bea should file her 2018 Form 1040 as Surviving Spouse.	○	○	○	○	○
2. Divorce decree—AGI A. Bea has AGI in 2018 of $59,920. B. Bea has AGI of $55,120. C. Bea has AGI of $48,000. D. Bea has AGI of $53,920. E. Bea has AGI of $49,120.	○	○	○	○	○
3. Preliminary Notice of Deficiency Once they receive the preliminary notice of deficiency for 2015, A. Bea and Bob have 90 days to file a written protest. B. Bea and Bob have 60 days to file a written protest. C. Bea and Bob have 30 days to file a written protest. D. Bea and Bob have 120 days to file a written protest.	○	○	○	○	○
4. Ninety-Day Letter Bea and Bob have now received a 90 day letter (Statutory Notice of Deficiency) for 2015 indicating that they owe a balance due plus penalty of $382 and interest of $176. Assuming these amounts are paid equally by them in 2018, A. They may deduct penalty of $382 and interest of $176 on their tax return. B. They may deduct penalty of $382 and interest of $0 on their tax return. C. They may deduct penalty of $0 and interest of $176 on their tax return. D. They may deduct penalty of $0 and interest of $0 on their tax return.	○	○	○	○	○
5. Balance Due on 2015 Tax Return Bea and Bob cannot currently pay their balance due in full for their 2015 tax return. A. Bea and Bob must pay their balance due in full immediately. B. If they owe less than $100,000, they may request an online Installment Payment Plan. C. If they owe less than $50,000, they may request an online Installment Payment Plan. D. Bea and Bob must pay their balance due within 30 days to avoid any penalty or interest. E. Bea and Bob must pay their balance due within 60 days to avoid any penalty or interest.	○	○	○	○	○

Answers and Explanations

Task-Based Simulation 1 Solution

```
┌─────────────────────┐
│ Document Review     │
│         ┌───────────────────────┐
│         │ Authoritative Literature │
│         │             ┌──────────────────┐
│         │             │ Help             │
└─────────┴─────────────┴──────────────────┘
```

	(A)	(B)	(C)	(D)	(E)
1. Divorce Decree	●	○	○	○	○

   A. Bea should file her 2018 Form 1040 as Head of Household.
   B. Bea should file her 2018 Form 1040 as Married Filing Jointly.
   C. Bea should file her 2018 Form 1040 as Married Filing Separately.
   D. Bea should file her 2018 Form 1040 as Single.
   E. Bea should file her 2018 Form 1040 as Surviving Spouse.

	(A)	(B)	(C)	(D)	(E)
2. Divorce decree—AGI	○	○	○	●	○

   A. Bea has AGI in 2018 of $59,920.
   B. Bea has AGI of $55,120.
   C. Bea has AGI of $48,000.
   D. Bea has AGI of $53,920.
   E. Bea has AGI of $49,120.

	(A)	(B)	(C)	(D)	(E)
3. Preliminary Notice of Deficiency	○	○	●	○	○

   Once they receive the preliminary notice of deficiency for 2015,
   A. Bea and Bob have 90 days to file a written protest.
   B. Bea and Bob have 60 days to file a written protest.
   C. Bea and Bob have 30 days to file a written protest.
   D. Bea and Bob have 120 days to file a written protest.

	(A)	(B)	(C)	(D)	(E)
4. Ninety-Day Letter	○	○	○	●	○

   Bea and Bob have now received a 90 day letter (Statutory Notice of Deficiency) for 2015 indicating that they owe a balance due plus penalty of $382 and interest of $176. Assuming these amounts are paid equally by them in 2018,
   A. They may deduct penalty of $382 and interest of $176 on their tax return.
   B. They may deduct penalty of $382 and interest of $0 on their tax return.
   C. They may deduct penalty of $0 and interest of $176 on their tax return.
   D. They may deduct penalty of $0 and interest of $0 on their tax return.

	(A)	(B)	(C)	(D)	(E)
5. Balance Due on 2015 Tax Return	○	○	●	○	○

   Bea and Bob cannot currently pay their balance due in full for their 2015 tax return.
   A. Bea and Bob must pay their balance due in full immediately.
   B. If they owe less than $100,000, they may request an online Installment Payment Plan.
   C. If they owe less than $50,000, they may request an online Installment Payment Plan.
   D. Bea and Bob must pay their balance due within 30 days to avoid any penalty or interest.
   E. Bea and Bob must pay their balance due within 60 days to avoid any penalty or interest.

1. **Divorce Decree—Filing Status**

   (A) Filing status is determined on the last day of the year. Bea filed for divorce in 2017, but it did not become final until 2018. Her filing status is determined on December 31, 2018. Because her divorce is final, she is considered Single. However, Bea maintains a home for at least one dependent child so she is allowed Head of Household status.

2. **Divorce decree—AGI**

   (D) Adjusted Gross Income is Gross Income less deductions for AGI (above the line). When a couple divorces, there is typically a division of assets. In addition, one spouse may have a legal obligation to support the other spouse. Alimony is includible in the gross income of the spouse receiving the payments. Alimony is taxable, but child support is not. Any payment made on behalf of support for a child is not includible in income of the recipient. Bea and Bob's divorce decree stipulated alimony of $400 per month be paid to Bea.

Wages	$48,000	Per divorce decree and tax return
Interest Income	120	Per tax return
Dividend Income	1,000	Per tax return
Alimony received	4,800	Per divorce decree
AGI	$53,920	

3. **Preliminary Notice of Deficiency**

   (C) In the federal system, at the conclusion of an audit, if the IRS believes there is a tax due and the taxpayer disagrees, the IRS will send the taxpayer a preliminary notice of deficiency. This is often referred to as a "30-day letter" because the taxpayer has 30 days to file a written protest of the IRS agent's findings. Or the taxpayer may agree to the changes on the return and sign Form 870. Or, if the taxpayer takes no action within 30 days, the IRS will mail a Statutory Notice of Deficiency.

4. **90-Day Letter**

   (D) The Statutory Notice of Deficiency is referred to as a "90-day letter" because its mailing date begins a 90-day period in which the taxpayer may do one of three things:

   1. Taxpayer files a petition in Tax Court to be heard by the Tax Court.

   2. Taxpayer takes no action and the IRS will begin the collection process.

   3. Taxpayer agrees and signs Form 870, which permits immediate assessment.

   Penalty and interest assessed are not deductible. Penalties or fines paid to any government agency or because of a violation of any law are not deductible. Likewise, interest assessed on a tax balance due is considered personal interest expense and not deductible.

5. **Balance Due on 2015 Tax Return—Installment Plan**

   (C) If the taxpayer is financially unable to pay their tax debt immediately, they can make monthly payments through an installment agreement. Before applying for any payment agreement, the taxpayer must file all required tax returns. The taxpayer is eligible to apply for an online payment agreement if the individual owes $50,000 or less in combined individual income tax, penalties, and interest. If the taxpayer is ineligible for an online payment agreement, the taxpayer can still pay installments by completing and sending in Form 9465, *Installment Agreement Request*, and Form 433-F, *Collection Information Statement*.

Compliance Responsibilities

Task-Based Simulation 2

tbs.TBSRCO0454

Research		
	Authoritative Literature	
		Help

Merill recently realized that she failed to report $20,000 of income on last year's last return. She is concerned that she may be subject to a substantial understatement penalty but is not sure how to determine this. Indicate the Internal Revenue Code section and subsection that provides the rules for the applicability of the substantial understatement penalty.

Choose a title from the list.

Select a title from the dropdown list below

IRC	§		·	

❶ Examples of correctly formatted IRC responses are IRC§1(a), IRC§12(a), IRC§12A(a), IRC§12AA(a), IRC§123(a), IRC§123A(a), IRC§1234(a), IRC§1234A(a), and IRC§1234A-5(a).

Answer

Task-Based Simulation 2 Solution

Research		
	Authoritative Literature	
		Help

IRC	§	6662	·	d

Federal Taxation of Property Transactions

Property Transactions

Section 1231 Assets — Cost Recovery

Task-Based Simulation 3

tbs.TBSRCO0369_2-18

Depreciation

Authoritative Literature

Help

Vanessa owns a consulting business that has always been reported as a sole proprietorship on her tax return. Assume that on February 19, 2018, Vanessa purchases a new computer for $5,000 that will be used solely for her business. Using the depreciation table below compute her depreciation expense for 2018. Assume no bonus depreciation and no Section 179 depreciation.

Enter the amount in the associated cells. Enter all values as positive numbers. If a value is zero, enter a zero (0).

Cost of asset	
Depreciation % from Table	
Months deemed owned in 2018	
Regular MACRS Depreciation for 2018	

Assume that Vanessa sells this computer on August 3, 2020. What would MACRS depreciation be for the computer for 2020?

MACRS Depreciation	

MACRS Accelerated Depreciation Table

	Property Class		
Recovery Year	**3-year**	**5-year**	**7-year**
1	33.33%	20.00%	14.29%
2	44.45	32.00	24.49
3	14.81	19.20	17.49
4	7.41	11.52	12.49
5		11.52	8.93
6		5.76	8.92
7			8.93
8			4.46

Answers and Explanations

Task-Based Simulation 3 Solution

Depreciation		
	Authoritative Literature	
		Help

Cost of asset	5000
Depreciation % from Table	20
Months deemed owned in 2018	6
Regular MACRS Depreciation for 2018	1000

MACRS Depreciation	480

Rationale:

Computers are classified as 5-year property under the MACRS rules. Therefore, first-year depreciation is $1,000, or 20% × $5,000.

The number of months that this asset is assumed to be owned for depreciation purposes is 6 months due to the half-year convention. The half-year convention assumes that personalty is owned for one-half of the tax year for the year the asset is purchased, regardless of when the asset is actually purchased during the year. For the year of purchase, the half-year convention is already built into the rates provided in the MACRS tables.

Cost of asset	$5,000
Bonus Depreciation	$0
Depreciation % from Table	20%
Months assumed owned in 2018 for depreciation purposes	6
Regular MACRS Depreciation for 2018	$1,000

Rationale:

The applicable percentage for 2020 (third year of the asset's life) is 19.20%. Note that this percentage assumes that the asset is owned for the entire year. However, the half-year convention provides that the asset is depreciated for one-half of the year for the year it is sold, regardless of when the asset is actually sold during the year. Therefore, 2020 depreciation is $5,000 × 19.2% × .5 = $480.

Federal Taxation of Individuals

Estate and Gift Taxation

Federal Gift Tax

Task-Based Simulation 4

tbs.TBSRWB0445_2-18

Type of Gift		
	Authoritative Literature	
		Help

During 2018, various clients went to Rowe, CPA, for tax advice concerning possible gift tax liability on transfers they made throughout 2018. For each client, indicate whether the transfer of cash, the income interest, or the remainder interest is a gift of a present interest, a gift of a future interest, or not a completed gift.

Assume the following facts:

Cobb created a $500,000 trust that provided his mother with an income interest for her life and the remainder interest to go to his sister at the death of his mother. Cobb expressly retained the power to revoke both the income interest and the remainder interest at any time.

Items to be answered

	(A)	(B)	(C)

1. The income interest at the trust's creation
  A. Present Interest
  B. Future Interest
  C. Not Completed
	○	○	○

2. The remainder interest at the trust's creation
  A. Present Interest
  B. Future Interest
  C. Not Completed
	○	○	○

Kane created a $100,000 trust that provided her nephew with the income interest until he reached 45 years of age. When the trust was created, Kane's nephew was 25. The income distribution is to start when Kane's nephew is 29. After Kane's nephew reaches the age of 45, the remainder interest is to go to Kane's niece.

	(A)	(B)	(C)

3. The income interest
  A. Present Interest
  B. Future Interest
  C. Not Completed
	○	○	○

During 2018, Hall, an unmarried taxpayer, made a $10,000 cash gift to his son in May and a further $12,000 cash gift to him in August.

	(A)	(B)	(C)

4. The cash transfers
   A. Present Interest
   B. Future Interest
   C. Not Completed
	○	○	○

During 2018, Yeats transferred property worth $20,000 to a trust with the income to be paid to her 22-year-niece Jane. After Jane reaches the age of 30, the remainder interest is to be distributed to Yeats's brother. The income interest is valued at $9,700 and the remainder interest at $10,300.

	(A)	(B)	(C)

5. The income interest
   A. Present Interest
   B. Future Interest
   C. Not Completed
	○	○	○

6. The remainder interest
   A. Present Interest
   B. Future Interest
   C. Not Completed
	○	○	○

Tom and Ann Curry, U.S. citizens, were married for the entire 2018 calendar year. Tom gave a $40,000 cash gift to his uncle, Grant. The Currys made no other gifts to Grant in 2018. Tom and Ann each signed a timely election stating that each made onehalf of the $40,000 gift.

	(A)	(B)	(C)

7. The cash transfers
   A. Present Interest
   B. Future Interest
   C. Not Completed
	○	○	○

Murry created a $1,000,000 trust that provided his brother with an income interest for 10 years, after which the remainder interest passes to Murry's sister. Murry retained the power to revoke the remainder interest at any time. The income interest was valued at $600,000.

	(A)	(B)	(C)

8. The income interest
   A. Present Interest
   B. Future Interest
   C. Not Completed
	○	○	○

9. The remainder interest
   A. Present Interest
   B. Future Interest
   C. Not Completed
	○	○	○

Answer and Explanations

Task-Based Simulation 4 Solution

Type of Gift

Authoritative Literature

Help

	(A)	(B)	(C)

1. The income interest at the trust's creation
  A. Present Interest
  B. Future Interest
  C. Not Completed
	○	○	●

2. The remainder interest at the trust's creation
  A. Present Interest
  B. Future Interest
  C. Not Completed
	○	○	●

3. The income interest
  A. Present Interest
  B. Future Interest
  C. Not Completed
	○	●	○

4. The cash transfers
  A. Present Interest
  B. Future Interest
  C. Not Completed
	●	○	○

5. The income interest
  A. Present Interest
  B. Future Interest
  C. Not Completed
	●	○	○

6. The remainder interest
  A. Present Interest
  B. Future Interest
  C. Not Completed
	○	●	○

7. The cash transfers
  A. Present Interest
  B. Future Interest
  C. Not Completed
	●	○	○

8. The income interest
  A. Present Interest
  B. Future Interest
  C. Not Completed
	●	○	○

9. The remainder interest
  A. Present Interest
  B. Future Interest
  C. Not Completed
	○	○	●

Rationale:

1. **(Not Completed)** Since Cobb expressly retained the power to revoke the income interest transferred to his mother at any time, he has not relinquished dominion and control and the transfer of the income interest is not a completed gift.

2. **(Not Completed)** Since Cobb expressly retained the power to revoke the remainder interest transferred to his sister at any time, he has not relinquished dominion and control and the transfer of the remainder interest is not a completed gift.

3. **(Future Interest)** Kane's transfer of an income interest to a nephew and a remainder interest to a niece are completed gifts because Kane has relinquished dominion and control. Since Kane's nephew was 25 years of age when the trust was created, but income distributions will not begin until the nephew is age 29, the transfer of the income interest is a gift of future interest and does not qualify for the annual exclusion.

4. **(Present Interest)** Since Hall's gifts of cash to his son were outright gifts, they are gifts of a present interest and qualify for the annual exclusion.

5. **(Present Interest)** Yeats's gift of the income interest to her 22-year-old niece is a gift of a present interest qualifying for the annual exclusion since Jane has the unrestricted right to immediate enjoyment of the income. The fact that the value of the income interest does not exceed $15,000 does not affect its nature (i.e., completed gift of a present interest).

6. **(Future Interest)** Yeats's gift of the remainder interest to her brother is a completed gift of a future interest since the brother cannot enjoy the property or any of the income until Jane reaches age 30.

7. **(Present Interest)** Tom's gift of $40,000 cash to his uncle is an outright gift of a present interest and qualifies for the annual exclusion. Since gift-splitting was elected and Tom and Ann would each receive a $15,000 annual exclusion, Tom and Ann each made a taxable gift of $20,000 − $15,000 exclusion = $5,000.

8. **(Present Interest)** Murry's gift of the income interest to his brother is a completed gift because Murry has relinquished dominion and control. It is a gift of a present interest qualifying for the annual exclusion since his brother has the unrestricted right to immediate enjoyment of the income.

9. **(Not Completed)** Since Murry retained the right to revoke the remainder interest transferred to his sister at any time, the transfer of the remainder interest does not result in a completed gift.

Task-Based Simulation 5

aq.tbs.ss.spec.corp.ded.001_2-18

Research		
	Authoritative Literature	
		Help

Sunshine Inc., a calendar-year corporation, has been profitable in recent years. In 2018, Sunshine has gross income from sales operations of $125,000 and expenses from operations of $65,000. Sunshine has made investments in four other corporations and has received dividend income from each. Sunshine's ownership percentage of each corporation is as follows:

GetFit, Inc.	5%
Yellow Inc.	19%
Sol, Inc.	15%
Orange, Inc.	10%

Please refer to the following Exhibits.

9191 [ ] VOID [ ] CORRECTED

PAYER'S name, street address, city or town, state or province, country, ZIP or foreign postal code, and telephone no.	1a Total ordinary dividends $ 5,000	OMB No. 1545-0110 2018 Form 1099-DIV	Dividends and Distributions
GetFit, Inc 200 West Energy Lane Valencia, CA	1b Qualified dividends $ 5,000		
	2a Total capital gain distr. $	2b Unrecap. Sec. 1250 gain $	Copy A
PAYER'S federal identification number: 36-12356489	RECIPIENT'S identification number 36-9721812	2c Section 1202 gain $	2d Collectibles (28%) gain $	For Internal Revenue Service Center
RECIPIENT'S name Sunshine, Inc.	3 Nondividend distributions $	4 Federal income tax withheld $	File with Form 1096.
Street address (including apt. no.) 100 Brightway Blvd.		5 Investment expenses $	For Privacy Act and Paperwork Reduction Act Notice, see the **2017 General Instructions for Certain Information Returns.**
	6 Foreign tax paid	7 Foreign country or U.S. possession	
City or town, state or province, country, and ZIP or foreign postal code Phoenix, AZ 85086	$		
	8 Cash liquidation distributions $	9 Noncash liquidation distributions	
	FATCA filing requirement [ ]	10 Exempt-interest dividends $	11 Specified private activity bond interest dividends $	
Account number (see instructions)	2nd TIN not [ ]	12 State	13 State identification no.	14 State tax withheld $ $	

Form **1099-DIV**   Cat. No. 14415N

Do Not Cut or Separate Forms on This Page — **Do Not Cut or Separate Forms on This Page**

www.irs.gov/form1099div   Department of the Treasury - Internal Revenue Service

---

9191 [ ] VOID [ ] CORRECTED

PAYER'S name, street address, city or town, state or province, country, ZIP or foreign postal code, and telephone no.	1a Total ordinary dividends $ 7,500	OMB No. 1545-0110 2018 Form 1099-DIV	Dividends and Distributions
Yellow, Inc. 1015 Healthy Way Atlanta, GA 30303	1b Qualified dividends $ 5,000		
	2a Total capital gain distr. $	2b Unrecap. Sec. 1250 gain $	Copy A
PAYER'S federal identification number: 36-0091008	RECIPIENT'S identification number 36-9721812	2c Section 1202 gain $	2d Collectibles (28%) gain $	For Internal Revenue Service Center
RECIPIENT'S name Sunshine, Inc.	3 Nondividend distributions $	4 Federal income tax withheld $	File with Form 1096.
Street address (including apt. no.) 100 Brightway Blvd.		5 Investment expenses $	For Privacy Act and Paperwork Reduction Act Notice, see the **2017 General Instructions for Certain Information Returns.**
	6 Foreign tax paid	7 Foreign country or U.S. possession	
City or town, state or province, country, and ZIP or foreign postal code Phoenix, AZ 85086	$		
	8 Cash liquidation distributions $	9 Noncash liquidation distributions	
	FATCA filing requirement [ ]	10 Exempt-interest dividends $	11 Specified private activity bond interest dividends $	
Account number (see instructions)	2nd TIN not [ ]	12 State	13 State identification no.	14 State tax withheld $ $	

Form **1099-DIV**   Cat. No. 14415N

Do Not Cut or Separate Forms on This Page — **Do Not Cut or Separate Forms on This Page**

www.irs.gov/form1099div   Department of the Treasury - Internal Revenue Service

9191 ☐ VOID ☐ CORRECTED

PAYER'S name, street address, city or town, state or province, country, ZIP or foreign postal code, and telephone no.		1a Total ordinary dividends $ 3,500	OMB No 1545-0110 2018 Form 1099-DIV	Dividends and Distributions
SOL, Inc. 2742 SOL Road Mexico City, Mexico 54720		1b Qualified dividends $ 0		
		2a Total capital gain distr. $	2b Unrecap Sec. 1250 gain $	Copy A For Internal Revenue Service Center
PAYER'S federal identification number 36-5006217	RECIPIENT'S identification number 36-9721812	2c Section 1202 gain $	2d Collectibles (28%) gain $	File with Form 1096.
RECIPIENT'S name Sunshine, Inc.		3 Nondividend distributions $	4 Federal income tax withheld $	For Privacy Act and Paperwork Reduction Act Notice, see the 2017 General Instructions for Certain Information Returns.
			5 Investment expenses $	
Street address (including apt. no.) 100 Brightway, Inc.		6 Foreign tax paid	7 Foreign country or U.S. possession	
City or town, state or province, country, and ZIP or foreign postal code Phoenix, AZ 85086		$		
		8 Cash liquidation distributions $	9 Noncash liquidation distributions $	
	FATCA filing requirement ☐	10 Exempt-interest dividends $	11 Specified private activity bond interest dividends $	
Account number (see instructions)	2nd TIN not. ☐	12 State	13 State identification no.	14 State tax withheld $ $

Form **1099-DIV**   Cat. No. 14415N   www.irs.gov/form1099div   Department of the Treasury - Internal Revenue Service

Do Not Cut or Separate Forms on This Page — Do Not Cut or Separate Forms on This Page

9191 ☐ VOID ☐ CORRECTED

PAYER'S name, street address, city or town, state or province, country, ZIP or foreign postal code, and telephone no.		1a Total ordinary dividends $ 4,000	OMB No. 1545-0110 2018 Form 1099-DIV	Dividends and Distributions
Orange, Inc. 555 Paradise Drive Ft. Myers, FL 33901		1b Qualified dividends $ 4,000		
		2a Total capital gain distr. $	2b Unrecap Sec. 1250 gain $	Copy A For Internal Revenue Service Center
PAYER'S federal identification number 36-1203406	RECIPIENT'S identification number 36-9721812	2c Section 1202 gain $	2d Collectibles (28%) gain $	File with Form 1096.
RECIPIENT'S name Sunshine, Inc.		3 Nondividend distributions $	4 Federal income tax withheld $	For Privacy Act and Paperwork Reduction Act Notice, see the 2017 General Instructions for Certain Information Returns.
			5 Investment expenses $	
Street address (including apt. no.) 100 Brightway Blvd.		6 Foreign tax paid	7 Foreign country or U.S. possession	
City or town, state or province, country, and ZIP or foreign postal code Phoenix, AZ 85086		$		
		8 Cash liquidation distributions $	9 Noncash liquidation distributions $	
	FATCA filing requirement ☐	10 Exempt-interest dividends $	11 Specified private activity bond interest dividends $	
Account number (see instructions)	2nd TIN not. ☐	12 State	13 State identification no.	14 State tax withheld $ $

Form **1099-DIV**   Cat. No. 14415N   www.irs.gov/form1099div   Department of the Treasury - Internal Revenue Service

Do Not Cut or Separate Forms on This Page — Do Not Cut or Separate Forms on This Page

For each item in column A, calculate the requested information and enter it in the associated cell in column B.

1. Calculate the dividend received deduction.	
2. Calculate taxable income.	
3. If Sunshine's gross income from sales operations is $60,000, what is Sunshine's dividend received deduction?	
4. If Sunshine's gross income from sales operations is $50,000, what is Sunshine's dividend received deduction?	

Answers and Explanations

Task-Based Simulation 5 Solution

Research		
	Authoritative Literature	
		Help

1. Calculate the dividend received deduction.	$11,550
2. Calculate taxable income.	$68,450
3. If Sunshine's gross income from sales operations is $60,000, what is Sunshine's dividend received deduction?	$10,500
4. If Sunshine's gross income from sales operations is $50,000, what is Sunshine's dividend received deduction?	$11,550

1. **Dividend received deduction.**

The purpose of the dividend received deduction (DRD) is to mitigate triple taxation of corporate income. The amount of the DRD depends on the percentage of ownership the receiving corporation has in the *domestic* corporation that issued the dividend distribution.

% of ownership	Deduction %
Less than 20%	70%
20% or more but less than 80%	80%
80% or more	100%

Follow these steps to calculate the DRD:

Step 1: Multiply the dividends received by the deduction percentage.

Step 2: Multiply the taxable income by the deduction percentage.

Step 3: The deduction is the lesser of step 1 or step 2, unless deducting the amount arrived in step 1 results in a net operating loss (NOL). If so, then the amount in step 1 is used.

Step 1:

Calculate DRD	Dividend Received	DRD %	DRD
GetFit, Inc.	$5,000	0.7	$3,500
Yellow, Inc.	7,500	0.7	5,250
Sol, Inc. (foreign)	3,500	0	0
Orange, Inc.	4,000	0.7	2,800
	$20,000		$11,550

Step 2:

Gross income from sales operations	$125,000
Expenses from operations	(65,000)
Dividend income received	20,000
Taxable income before DRD	$80,000

Dividend income must be included in the calculation of taxable income. No DRD is allowed for the dividend income received from Sol, Inc. because it is a foreign corporation.

Taxable income $80,000 × 70% deduction percentage = $56,000

Step 3:

The DRD is the lesser of step 1 or step 2. The correct DRD is $11,550.

2. **Calculate Taxable Income.**

Gross income from sales operations	$125,000
Expenses from operations	(65,000)
Dividend income received	20,000
Taxable income before DRD	$80,000
Dividend received deduction	(11,550)
Taxable income after DRD	$68,450

3. **Calculate DRD if gross income from sales operations is $60,000.**

Step 1:

Calculate DRD	Dividend Received	DRD %	DRD
GetFit, Inc.	$5,000	0.7	$3,500
Yellow, Inc.	7,500	0.7	5,250
Sol, Inc. (foreign)	3,500	0	0
Orange, Inc.	4,000	0.7	2,800
	$20,000		$11,550

Step 2:

Gross income from sales operations	$60,000
Expenses from operations	(65,000)
Dividend income received	20,000
Taxable income before DRD	$15,000

Taxable income $15,000 × 70% deduction percentage = $10,500

Step 3:

The DRD is the lesser of step 1 or step 2. The correct DRD is $10,500.

4. **Calculate DRD if gross income from sales operations is $50,000.**

Step 1:

Calculate DRD	Dividend Received	DRD %	DRD
GetFit, Inc.	$5,000	0.7	$3,500
Yellow, Inc.	7,500	0.7	5,250
Sol, Inc. (foreign)	3,500	0	0
Orange, Inc.	4,000	0.7	2,800
	$20,000		$11,550

Step 2:

Gross income from sales operations	$50,000
Expenses from operations	(65,000)
Dividend income received	20,000
Taxable income before DRD	$5,000

Taxable income $5,000 × 70% deduction percentage = $3,500

Step 3:

The deduction is the lesser of step 1 or step 2, unless deducting the amount arrived in step 1 results in a net operating loss (NOL).

Gross income from sales operations	50,000
Expenses from operations	(65,000)
Dividend income received	20,000
Taxable income before DRD	5,000
Dividend received deduction	(11,550)
Taxable income after DRD	(6,550)

Therefore, the correct DRD is $11,550 since the deducting the full DRD creates an NOL.